Nicholas Witchell was born in 1953 in Cosford, Shropshire. His father was an officer in the Royal Air Force.

He lived most of his childhood in Surrey. He went to school at Epsom College and then to Leeds University where he completed a law degree. He had intended to become a lawyer but at university, where he edited the student newspaper, he decided instead to be a journalist.

He joined the British Broadcasting Corporation in 1976. For several years he was a television news reporter in Northern Ireland; later assignments took him to places such as Beirut and the Falklands.

In 1984 he became a BBC newscaster, presenting the nightly 'Six O'Clock News'. In September 1989 he launched BBC Television's new 'Breakfast News' programme.

Nicholas Witchell is single and lives in Kensington, West London.

THE LOCH NESS STORY

Revised and Updated Edition

Nicholas Witchell

With Forewords by
Gerald Durrell and Sir Peter Scott

CORGI BOOKS

THE LOCH NESS STORY
A CORGI BOOK 0 552 99349 2

Originally published in Great Britain by
Terence Dalton Ltd.

PRINTING HISTORY
Terence Dalton edition published 1974
Corgi edition published 1982
Corgi revised edition published 1989
Corgi revised edition reprinted 1989
Corgi revised edition reprinted 1991
Corgi revised edition reprinted 1993

This book is set in Times 11/12pt by
Chippendale Type, Otley, West Yorkshire

Corgi Books are published by Transworld Publishers Ltd.,
61–63 Uxbridge Road, Ealing, London W5 5SA, in Australia by
Transworld Publishers (Australia) Pty. Ltd., 15–25 Helles
Avenue, Moorebank, NSW 2170, and in New Zealand by
Transworld Publishers (N.Z.) Ltd., 3 William Pickering Drive,
Albany, Auckland.

Printed and bound in Great Britain by
Cox & Wyman Ltd., Reading, Berks.

To my Mother and Father

CONTENTS

LIST OF ILLUSTRATIONS

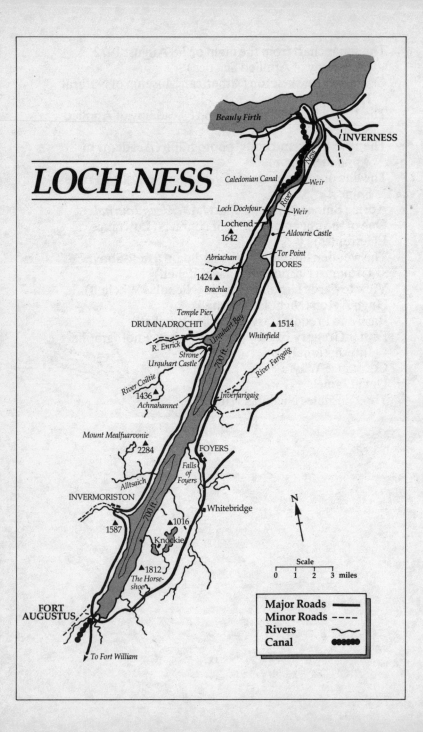

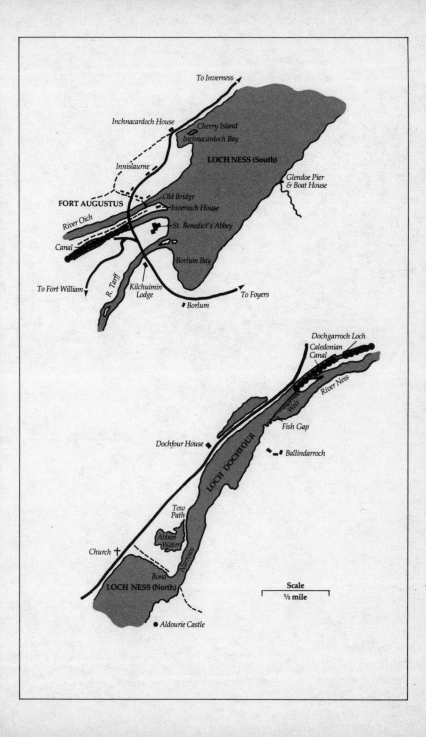

FOREWORD

by Gerald Durrell

It has always seemed very curious to me that anybody faced with reasonably good evidence (supplied by witnesses of guaranteed probity and sobriety) as to the possible existence of a creature as yet unknown to science, should not throw up his hands in delight at even the faintest chance of such a windfall in this shrinking world. Unfortunately, as Mr Witchell's book shows, the opposite is generally the case. Man, whose intelligence you had no cause to doubt, suddenly leaves you bereft of speech at the lengths to which he will go to prove that nothing new can exist under the stars. It was Cuvier who produced the arrogant statement that there were no new large animals to be discovered for, as he pointed out, he knew them all. Since that date, there has been an endless succession of equally arrogant people who adopt the same blinkered attitude.

In this book Mr Witchell has collected and clearly set out the saga of the Loch Ness Monster and it makes fascinating reading, but, as he rightly points out, 'It seems a puzzling reflection on our capacity to be fair and logical that the testimony of so many reliable witnesses, often offered under oath, should have been considered inadmissible as proof that there is something unknown in Loch Ness.'

I am not suggesting for a moment that one accepts the existence of an unknown creature without sifting the evidence with great care, but what I am advocating – and surely this should not be too much to hope for in scientific circles – is a reasonably open mind. There are after all sufficiently strange things in the world which we now accept but which at one time were considered very dubious indeed. Think of the courage it must have taken to set out to describe to the scientific fraternity the first duck-billed platypus.

So many people state that a prehistoric monster (that loose generic term so beloved of the press) could not exist today. Yet they have only to travel to New Zealand, where they will find the Tuatara (*Sphenodon punctatus*) which has, with scant consideration for science, come down from the Triassic age unchanged; and this is not the only survivor, as Mr Witchell points out. The coelacanth could not be more of a prehistoric creature if it tried.

In these pages we have the extraordinary cross section of observant intelligent witnesses who are above reproach being virtually told by the scientists that they are either drunk, insane, hoaxers or partially blind and all definitely mentally retarded. Faced with evidence that seems to me incontrovertible, that something large and unknown exists in the loch, the scientific fraternity nervously takes refuge behind a barricade of ripples, leaping salmon, shadows, dead stags, logs of wood, branches, and what must surely be the most agile and acrobatic strings of otters ever seen, rather than admit that there is something large, strange and unknown to science in the dark waters of the loch.

It seems incredible also that all the research to date has had to be done virtually on a shoestring by dedicated amateurs who, when they were helped at all, received assistance from places like America while receiving precious little but a petulant moue from the disbelieving ranks of British Science. You would have thought that even the British Tourist Board could have spent a little less money in sending mini-kilted young ladies and out-of-focus coloured pictures of heather around the world, in an attempt to attract tourists to the Highlands, and, instead, back to the hilt an expedition or a series of expeditions finally to identify the creature or creatures in Loch Ness once and for all. Surely, even a public relations officer, lowly species of animal life that it is, could appreciate what an enormous attraction it would be to prove that Scotland supports a living group of Plesiosaurs. Mr Philip Stalker, writing about the Loch Ness Monster in 1957, pointed out that 'If medical science had shown as little enterprise and as little courage, in its various fields, as marine zoologists have shown in regard to the Loch Ness animal, the Gold Coast would still be the White Man's Grave, appendicitis would still be a fatal illness and tuberculosis would be killing millions every year in Britain.' It seems to me fair comment.

I hope that this excellent and lucid account may prod the powers-that-be into doing two things. Firstly, giving financial support to an all-out effort to find out exactly what *does* exist in Loch Ness, and secondly (before this is done) to pass some sort of legislation completely protecting whatever it is that may be found from any harm that could come to it. It would be a sad (but perhaps not altogether surprising) comment on human beings if a creature which had come down unchanged and unharmed from prehistory was to be finally exterminated by modern man.

Gerald Durrell, O.B.E., L.H.D., F.I.Biol.

FOREWORD

by Sir Peter Scott

The story of the Loch Ness Monster never ends. Only by draining the loch could it ever be proved that no such animal exists. Although no specimen has so far been available for examination, it is still possible to keep an open mind.

Of course from a zoological point of view the existence of a population of very large animals in Loch Ness is extremely improbable. No less improbable, however, is the alternative hypothesis that all the people who have, down the years, seen very large animals in the loch, of the same general appearance and behaving in a broadly similar manner, are either victims of error or hallucination or are simply telling lies.

I hope that all new evidence will continue to be recorded regularly, for all who have studied Nessie down the years to consider and assess, and for historians to evaluate. The name *Nessiteras rhombopteryx* (Rines and Scott) is still available. Without a scientific name it would be impossible to protect the species should it prove to exist.

I am delighted to be associated with this further edition of Nicholas Witchell's searching and informative book on the subject.

Sir Peter Scott, C.H., C.B.E., D.S.C., F.R.S.
Slimbridge

The Blind Men and the Elephant

A Hindoo Fable

by John Godfrey Saxe

I

It was six men of Indostan
    To learning much inclined,
Who went to see the Elephant
    (Though all of them were blind),
That each by observation
    Might satisfy his mind.

II

The *First* approached the Elephant
    And happening to fall
Against his broad and sturdy side,
    At once began to bawl:
'God bless me! but the Elephant
    Is very like a wall!'

III

The *Second*, feeling of the tusk,
    Cried, 'Ho! what have we here
So very round and smooth and sharp?
    To me 't is mighty clear
This wonder of an Elephant
    Is very like a spear!'

IV

The *Third* approached the animal,
    And happening to take
The squirming trunk within his hands,
    Thus boldly up and spake:
'I see,' quoth he, 'the Elephant
    Is very like a snake!'

V

The *Fourth* reached out his eager hand,
　　And felt about the knee.
'What most this wondrous beast is like
　　Is mighty plain,' quoth he:
' 'T is clear enough the Elephant
　　Is very like a tree!'

VI

The *Fifth*, who chanced to touch an ear,
　　Said: 'E'en the blindest man
Can tell what this resembles most;
　　Deny the fact who can,
This marvel of an Elephant
　　Is very like a fan!'

VII

The *Sixth* no sooner had begun
　　About the beast to grope,
Than, seizing on the swinging tail
　　That fell within his scope,
'I see,' quoth he, 'the Elephant
　　Is very like a rope!'

VIII

And so those men of Indostan
　　Disputed loud and long,
Each in his own opinion
　　Exceeding stiff and strong,
Though each was partly in the right,
　　And all were in the wrong!

MORAL

So oft in theologic wars,
　　The disputants, I ween,
Rail on in utter ignorance
　　Of what each other mean,
And prate about an Elephant
　　Not one of them has seen!

Chapter One

A MONSTROUS TALE

The German coach driver was having problems. His way was blocked by the car belonging to the French television cameraman. And the queue of traffic was growing ever longer. Not that anyone was in a hurry. Because from every vehicle people were peering out from their windows towards the water below.

It was a Saturday afternoon in October. Nineteen well-marshalled motor cruisers were strung out in line abreast across Loch Ness, moving forward slowly and throwing down an invisible curtain of sound into the water below.

Occasionally the advance would slow. Other boats which had been shadowing the main line would accelerate forward. Technicians down in their cabins bent over shimmering sonar screens and stared at the shapes which were appearing on them.

They'd been at it for two days. Twice the line of boats had trailed its sonar net along the length of the loch. Three times traces had appeared on the sonar charts: faint shapes, insignificant-looking curls etched by the graphite pencils. They were there because the sound waves being radiated into the water had been reflected back by objects a long way beneath the surface; by objects which were in midwater and which were moving; by objects, one of which had been tracked by the sonar operators for two minutes and ten seconds before it had been lost.

To the sonar experts, the marks left by the objects on the charts had meaning. The American engineer whose career had been spent building and understanding sonar studied the traces and said that, in his opinion, each one had been

1

caused by a target which was larger than a shark but smaller than a whale.*

And yet, in Loch Ness, there is supposed to be virtually nothing which could not be landed by a fly fisherman.

For more than fifty years people the world over have associated the words Loch Ness with only one thing. With something we call a 'Monster'. And for more than fifty years most of the people in Britain's museums have turned their heads to look the other way; closed their ears to the eyewitnesses who've stood and watched this mythical monster turn into a flesh and blood creature; closed their eyes to the findings of the privately-sponsored expeditions which, time and again, have played their sonar fingers through the loch and found things which, by rights, should not be there; and closed their minds to a phenomenon which has managed not merely to slip through our neatly arranged intellectual and technological nets, but which threatens to tear a great hole in them.

But perhaps it is unfair to blame the scientists. Because, after all, the proposition is a pretty preposterous one. It is that in one of the most thoroughly explored and heavily populated corners of the world there exists a species of large animal which has eluded the best efforts of man to be found and identified. And the proposition is little short of ludicrous when one considers what some people suggest: that in Loch Ness – a mere five hundred miles from London – there are creatures which are relics from a generation which was supposed to have become extinct millions of years ago.

Daft really. No wonder psychiatrists insist it's all in our minds: that the sight of or belief in Nessie stems from a deep-seated need to have monsters and mysteries because they allow us to step out of our basically rather boring lives and touch something utterly fantastic. They offer an escape from the routine to the romantic, say the experts, and at Loch Ness it's all so terribly convenient: no jungles to

* See Chapter Ten: 'Operation Deepscan'.

2

thrash through or mountain ranges to struggle up in search of our legend. And what is more, they say, it's a playground for every amateur to act out his dream of putting one over on the professional panjandrums who sit atop their ivory towers and scoff.

Yes, probably most of this is true. Loch Ness has, over the years, attracted more than its share of bizarre characters: publicity-seekers and pranksters; charlatans and crooks; the inadequate and the incompetent. Very often it has been individuals such as these who've provided the headlines to satsify the news media's perpetual curiosity about Loch Ness.

But there is more. There would need to be to sustain a story for more than half a century and bring no fewer than 230 journalists and 22 television crews to the loch that autumn weekend in 1987. My own colleagues from BBC Television News were there, so too were our friends from ITN, and teams from the American networks, from most of Europe, Australia, Japan, Brazil and beyond. The London correspondent from *Pravda* was even there.

It was a curious spectacle. The line of boats out on the loch and on the shore above them a pack of televison news cameramen, weighed down with their electronic equipment; reporters with their portable cellular telephones – a babble of a dozen different languages, and along the road the cars and coaches of passers-by pulled onto the grass verge to witness this latest attempt to unlock the loch's secret.

As a scene it was not so different from how it must have been fifty-four years before, in the late autumn of 1933, when the world first became aware of Loch Ness and first heard about its monster. Then the newspapermen hurried north on the night sleeper to Inverness. And on the very same motor road above the loch people had stood by their cars and charabancs to watch the early searchers put out by boat.

In the intervening years the mystery has lapped away at our consciousness. Few summers have passed without

3

Nessie making a splash in stories which frequently have had the ring of well-rehearsed formula writing to them: 'A sure sign of the start of the silly season . . .' and so on. The same clichés and cartoons are dusted off and served up again and again!

My own interest in Loch Ness began when I was about thirteen. I can remember browsing through a magazine article, and having a school project to write. With perhaps the embryonic journalist even then starting to stir, I decided that this excellent story would be my subject. Books and cuttings were gutted: the project written. I seem to remember I even won some minor school prize for it.

Nothing more happened until I was sixteen and looking for somewhere to spend a summer camping holiday with two schoolfriends. I remembered Loch Ness and suggested it: my friends agreed. It would not simply be a camping holiday, we decided, but an expedition – so I wrote off to every local company I could think of to try to enlist some sponsorship. Several months and one much-prized crate of baked beans later we found ourselves in a field a few miles south of the lochside village of Dores.

For two weeks I watched obsessively, saw absolutely nothing but began to talk to some of the people who've lived their lives by the loch. I remember in particular a conversation with Hugh Ayton, the farmer on whose land we stayed. A quiet, softly-spoken Highlander, the first time I asked him whether he'd ever seen anything unusual in the loch he indicated that he hadn't. It was only a few days later, when I think he'd realised that our interest was a genuine one, that he recounted how one night he and three other men had followed one of the animals down the loch in a small boat.* The details were slow in coming: offered with a mixture of diffidence and matter-of-factness which seemed to say a great deal about Hugh Ayton's straightforward honesty. They were characteristics which I was to come across many times in the next few years as I

* See Chapter Four

4

interviewed more and more eyewitnesses and asked them to describe what they'd seen.

It was this testimony, the straightforward accounts of the eyewitnesses – most especially of the local farmers who were set apart from the tourist industry – which persuaded me that the Loch Ness story was more than a mirage, more than the figment – so beloved by the comics and the columnists – of some thirsty Highlander's or money-grubbing Scotsman's imagination.

In 1972, during a year off between school and university, I took myself back to Loch Ness and built a wooden hut high in a field overlooking Urquhart Castle and the bay beside it. I lived alone in it for five months. I had a large 35mm. cine camera and powerful telephoto lens loaned to me by the Loch Ness Investigation Bureau and a still camera and lens of my own. Most days, if the weather was reasonably calm, I would start to scan the loch's surface at dawn. They are precious memories: of the sun rising over the mountain tops: the loch totally still and silent and the fishing boats scudding along its surface through the soft early morning mists. I was nineteen: in a hut I'd built for myself, overlooking the ruins of an ancient castle and convinced it would be only a matter of time before one of these animals so many people had told me about would appear and allow itself to be filmed and photographed.

It was not to be, of course. In the many months I spent at Loch Ness in the early seventies, living in my hut and gathering material for the orginal edition of this book, I never saw any sure sign of any unknown species in the loch. It was disappointing, but I had come to know and trust many local people who had seen something and that was good enough.

I orginally wrote *The Loch Ness Story* when I was twenty: it was first published in 1974. Two years later, after I'd finished a law degree at Leeds University, I joined the BBC as a graduate entrant on its News Training scheme. Loch Ness started to recede in importance. The rudimentary journalistic impulses it had stirred some years earlier had, by now, overtaken my ambition to become a lawyer and grown into the beginnings of a full-time career.

For a year I was a scriptwriter in BBC Television's national newsroom in London. But I wanted to cover the stories myself rather than help to write them up for the announcers and others who then read the bulletins and who, in those days, played no part in their preparation. So in 1978 I transferred to BBC News in Northern Ireland. In all, I lived in Belfast for the best part of four years, reporting on the Troubles for regional programmes in the Province and for the network news in London. After Northern Ireland came a spell as a reporter based in London and a number of assignments to places like Beirut and the Falklands, and the 1983 General Election when I was the BBC TV News correspondent on the campaign trail with the Prime Minister, Margaret Thatcher. It was great fun: I loved life on the road: the endless variety and the television news reporter's challenge of distilling stories quickly and using images and words together to try to tell them sharply and well, fairly and accurately. On two or three occasions I covered stories at Loch Ness: no longer there as the teenage enthusiast in his wooden hut (which, incidentally, is still standing, though now very dilapidated and overgrown!) but as the professional gatherer of facts with a duty to stand back and be objective, and perhaps to be cynical.

It is now nearly twenty years since I first went to Loch Ness and heard Hugh Ayton describe how he'd followed an unknown creature along its waters in his boat. There have, I must admit, been moments in recent years when that cynicism which is a necessary part of every journalist's outlook has touched my attitude to Nessie. Once I was so certain: then I went off and became preoccupied with the sorts of stories which have no romance, which are no escape – which are simply raw, tragic and awful. Their contrast with the story at Loch Ness could hardly be greater.

6

But despite the time away and the bouts of cynicism, I still believe that the saga of Nessie, as it will unfold in the ensuing chapters, DOES bear witness to the integrity of people like Hugh Ayton and the hundreds of others who've seen something unusual. They have reported in good faith, and increasingly their testimony has been backed up by the small teams of scientists who've gone to the loch with their instruments and whose results must – after the coldest and most clinical of examinations – be accepted as supporting the view that in Loch Ness there is something which we do not fully understand and which deserves to be taken seriously.

What has happened at Loch Ness over the past half century is not something of shattering significance. But it is intriguing, and it does surely offer a few lessons which we might want to remember. The main one is to keep an open mind: to be willing to inquire: to discover and check the facts before making a judgement. That, I would suggest, is what many British scientists have rather ostentatiously failed to do where Loch Ness is concerned. They have rejected out of hand, without even taking the trouble to go there and meet the people who have made the sightings. That, I think, is the most unfortunate aspect of their behaviour, because they have by implication damned hundreds of well-meaning people as either fools or liars. And that is unfair.

Loch Ness is also an example of how difficult it is to persuade some sections of the mass media to broaden their preconceived perceptions of a subject. Nessie was filed away under facetious years ago and despite its best efforts to be taken more seriously, it's never quite made it. It and some of the people who've been to the loch must bear a lot of the blame, but sometimes the way this subject's been written about has seemed rather less than fair. It's been an excellent example of the gulf which often exists between image and reality and which extends to so many subjects – usually people but sometimes things – occupying a regular place in our diet of news consumption.

So before a judgement is made about Loch Ness I hope the details and stories of which this book consists may be taken into account. I still remember my irritation at a review of an early edition which was written by one of Scotland's most eminent zoologists. He pooh-poohed the whole subject. Fair enough, but out of curiosity I wrote to ask him his private opinion of the research done in 1972 by the American scientist, Dr Robert Rines. He replied that he could not recall reading about it when he had prepared his review. This seemed rather strange since the 1972 underwater results were highlighted in the opening paragraphs of that edition and formed the climax to the book. But this distinguished gentleman concluded, rather curtly, that ' . . . this new "evidence" is all on a par with so much in the past,' (a puzzling observation since, by his own admission, he didn't know what this new evidence was) ' . . . it is just a very good tourist attraction and satisfies the human need for "monsters".'

Quite so. It is rather as the Soviet news agency said in 1968, that 'When it becomes necessary to distract readers from real problems, Western leaders have three sensational stories which never fail: flying saucers, the Loch Ness monster and the abominable snowman.'

I suppose, if nothing else, the fact that the man from *Pravda* was at the loch that weekend in October 1987 was an indication that understanding may have moved forward a little! All I can ask you to do now is to consider the rest of the Loch Ness story and then form your own opinion.

Chapter Two

BACKGROUND TO A MYSTERY

From either end it stretches for as far as the eye can see: a narrow trench of dark water greater in length than the narrowest point of the English Channel. On either side tree-clad mountains rise to heights of over 2,000 feet. This is Loch Ness: moody and secretive, in terms of volume the largest freshwater lake in Great Britain and the third deepest in Europe. A writer in 1808 observed: 'Travelling down the North side of Loch Ness a person of any taste must be struck with the sublimity of the scene.'

The loch lies in the northernmost sector of the Great Glen, the scar-like fault which traverses the North of Scotland from the Moray Firth to Loch Linnhe. Between 300 and 400 million years ago, in a succession of tremors, the land cracked open and the area to the north of the fault slowly moved some sixty-five miles in a south-westerly direction.

The landform, lying like an open wound, was at the mercy of nature's erosive forces, and during the period of glacial action 25,000 to 10,000 years ago Loch Ness was gouged out by north-eastward-flowing glaciers of up to 4,000 feet in thickness. The whole of the Highland area was enveloped in ice, all, that is, except Britain's highest mountain, Ben Nevis, sixty miles southwest of Loch Ness.

The glaciers created a narrow steep-sided loch, 14,000 acres in surface area, twenty-two and a half miles long, and up to one and a half miles wide. For much of its length Loch Ness is over 700 feet deep, and for many years the maximum depth was believed to be 754 feet. However, in 1969 a miniature submarine went down to a depth of 820 feet and recorded 975 feet on its depth-sounding apparatus. Such a reading has never been repeated: so the true maximum depth of Loch Ness is still uncertain.

Judged by its estimated cubic capacity of 263,000 million cubic feet, the loch is easily the largest freshwater body in the British Isles. Its volume contrasts with that of Loch Lomond, its superior in surface area but with a volume of only 93,000 million cubic feet; and Loch Morar, at 1,017 feet the deepest lake in Britain, which has a volume of only 81,000 million cubic feet. Compared to, say, America's Great Lakes Loch Ness is, of course, relatively small but it supports an abundant quantity of life.

Its waters are fresh and unpolluted and for the greater part of the year it is fished for salmon and sea trout; the record salmon for the loch is 52lb., caught by a resident of Fort Augustus in the 1950s. In addition to these two migratory fish there are brown trout, an added attraction for the angler and perhaps also for any large predators in the loch. In the deeper water of the main loch are arctic char and an enormous quantity of eels, some of which are known to be quite large. No one has ever calculated the size of Ness's fish population, but since netting is prohibited there is no reason why it should not be very large.

The only major survey of the loch was carried out in the early years of this century. Its results, published in the Bathymetrical Survey of 1911, describe it as a long V-shaped rock-basin, the northern end of which is ponded by glacial and fluvio-glacial and raised beach deposits. The bottom was said to be 'as flat as a bowling green', although the subterranean sides are very steep. At Horseshoe Crag on the south-eastern side, a depth of 236 feet was recorded just 100 feet from the shore, and at Cormorant Rock a similiar depth was found only fifty feet from the shore, indicating an angle only 15° from the perpendicular.

Although the water is fresh it has a low pH factor, because of the suspension of peat particles brought down from the mountains by the numerous rivers and burns. At a depth of about fifty feet the water is opaque and, judging

10

by divers' accounts, rather eerie. Its acidity, combined with the steep sides, prevents any substantial plant growth in the water; it may also be the reason why an eighteenth-century writer recorded that the loch waters caused biliousness when drunk.

The temperature of the water is low. Research just after the turn of the century by Sir John Murray, and in 1953 by Dr C.H. Mortimer of the Freshwater Biological Association indicated the presence of a surface warm layer about 150 feet in depth, the temperature of which varies according to the prevailing weather conditions. Below this layer, the loch contains colder, heavier water which remains at a fairly constant temperature of 42–44°F.

The climate is mild and damp and not terribly enticing. From 1921 to 1950 Fort Augustus, at the southern end of the loch, is recorded as having enjoyed the lowest annual amount of sunshine in Britain! Mist and squalls are channelled in from the sea along the length of the Great Glen, and the loch's placid surface can be whipped into a turmoil within minutes. Its catchment area is extensive, and during periods of heavy rain the loch surface can rise rapidly.

However, the loch itself never freezes, partly because of its great depth and its sheer volume of water. This acts as an enormous storage heater during the winter months, preventing snow from lying in the immediate vicinity for any length of time. It has been calculated that the heat released from the loch during winter is equivalent to that given off by the combustion of two million tons of coal.

So much for the basic geographical details of the setting. Imagine an area of mountain, forest and lake into which twentieth-century development has infiltrated slowly. This is the area where Britain's largest known animal, the red deer, is to be found; where her largest bird, the golden eagle, and her wildest animal, the wildcat, live, and where the wolf roamed until the last one was shot in Inverness-shire in 1743.

It is set in a country which retains its proud independence

11

from the rest of Britain; where the native language, Gaelic, is still spoken by many of the older generation and where the ancient tribal ties of the clan are still venerated. In such an area, where superstition has clearly manifested itself within modern times, one would expect there to be a legend concerning the source of the great lake.

Such a legend is recorded in William Mackay's book *Urquhart and Glenmoriston* (published privately in 1914); it is with the kind permission of his son that the following extract is included.

Legend says that the great glen which now lies under the waters of Loch Ness was a beautiful valley, sheltered from every blast by high mountains and clothed with trees and herbs of richest hues . . . There was a spring in this happy vale which was blessed by Daly the Druid and whose waters were ever afterwards an unfailing remedy for every disease. This holy well was protected by a stone placed over it by the Druid who enjoined that whenever the stone was removed for the drawing of water it should be immediately replaced. 'The day on which my command is disregarded,' said he, 'desolation will overtake the land.' The words of Daly were remembered by the people and became a law among them: and so day followed day and year gave place to year. But on one of the days a woman left the child of her bosom by the fireside and went to the well to draw water. No sooner did she remove the stone from its place than the cry reached her ear that the child had moved towards the fire. Rushing to the house, she saved the infant – but she forgot the word of the Druid and omitted to replace the stone. The waters rose and overflowed the vale, and the people escaped to the mountains and filled the air with lamentation, and the rocks echoed back the despairing cry – 'Tha loch 'nis ann, tha loch 'nis ann!' – 'there is a lake now, there is a lake now!' And the lake remained and it is called Loch Nis to this day.'

The Highlands of Scotland were shrouded in the mists of obscurity until the beginning of the Middle Ages, when English troops first occupied the area. Legends abounded and one of these concerned the water horse or kelpie ('Each Uisge' in Gaelic). Its favourite haunts were supposed to be lonely lochs, and the abundance of Highland lochs baptised 'na beiste' indicates the widespread belief in this mythical creature. It was said to be an evil spirit which lured weary travellers to their deaths, and it is undoubtedly this belief and subconscious association with the kelpie that accounts for much of the historical reluctance of the Highlanders to talk about any real experiences with the creatures believed to be inhabiting Loch Ness.

Not until 1933 did the world hear about the Loch Ness 'Monster', and since then there have been regular reports of sightings every year. Before that date there were, by comparison, only a handful. The reason usually put forward for the lack of publicity before 1933 is that the area was remote and isolated and that the construction of an A-class road along the whole northern shore of the loch in 1933 was the spark which sent news of the animals spreading around the world.

This is largely true. And yet the Highlands were populated by many more people in past centuries than they are now. Furthermore, after the construction in the early nineteenth century of the Caledonian Canal, which itself brought hundreds of workers to the loch, the Great Glen became a fashionable area for the Victorian aristocracy, and paddle steamers plied up and down the loch daily. Yet there are comparatively few reports of a large animal being seen, certainly not sufficient for the loch to be associated with strange creatures in the minds of any but the local residents.

If a herd of large animals does exist in Loch Ness, one would expect visitors of past centuries, few in number though they may have been in comparison with the contemporary hordes, to have noticed and reported the

13

fact. Before trying to explain this apparent paradox, here, in chronological order, are some of the pre-twentieth-century reports of Loch Ness animals that have come to light.

The first known record of a 'Monster' in the loch, as all students of the subject know so well, dates from 1,400 years ago. The year was 565, and the witness outstrips any of his modern counterparts in terms of social standing, since he was a saint.

St Columba, the man who brought the Christian religion to Scotland (there is a stone at the lochside village of Abriachan from which it is said he baptised the heathen Picts), was on his way to visit Brude, King of the Northern Picts in Inverness. His biographer, Adamnan, writes in his *Life of St Columba* (Volume 6, Book II, Chapter 27): 'Of the driving away of a certain water monster by the virtue of the prayer of the holy man.'

The saint had arrived on the banks of Loch Ness at a place where there was a ferry coble. (It has been suggested that this was either at the mouth of the River Ness or near Urquhart.) There he found the Picts burying a man who had been bitten to death by a water monster while he was swimming. According to one version of the story, St Columba laid his staff upon the man's chest and brought him back to life. Another version relates that one of the Picts, rather than listen to the saint's sermon, had swum off across the river or loch and was attacked and killed by the monster. When he heard of the man's death, St Columba ordered one of his men to swim across the water and return with the coble moored on the far side. Adamnan continues the story thus:

> On hearing this direction of the holy and famous man, Lugne Mocumin, obeying without delay, throws off all his clothes except his tunic and casts himself into the water. But the monster, perceiving the surface of the water disturbed by the swimmer,

14

suddenly comes up and moving towards the man rushed up with a great roar and open mouth. Then the blessed man, observing this, raised his holy hand . . . invoking the name of God, formed the saving sign of the Cross in the air and commanded the ferocious monster saying, 'Thou shalt go no further nor touch the man; go back with all speed.' Then at the voice of the saint the monster was terrified and fled more quickly than if it had been pulled back with ropes.

St Columba is also credited with another brush with the animals; there is a legend that the beast towed the saint's boat across the loch and was granted the perpetual freedom of the loch as a reward.

The St Columba story is a striking curiosity, and no more. But it is a remarkable coincidence that Adamnan should record that St Columba encountered a 'water monster' in, of all the Scottish lochs, Loch Ness. Perhaps the story became exaggerated during its transmission to Adamnan, who wrote this biography a century after the event is said to have occurred. Perhaps it is an embellished version of a real incident involving a sighting of a large animal in the loch which was designed to demonstrate the power of Christian prayer. All we can do is note the story as an auspicious start to the mystery which was to develop more than a thousand years later.

The source of the next report of a 'Monster' in Loch Ness is a letter dated 17 October 1933 to *The Scotsman* newspaper from a Mr D. Murray Rose. He wrote:

The next reference to the monster of Loch Ness (i.e., after St Columba) appears in an old book dealing with curiosities – such as dragons, dog-devils, the dwarfs of Dalton. It mentions that the monster appeared in the year when Fraser of Glenvackie, after a 'sair tussle', killed a fire-spouting dragon . . . It goes on to say that Fraser killed the last known dragon in Scotland. But 'no one has yet managed to slay the monster of Loch Ness, lately seen'. We have independent reference to Fraser of Glenvackie's fight with the dragon, and the date is known to be about 1520. The 'beast' of Loch Ness was seen twice between 1600 and 1700. Patrick Rose of Rosehall, Demerera, who was born in the district, wrote some notes about his youthful adventures when fox-hunting or after wild-cats in the country above Loch Ness. People told him that in the year when Sir Ewen Cameron of Lochiel had a fight with wildcats on the shores of Loch Ness, a monster was seen in the loch . . . It appeared again in 1771 and people were convinced it was the 'water-kelpie.'

In the mid-seventeenth century, during the eleven years when Great Britain's monarchy was replaced by Oliver Cromwell's Commonwealth, a garrison of English soldiers was stationed in Inverness. Their task was to control the Highlands, and one of the steps taken to improve communications was to transport a ship from Inverness to Loch Ness on wooden rollers. The ship was launched on the loch in about 1655 and for years after that it used to patrol it.

Amongst the men stationed in the Highlands at the time was Richard Franck, a literary trooper in Cromwell's army. He wrote: 'The famous Lough Ness, so much discours'd for the supposed floating island, for here it is, if anywhere in Scotland.'

'The floating island.' Could this reference to unidentified floating objects on the surface of Loch Ness relate to the animals? Franck said that it was merely a mat of vegetation blown across the loch's surface. And yet vegetable mats do not exist on Loch Ness, because there is no vegetation in the water to form them. An interesting corollary to this appears in Blaeu's Atlas, which was published in 1653. It contains the following note against Loch Lomond: 'Waves without wind, fish without fin and a floating island.'

The eighteenth century was a period of great upheaval in Scottish history. The two Jacobite rebellions, in 1715 and

1745, and the subsequent victory of the English at the Battle of Culloden in 1746 led to widespread social and geographical changes throughout the Highlands. The Commander-in-Chief of the English army in Scotland, General Wade, was responsible for the construction of the first proper road along the loch side, from Fort Augustus up into the mountains behind the loch and back down through Foyers, Inverfarigaig and Dores and into Inverness. Work started in 1731, and several hundred soldiers were employed on a task which required considerable engineering skill. The miners who blasted away the terraces had to hang on the end of ropes so that they could bore into the rock and place the explosive charges.

In 1964, a correspondent in New Zealand claimed to have come across a book published in 1769 describing how 'Two Leviathan creatures were sighted upon several occasions in the loch by the road builders. It was thought these may have been one of the whale variety or some huge unknown sea species which had made their way through some subterranean passage and grown too large to return.' Attempts to trace the book from which the passage was taken have been unsuccessful, and so we are unfortunately left with unsubstantiated historical evidence of events which we can only say may have taken place.

Another claim which is similarly unsubstantiated so far has been made by an American writer, Mr John A. Keele. A few years ago he was browsing through the files of *The Atlantic Constitution*, a widely read newspaper on the eastern coast of the U.S.A., when, he claims, he came across a long feature article on the Loch Ness animals in a copy of the newspaper dated some time in the 1890s. At the time he paid little attention to it, since it was not the subject he was researching. Mr Keele writes: 'I did not read the piece in toto since it was a full page illustrated with a drawing very similar to the modern drawings . . . ' Attempts to trace the article have, again, so far been unsuccessful.

As we move nearer to the present day, greater reliance

17

can be placed on the eyewitness accounts, since they are more specific in their details and less uncertain as to their sources. In 1802, Alexander MacDonald, a crofter in the village of Abriachan, told one of the ancestors of Loch Ness' former water bailiff, Alexander Campbell, that he had several times seen a strange animal in the loch. On one occasion he was rescuing a lamb that had fallen down the hill when a creature surfaced and swam to within fifty yards of him. He could see that it had short appendages with which it was propelling itself. Then it turned and proceeded out into the open loch until it submerged with a great commotion at a range of about 500 yards. Mr MacDonald said the animal appeared to be about twenty feet long and reminded him of a salamander. It is said that until he died he often referred to the animal as 'the great salamander.'

This is interesting because right into the early years of the present century, when the ferries used to put into Abriachan pier, the skipper would regularly hail the piermaster by shouting: 'Seen the salamander today, Sandy?'

Mr D. Mackenzie of Balnain wrote in 1934 to Commander Rupert T. Gould, author of *The Loch Ness Monster and Others* (Geoffrey Bles, 1934), the first book written on this subject: 'I saw it in about 1871 or 1872 as near as I can remember now – about 12 o'clock on a grand sunny day, so that it was impossible to be mistaken. It seemed to me to look rather like an upturned boat and went at great speed wriggling and churning up the water. I have told the same story to my friends long before the present Monster became famous.'

Then there is the dramatic story of a diver, Duncan MacDonald, who was sent to examine a sunken ship off the Fort Augustus entrance to the Caledonian Canal in 1880. Soon after MacDonald was lowered into the water the men on the surface received frantic signals from him to be pulled up. When he did surface it is said his face was like chalk and he was trembling violently. It was several days before he would talk about the incident, but eventually he described how he had been examining the keel of the ship when he saw a large animal lying on the shelf of rock on which the wreck was lodged. 'It was a very odd-looking beastie,' he said, 'like a huge frog.' He refused to dive in the loch again.

In 1933 the late Duke of Portland wrote to *The Scotsman* (20 October) and *The Times* (10 November): 'I should like to say that when I became, in 1895, the tenant of the salmon angling in Loch Oich and the River Garry, the forester, the hotelkeeper and the fishing ghillies used often to talk about a horrible great beastie as they called it, which appeared in Loch Ness.'

In the summer of 1896 the animals are reported to have been seen on several occasions by the residents of Fort Augustus. Amongst the witnesses was James Rose, a local shopkeeper, who saw a large hump-like object moving at speed along the loch.

And so the shreds of an historical record of strange animals in Loch Ness do exist, although the details are frequently clouded or lost through the passage of time. The local residents had neither any reason nor any desire to broadcast their superstitions and beliefs about the contents of the 'great water'. Often the borderline between super-stition and objective belief was obscured. The local people knew that the loch contained something – but what was it? Their ignorance about its true nature bred fear. Some, I have been told by an elderly resident, used to believe that the loch contained the devil itself and that the sight of one of its denizens was an evil omen.

Alex Campbell, the retired water bailiff who has himself had many sightings of the animals (as will be described later), was strictly instructed as a boy never to swim in the loch in case the kelpie took him. No wonder, therefore, that in such an atmosphere the local Highlanders displayed their traditional reticence and refrained from talking about what, to the small closely-knit communities, must have been a rather confidential subject and certainly not one to be bandied about amongst the frivolous nineteenth- and early-twentieth-century visitors brought to the area by the Caledonian Canal.

Information about the early sightings emerges only now, in a trickle of hard fact and hearsay conviction. Now that the subject has acquired a certain amount of fame and respectability, and Loch Ness has adjusted to its annual cosmopolitan atmosphere, the witnesses of older generations are more ready to place their experiences on record.

The *Inverness Courier* reported on 6 November 1962 on an outing of pensioners of the Caledonian Canal Authority. Conversation turned to the 'Monster', and under the heading 'Monster sightings recalled', the correspondent wrote:

> As long ago as 1926, Mr Simon Cameron of Invergarry saw it for the first time near Cherry Island, at the Fort Augustus end of the loch. 'It was while I was watching two gulls skimming the loch's surface that my attention was fixed when the gulls suddenly rose screaming into the air,' he said. 'Then before my eyes, something like a large upturned boat rose from the depths and I can still see the water cascading down its sides. Just as suddenly, though, it sank out of sight, but it was an extraordinary experience.' Much older, however, is the experience that Mr Duncan Chisholm of Inverness told of. It goes back to the time of the Battle of Waterloo, when his mother's grand-aunt, Miss Bella MacGruer, at that time living at Markethill, Fort Augustus, warned the youth of the village not to go bathing in Loch Ness where she and others had frequently seen the 'water horse'.

The following two extracts from letters written to *The Scotsman* provide valuable additional information. The first takes us far back into the nineteenth century, and the second gives an insight into the oppressive superstition prevailing at the turn of the century. The first letter is dated 11 September 1950.

The late Dr Galbraith of Dingwall used to tell of how he was visiting on the west coast of this country, and while in a house there, a paper came in with an account of the Loch Ness Monster. With them in the house was a man who had returned home after spending most of his life in New Zealand. This New Zealander quietly said: 'I have seen the Loch Ness Monster.'

As a boy he had gone to help to take a boat from Plockton to Inverness. While they were sailing (there were no engines in those days) through Loch Ness with a steady wind behind them the Monster had suddenly 'heaved up alongside' and it continued on a parallel course for a very short distance.

I once met John MacGillivray from Invergarry at Inverness. I translate our talk about the Monster (we spoke in Gaelic) word for word.

'Did you come from Invergarry today?'

'I did.'

'Did you come by Loch Ness?'

'I did.'

'Did you see the Monster?'

'I did not. How old do you think I am?'

'You are about seventy years old, I imagine.'

'I am eighty-three years old,' he said, and drawing himself up, with a touch of assurance he added, 'and the Monster was in the loch before I was born and that was not yesterday.'

The second correspondent, who signed himself 'H.F.W.', wrote the following on 6 September 1957:

There is no doubt in my mind, and never was, that there was 'something odd' in Loch Ness, as the Fort

21

Augustus Monastery people knew about it and I heard from them during the years of the South African War. It was common knowledge; but people did not like being laughed at and you only heard little bits as you got to know the people.

However, one night I got something to think about. I had been out on the hills after deer at Inchnacardoch with the keeper, and when we got to his house the three children were crying – a sort of hysterical crying. Husband and wife spoke Gaelic and I only had a fair smattering. He told his wife in no uncertain tones that he had warned her time and time again that the children were not to go near Cherry Island in the gloaming. Later in the evening I tried to 'draw' him about it, but beyond saying that no one ever knew what might be in a loch like that, I was left guessing . . . but it was clear that they knew or thought something was in the loch. The odd thing was that no one ever thought of not going fishing in the loch for salmon: and it might have been that they did not wish the visitors to know. I subsequently, after the first war, had a talk with a priest with whom I had been friends for years, and he frankly said that the story had been going around to his knowledge since before the monastery was built.

From these accounts it would appear that the belief in the existence of unknown animals in Loch Ness is as old as the Christian religion in the Highlands of Scotland. The animals have existed in obscurity, roaming the black depths of the loch, occasionally showing themselves and adding a new strand to be woven into the fabric of Highland legend. It is understandable that many of the eyewitness stories have been lost, since the subject was suppressed by the local people for fear of its unpleasant consequences and associations.

The opening up of the Highlands and, in particular, of the Great Glen was a gradual process from the beginning of the nineteenth century. Until just two hundred years ago visitors ventured into the Highlands at their peril. The construction of General Wade's military road has already been mentioned. On the other bank, the northern, which now carries the A82 major route, a track ran along the hilltops from Inverness to Castle Urquhart and from there across the flank of Mealfuarvonie and into Glenmoriston. This was the route taken by the English and Scottish soldiers in the thirteenth century as they fought for control of the Highlands.

Credit for the first step in opening the Great Glen as an attraction to visitors is undoubtedly due to Thomas Telford, the designer and engineer of the Caledonian Canal. The Canal links the three freshwater lochs in the Great Glen (Ness, Oich and Lochy) to form a sixty-mile-long waterway joining the North Sea to the Atlantic Ocean. It took nineteen years to build and was opened in 1822. Its construction raised the level of Loch Ness by about six feet.

Several hundred men were employed on building the Canal and in 1818 over 200 of them were working in Fort Augustus. With so much activity near the loch one would expect there to be some mention of the animals; and in a letter to *The Scotsman* dated 10 September 1957 a Mrs Joan Grieve wrote: 'I would like to say that my grandfather was for some time employed by the company which built the Caledonian Canal. He repeatedly referred to a strange creature living in Loch Ness, having seen it himself. He lived to be a centenarian and died over 60 years ago.' It is not clear whether the writer's grandfather saw the creatures while he was working on the Canal. One can presume that since many of the Canal workers were local men they must have been aware of the stories.

The journey through the lochs on one of the paddle steamers became a fashionable leisure activity for rich visitors to the Highlands. In 1873 Queen Victoria travelled down the Canal and remarked: 'The Caledonian Canal is a very wonderful piece of engineering but travelling on it is very tedious.' In the same year a certain Gordon Cumming, a well-known big-game hunter, regularly made the

23

trip through the Canal accompanied by his servant and long-bearded goat. He was himself quite an attraction – on hot days he often paraded without his kilt. Presumably he was unaware of the greatest of all potential quarries beneath his very feet as the steamers pounded their way along Loch Ness.

The summer at Loch Ness today is a flurry of visitor activity. Cars, coaches and caravans ring the loch with steel and glass; motor cruisers and yachts vie for space on the water. Five miles north-east of the loch is the small city of Inverness, the 'Capital of the Highlands' which each year copes with the tourist invasion with increasing difficulty. From Inverness the traveller to Loch Ness has a choice of either the modern highway, the A82, or a greatly improved version of General Wade's old road. Each leads to one side of the loch and they eventually join again at Fort Augustus at its southern tip.

Between Inverness and Fort Augustus the A82 clings to the loch's side apart from two detours at the villages of Drumnadrochit and Invermoriston. For most of the distance the traveller's view of the water from the road is obscured by bushes and trees which exasperate the many watchful eyes peering anxiously from speeding cars.

Drumnadrochit was a popular resting place for nineteenth-century travellers, and lines in the old visitors' books of the village inn attest to the popularity of the place. In 1860, Shirley Brooks wrote in a letter to *Punch* magazine: 'If there were many places like Drumnadrochit persons would be in fearful danger of forgetting that they ought to be miserable.'

South of Drumnadrochit and its neighbour Lewiston, the road returns to the lochside and runs on – past Strone, 'the nose', where the ancient ruins of Castle Urquhart are perched below the road – past the stone memorial to John Cobb, who died on Loch Ness in 1952 whilst attempting to break the world water speed record in his boat *Crusader* – past Achnahannet, until 1972 the headquarters of the Loch

Ness Investigation Bureau, and on through Forestry Commission pine forests and under the eaves of Mealfuarvonie.

At Invermoriston the road makes another loop through the village. A few miles up Glenmoriston, away from Loch Ness, is Dundreggan, which means the 'Hill of the Dragon'. Here too are 'The Footprints'. These are said to date from 1827 when a travelling preacher tried to conduct a sermon at the spot. A couple of young men started to heckle and throw things at him, at which the preacher is said to have retorted that the ground on which he stood would bear witness to the truth of what he said until the Day of Judgement. Marks in the solid rock, visible today, are said to be his footprints.

It was across these mountains and moors that Bonnie Prince Charlie made his escape after the defeat at Culloden. For a time he lived in a cave near Glenmoriston, protected by the celebrated 'Seven Men of Glenmoriston', who carried on a private guerrilla war against the English Redcoats swarming over the mountains in search of the Prince.

These were desperate times for the Highland people. William Augustus, the Duke of Cumberland, youngest son of King George II, after whom Fort Augustus was named in 1742 (its old name was Kilcumein, meaning the Church of Cumein, one of St Columba's successors), moved his entire army to Fort Augustus and ordered his men to spread out through the glens and show no mercy in suppressing the native population. Houses were destroyed and people murdered in their hundreds. Cattle and sheep were herded together and driven back to Fort Augustus to be sold to dealers from the south. The local people took refuge in the mountains, where many died of hunger and disease. Others left their homes for good and emigrated to America and the other colonies. Those that remained found themselves deprived of their land as clan chiefs rented vast stretches to southern sheep farmers. They were even prevented from wearing their traditional dress, the plaid; an Act of Parliament prohibited it in 1746.

Fort Augustus, the scene of so much brutality and bloodshed two hundred years ago, is now the largest settlement on the shores of Loch Ness. The fort from which the town's new name derived was completed in 1742 by General Wade and played a significant part in the troubles described above. Today the fort is gone: and in its place stands a monastery. The fort was sold in 1876 for £5,000 to Lord Lovat, whose son bequeathed it to the English congregation of Benedictine monks who converted the site.

Northwards from Fort Augustus, General Wade's old route makes a precipitous climb up the mountains to the east of the loch, from the top of which one gains an imposing panoramic view of the town and of the loch stretching into the far distance, before the road plunges away from the lochside across an area of barren Highland landscape. For fourteen miles the route meanders across moorland, dodges tiny lochs and scales hills before dropping down a narrow, perilously winding track to Foyers and the loch again.

The village of Foyers is famous for two things. First the aluminium works, started in 1896 and which at one time produced the greatest quantity of aluminium in the world. The smelting was made possible by the use of hydro-electric power (the first in Great Britain), which in turn was made possible by the River Foyers and the village's second claim to fame, the Falls of Foyers.

The river makes two falls during its thirteen-mile run across the mountains, one of forty feet and the other of ninety feet. The spray rising from the latter has given it the name of 'Eas na-smud' – 'The Fall of Smoke' – and inspired the great Scottish poet Robert Burns to verse:

Among the heathy hills and rugged woods
The foaming Foyers pours his mossy floods,
Till full he dashes on the rocky mounds
Where through a shapeless breach his stream
resounds.

As high in air the bursting torrents flow
As deep recoiling surges down below.
Prone down the rock the whitening sheet descends
And viewless Echo's ear, astonished rends.
Dim seen through rising mist and ceaseless showers
The hoary cavern wide resounding low'rs
Still through the gap the struggling river toils
And still below the horrid cauldron boils.

The aluminium works closed in 1967. After that, extensive work was done on a £10-million hydro-electricity scheme designed to provide power for Inverness. The scheme involved driving a tunnel through the rock from Foyers to Loch Mhor, nearly 600 feet up in the mountains, and sinking the power station into the ground below the surface of Loch Ness. About 500 men were employed on the work and many sightings of the animals were reported by them.

One mile north of Foyers lies the hamlet of Boleskine, recognisable by the tiny graveyard below the road and Boleskine House immediately above it. From 1900 to 1918 this was the home of the infamous Aleister Crowley, the self-styled 'Great Beast' of black magic and 'the wickedest man in the world', according to the tabloid press of the day. It is said that Crowley terrorised the local people and drove several of his servants mad. Nowhere in his writings is there any reference to unknown animals in Loch Ness.

Another mile further north is the village of Inverfarig-aig, a tiny cluster of houses and cottages nestling in a clearing above the loch. Running east from the village is Inverfarigaig Pass, a narrow cleft in the mountains, on one side of which is a granite outcrop known as Black Rock. The summit of this crag bears the remains of a 2,000-year-old vitrified fort called Dunn Dear-dail. This is said to have been the residence of an Irish folk hero called Nysus who was the first person ever to set out by boat and explore Loch Ness, thereby ensuring that the loch would bear a modified version of his own name.

Continuing on our imaginary tour we pass special

clearances on the loch side of the road where brief uninterrupted views of the water can be enjoyed. Elsewhere the undergrowth is thick and the terrain largely inhospitable both below and above the road. Finally we come to the village at Dores, situated on the north-eastern corner of the loch, from where the shore leads around a shallow, sandy beach consisting of the deposits left by the ancient glaciers. Here the whole vista of Loch Ness spreads out before one. The dome-shaped cap of Mealfuarvonie protrudes from the mountain line on the right, and in the distance the water rises to meet the sky. On a calm day the surface resembles a sheet of darkly stained glass, reflecting the mountains and sky and giving a deceptively innocent impression of its plunging depths.

This then is the scene of our mystery: an enormous volume of water situated in a corner of Britain which retains much of the atmosphere of wild remoteness of former ages despite the regular flow of traffic along the arteries on its banks and the yearly influx of visitors.

We have travelled rapidly from the distant past right into our own century and found a history of unknown creatures in Loch Ness throughout. Next we turn to the near past and the events which transformed the intermittent trickle of 'Monster' stories into a raging torrent that overflowed the confines of the Loch Ness district and seized the world's attention in the winter of 1933–34.

In 1773, Dr Samuel Johnson rode along Loch Ness and wrote: 'Natural philosophy is now one of the favourite studies of the Scottish nation and Loch Ness well deserves to be diligently studied.'

Loch Ness has surely lived up the doctor's wish!

Chapter Three

THE 'MONSTER' IS BORN

The 1930s dawned in an atmosphere of grave international depression. In Britain, millions were out of work; so too in the United States, where many had been driven to despair by the collapse of the stock market. And in Germany, a rising politician was beginning to gather support and spread doctrines which were to create the greatest tyranny of the twentieth century and lead the world, once again, into war.

This was the world in which another monster made its newspaper headline debut in 1933. It began as a seven-week-wonder: an intriguing talking point which seemed to be an amusing distraction from the world's other, gloomier stories.

Along the northern shore of Loch Ness the new road was being completed. Vast amounts of rock had been blasted out of the mountainsides and pitched into the water below. Extensive areas of forest and scrubland had been cleared away to allow the road's passage, and unhampered views of the loch surface could now be obtained with ease and in comfort.

It was along this new road on the spring afternoon of 14 April 1933 that Mr and Mrs John Mackay set out for a peaceful drive from Inverness back to their home in Drumnadrochit. As they approached Abriachan Mrs Mackay, who was gazing out across the loch's serene surface, suddenly cried in surprise to her husband; 'Look, John, what's that – out there?'

She pointed to where, in the centre of the loch, the

tranquility had been replaced by a surging mass of water. Mr Mackay jammed on his brakes and for several minutes both of them watched 'an enormous animal rolling and plunging' until it disappeared with a great upsurge of water.

Mr and Mrs Mackay were the owners of the Drumnadrochit Hotel, a fact which will no doubt provoke wry grins among a good many sceptics. However, they never sought publicity for their story and nothing more would have been heard of it had it not come to the attention of Alex Campbell, then a young water bailiff in Fort Augustus and the local correspondent for the *Inverness Courier*. He knew Mr and Mrs Mackay personally and therefore had no hesitation in writing the story up and delivering the copy to the *Courier's* then editor, Dr Evan Barron.

The tale goes that when Dr Barron saw Alex Campbell's report he said 'Well, if it is as big as Campbell says it is we can't just call it a creature; it must be a real monster.' Thus the animals were christened with a title that has stuck ever since. The report of the sighting finally appeared as one of the *Courier's* leading stories in its issue of 2 May 1933, and this is traditionally credited with being the start of the 'Monster' saga.

However, this was not the first occasion on which the local press had reported the sighting of an unidentified animal in Loch Ness. On 27 August 1930 the *Northern Chronicle* had reported how 'Three young men from Inverness, the sons of well-known businessmen, had a curious experience the other evening on Loch Ness.' One of the young men was Ian Milne, later the manager of a gunsmith's shop in Inverness. He described to me what happened:

It was about 7 p.m. on 22 July 1930 when three of us were in a boat fishing off Tor Point near Dores. The loch was very calm, too calm for fishing to be worthwhile in fact, and I was amusing myself trying to see how far I could cast when I heard and saw a

30

commotion about 600 yards up the loch. I saw spray being thrown up into the air to a considerable height . . . it continued until it was about 300 yards away and then whatever was causing it turned southwards in a large half circle and moved away from us. It must have been travelling at about fifteen knots. My estimation of the length of the part of it we saw would be about twenty feet, and it was standing three feet or so out of the water. The wash it created caused our boat to rock violently . . . It was without doubt a living creature and since I spend a good deal of time in contact with wildlife I can say that it was certainly not a basking shark or seal or a school of otters or anything normal.

Under its account of this sighting the *Northern Chronicle* published an appeal for further information on the phenomenon. A week later, on 3 September 1930, it printed several letters from people who described their own or other people's experiences on the loch. One correspondent, an 'Invernessian', wrote that about forty years earlier the skipper and crew of a canal steamer had seen a monster animal or fish while on passage through the loch.

Loch Ness was in the national news in 1932, though not because of any association with unidentified animals of which there was no mention. On Sunday 28 August of that year Mrs Olaf Hambro, wife of a famous London banker, drowned in the loch whilst trying to swim to safety after an explosion on the boat on which she was travelling. The tragedy occurred off Glendoe boathouse, just south of the remote Horseshoe area of the loch's shoreline.

A couple of days later three professional divers were hired to try to recover the body, and it was the activities of these divers which were largely responsible for the alarming stories of vast underwater caverns and treacherous currents. It is said that the divers were hauled to the surface in a state of shock, with their hair suddenly turned white and full of stories about caves like the interiors of great cathedrals. The truth is that the divers went down to about

150 feet, where they found they could see nothing because of the loch's impenetrable gloom. They returned to the surface, shaken and no doubt determined to avoid excessive work in such an eerie atmosphere.

Tracing the development of the 'Monster' story in the summer, autumn and winter of 1933 provides an interesting example of the news media at work. Here was an immediately attractive story coming at a time when the press badly needed relief from the otherwise gloomy news diet. At first the approach was serious, but this soon gave way to facetiousness.

Since 1933 several newspapers have vied with each other for the credit of having discovered 'Nessie'* in the summer of 1933. Although the *Inverness Courier's* report of the Mackay sighting can claim to have been the original catalyst, the publicity was nevertheless slow in gathering momentum. By June the Scottish *Daily Express*, then operating from Glasgow, was carrying regular but rather cautious reports of events at the loch. The following are extracts from some of them.

9 June 1933:

Mystery fish in Scottish loch – Monster reported at Fort Augustus. A monster fish which for years has been somewhat of a mystery in Loch Ness was reported to have been seen yesterday at Fort Augustus.

28 June 1933:

Two men and two women who were boating on Loch Ness had an unpleasant and exciting experience today. The 'monster' rose out of the water about 50 yards from where the boat was drifting. One of the women fainted.

* Nessie is the affectionate nickname bestowed upon the animals by the press in 1933.

12 August 1933:

An effort to photograph the Loch Ness Monster is to be made by Captain Ellisford, a well known amateur photographer. He arrived in Inverness today with a large box of modern photographic material. He will use a telephoto lens.

Evidence that the mystery had not really caught the public eye by the end of the long and very hot summer of 1933 (it was the hottest on record) is afforded by the absence of any reference to the 'Monster' in a report, published on 13 September, by the local Tourist Board stating that the season had been a record one for visitors to the loch.

The excitement really began in October. By this time one of the animals had been seen crossing a lochside road (see Chapter 6), and over twenty accounts of water sightings had been reported since the Mackay sighting. One such occurred at about 11 a.m. on the morning of 22 September 1933, when the Reverend W.E. Hobbes of Wroxeter arrived at the Halfway tea-house near Altsigh (now a Youth Hostel) with his wife and sister-in-law. They walked in and found the room deserted. They called out and a voice from upstairs replied: 'We can't come down yet – we are looking at the Monster.'

The three visitors hurried up the stairs and found three other people, Miss Janet Fraser, Mrs G. Fraser and Miss M. Howden, standing on a balcony watching an object moving in the loch about half a mile away. At the front was a snake-like head and neck which was moving up and down and turning from side to side. Miss Fraser remarked that the head, in profile, was hardly wider than the neck. She thought she could see a large, glittering eye on its near side. The rest of the party all saw two low humps sitting in the water and a tail of indefinite length which splashed on the surface. The animal – for none of the witnesses was in any

33

doubt that they were watching a live object – remained in view for about ten minutes before moving slowly away and sinking.

Distance deterred any attempts at estimating size but for it to have been visible at that range its proportions must have been quite considerable. Mr Hobbes wrote: 'My wife and her sister were naturally excited at beholding this marvellous sight, but the proprietress of the teashop (Miss Fraser) took the matter quite calmly, remarking that she had seen the "Monster" three times before.'

In the second week of October 1933 *The Scotsman* became the first newspaper to send its own correspondent to the loch. The journalist assigned was P.A. Stalker, who was with the Home Fleet at Invergordon when he received a message from the paper's chief reporter, J.W. Herries, to go to Loch Ness and carry out his own investigation. Stalker recalls that the news caused 'more merriment than serious interest' in the wardroom of the destroyer at the time (*The Scotsman*, 16 June 1956). Nevertheless, he journeyed to Loch Ness and there spoke to a number of the people who claimed to have seen one of the animals. 'It didn't take me long to decide that, with one or two probable exceptions, the witnesses were telling the truth,' he reported.

The first of his three long articles appeared in *The Scotsman* on 16 October. London newspapers immediately sent teams of correspondents galloping north. By 18 October the *Daily Mail* and the *Daily Express* had begun their own inquiries, and on 23 October both carried special reports. The *Daily Express* gave theirs the whole of the back page, under the chilling headline 'Loch Ness Monster Hunted in Its Watery Lair.' Percy Cater, the *Daily Mail*'s man-on-the-spot, wrote breathlessly:

In Inverness, the Highland Capital, there is one topic of conversation – 'the beast' as by one accord everybody dubs the uncanny denizen of the loch by this sinister title. Some think the loch harbours a survivor of some prehistoric creature which may have been released from the earth's recesses by the great blasting operations required for the making of the new Inverness-Glasgow motor road.

Radio programmes were interrupted to accommodate the latest news from the loch. Letters began to pour into the offices of the Fishery Board for Scotland suggesting methods of capturing the creature. The Traffic Commissioners granted special permission for an express coach service to be run between Glasgow and Inverness to convey the inquisitive to the lochside. The Caledonian Canal, which had been losing a lot of traffic in recent years, suddenly found itself swamped by people wanting to tour the loch by boat. A special passenger steamer, *Princess Louise*, was laid on to travel between Inverness and Fort Augustus and was an immediate success.

Pleasing as this undoubtedly must have been to the local traders, the loch's sudden popularity was not to everybody's liking. In particular the local kirk complained about 'monster-hunters' breaking the Sabbath. The Rev. Murdo Campbell of Fort Augustus' Free Church complained indignantly:

> One of the most pathetic sights which came under the observation of sane people in these parts within recent months was the presence of a number of people who arrived from the South last Lord's Day with a view to seeing a harmless animal which is supposed to reside in the depths of Loch Ness. It now appears that a wise Providence prevented the animal from gratifying the eyes of these breakers of the Lord's Day. This leads me to say that the word 'monster' is really not applicable to the Loch Ness animal but it is truly applicable to those who deliberately sin against the light of law and revelation. (Scottish *Daily Express*, 2 November 1933)

*

Undaunted, the monster-hunters persisted in their investigations. Parties of boy scouts and ramblers and other diverse collections broke out their box cameras, lit their lochside camp fires, set up their deck-chairs and waited hopefully.

Looking back to the press reports of the almost carnival-like atmosphere of fifty years ago it is hard not to be touched by the earnest optimism of the searchers. For instance, there is a report of a group of forty Glasgow ramblers who spent six hours tramping through rain and mist. 'They then gave up the search, but three of them are to remain at Loch Ness for the next two or three days to see if they can trace any sign of the Monster.'

His Majesty's Goverment became involved when Sir Murdoch Macdonald, M.P. for Inverness-shire, wrote to the Secretary of State for Scotland, Sir Godfrey Collins, on 13 November:

As I have no doubt you are aware, some animal or fish of an unusual kind has found its way into Loch Ness. I think I can say the evidence of its presence can be taken as undoubted. Far too many people have seen something abnormal to question its existence. So far, there has been no indication of its being a harmful animal or fish and until somebody states the genus to which it belongs, I do hope you can authorise the police in the district to prevent pot-hunters deliberately looking for it. I have indeed been asked to bring a Bill into Parliament for its protection. I do not suggest this now because nobody yet knows what the animal or fish really is.

Sir Godfrey replied two days later:

I have been in communication with the Chief Constable of Inverness-shire who has informed me that five constables are stationed at different places on

36

the loch, but that none of them has seen the Monster. The Chief Constable has, however, offered to cause warning to be given to as many of the residents and visitors as possible, for the purpose of preventing any attempt on the animal, if sighted, and I have told him that I shall be glad if he will do so.

This attempt to protect the animals seemed to be justified when Bertram Mills' Circus announced the offer of a £20,000 reward for the live capture of the 'Monster'. They apparently considered that there was a real risk of having to pay the reward, since they took out an insurance policy with Lloyds of London which cost them £80. Their offer was soon followed up by one of £5,000 from the New York Zoological Park and a private offer of £1,000.

However, 'Nessie' was not being taken seriously by everybody. Disparaging snorts were starting to come from the upper tiers of the scientific community.

Professor D.M.S. Watson of University College, London, suggested that the 'Monster' was: 'a large lump of waterlogged peat floating round Loch Ness at the mercy of wind and currents'. Mr P.C. Grimshaw of the Royal Scottish Museum wrote: 'In our opinion the creature will probably turn out to be a young beluga or white whale.' Professor James Ritchie wrote to say that since the Stronsay Sea Serpent of a hundred years ago had turned out to be a decomposed shark, the Loch Ness Monster obviously could not be what it was claimed to be.

Perhaps the classic example of the pawky impotence of the Establishment's sense of inquiry came from the Director of the Aquarium at the London Zoo, Mr E.G. Boulenger. He wrote:

The case of the Monster of Loch Ness is worthy of our consideration if only because it presents a striking example of mass hallucination. For countless centuries a wealth of weird and eerie legend has centred

37

round this great inland waterway . . . Any person with the slightest knowledge of human susceptibility should therefore find no difficulty in understanding how the animal, once being said to have been seen by a few persons, should have shortly after revealed itself to many more . . .

(*Observer,* 29 October 1933)

There is, one must admit, an element of truth in what Mr Boulenger wrote. Auto-suggestion, the preconceived idea brought to life by the desire to see something, does indeed play its part in Loch Ness sightings. However, it is significant that none of those who criticised well-meaning witnesses ever visited the loch to examine either them or the environment at first hand.

One man who did visit the loch was Commander Rupert T. Gould, a prominent member of the BBC's *Brains Trust* radio programme, a man whose insatiable curiosity had made him an authority on subjects as diverse as the identity of the Man in the Iron Mask and Arctic exploration. He arrived at Loch Ness in November and began the research which eventually led him to write *The Loch Ness Monster and Others* (1934), a careful documentation of all the evidence available at that time.

In the absence of a specimen to parade triumphantly under the raised eyebrows of the sceptics, all efforts at the loch were being directed towards obtaining photographic evidence of the animals' existence. It is a humbling thought that the same search is still going on.

The first known photograph which claimed to show one of the animals was taken on 13 November 1933 by Hugh Gray, an employee of the British Aluminium Company at Foyers. Mr Gray was later interviewed by Bailie Hugh MacKenzie, J.P., in Inverness, when he swore the following statement:

Four Sundays ago after church, I went for my usual walk near where the Foyers river enters the loch. The loch was like a mill pond and the sun shining brightly. An object of considerable dimensions rose out of the water not so very far from where I was. I immediately got my camera ready and snapped the object which was then two to three feet above the surface of the water. I did not see any head, for what I took to be the front parts were under the water, but there was considerable movement from what seemed to be the tail, the part furthest from me. The object only appeared for a few minutes then sank out of sight.

Mr Gray had seen and photographed the object from a distance of an estimated 200 yards and from a height of thirty to forty feet above the water. He declined to estimate its size, except that it was 'very great'. The surface of it appeared to be smooth and glistening and to be a dark grey colour. It created a considerable disturbance in the water, which obscured a clear view of it.

Mr Gray took five shots of the object and then went home, where he put the camera and film away. It wasn't until a fortnight later that his brother removed the film and took it to an Inverness chemist for processing. My Gray explained his reluctance to take the film in himself: 'From the brief view I had of the object so far as the photo was concerned I thought nothing would show . . . I might have had it developed long before I did but I was afraid of the chaff which the workmen and others would shower upon me.'

The photograph appeared in the *Daily Record* and *Daily Sketch* on 6 December, accompanied by statements by staff of the Kodak Company that the negative was untouched. Reaction from the scientific community was predictable. As the late F.W. Holiday wrote in his book *The Great Orm of Loch Ness*: 'Like a street musician, zoologists seemed limited to the one tune, and given a heaven sent chance to play at the Carnegie Hall, their limitations became plain.'

J.R. Norman of the British Museum (Natural History) remarked: 'I am afraid that the photo does not bring the mystery any nearer to a solution. It does not appear to me to be the picture of any living thing. My personal opinion is that it shows a rotting tree trunk which rises to the loch surface when gas has generated in its cells.' One wonders where our 'experts' would be without the ubiquitous rotting tree trunk and the decaying mat of vegetation!

With the publication of Hugh Gray's photograph, monster-fever swelled to unprecedented proportions. For the next six weeks not a day passed without some fresh news about the subject in the press. The first film which was claimed to show one of the animals was taken on 12 December by Malcolm Irvine of Scottish Film Productions. He had deployed a small team of cameramen around the loch for two weeks before taking the film himself from the hillside opposite Urquhart Castle. He described what happened: 'We were so excited and elated when the Monster appeared that we had no time to think of the still cameras. What you actually see of the Monster on the screen lasts less than a minute, but it seemed hours when we were taking it. It definitely is something with two humps – that much is clear from the picture.'

The film was shot at a range of about one hundred yards with a cine camera fitted with a three-inch lens. The object, according to Mr Irvine, 'sailed along the surface at nine to ten m.p.h., leaving a trail of foam. We could see two portions of its back.'

By now there were scores of newsmen at the loch from all over the world, falling over each other in desperate attempts to find an exclusive scrap of information. In a review of the events of 1933, the French press decided that the year's only bright spot was the 'discovery' of the 'Monster.' The Austrian government expressed indignation and claimed it was all an ingenious Scottish trick to keep tourists away from Austria. The British Prime Minister, Ramsay MacDonald, was reported to have been so keenly interested in the phenomenon that he planned a special trip to the loch in the hope of catching a glimpse himself. At Loch Ness fishermen complained that salmon had been scarcer than normal; 'Nessie' was naturally blamed.

On the same day that Malcolm Irvine was filming a moving object in the loch, the animals were the topic of a short debate in Parliament. Sir Murdoch Macdonald and William Anstruther-Gray asked the Government what steps they proposed to take to investigate and resolve the matter. Sir Murdoch proposed trawls of the loch; Mr Anstruther-Gray favoured Air Force patrols.

Their suggestions caused temporary amusement and no more. The Government had more pressing problems, and Sir Godfrey Collins declared that he felt the search was a matter for private individuals and for the private enterprise of scientists, 'aided by the zeal of the press and photographers'.

One British newspaper in particular determined to rise to the occasion. The *Daily Mail* announced that it was to engage a famous big-game hunter to track 'Nessie' down. Sadly, and through no fault of the sponsors, it was perhaps this expedition more than anything which was to destroy whatever credibility the animals had established.

M.A. Wetherall, a Fellow of the Royal Geographical Society and the Zoological Society of London, arrived in Inverness with his photographer, Gustave Pauli, and a *Daily Mail* journalist, F.W. Memory, in mid-December. They hired a boat and within a few days of their arrival they stumbled across strange footprints on the loch shore near Dores.

The 21 December edition of the *Mail* carried a large headline: 'Monster of Loch Ness is not a Legend but a Fact.' Mr Wetherall was quoted as saying:

It is a four-fingered beast and it has feet or pads about eight inches across. I should judge it to be a very powerful soft-footed animal about 20 feet long. The spoor I have found clearly shows the undulations of

41

the pads and the outlines of the claws and nails . . . I
am convinced it can breathe like a hippopotamus or
crocodile with just one nostril out of the water.

The spoor I found is only a few hours old, clearly
demonstrating that the animal is in the neighbourhood where I expected to find it.

Mr Wetherall was unwise enough to say that he pledged his
reputation that the spoor was genuine. On 23 December he
broadcast his findings on the BBC. His talk was introduced
as being 'something to freeze your blood' and was preceded (appropriately as it turned out) by a comic newsreel.

Just as thirty-nine years later the BBC television newsroom was to show discretion over the apparent discovery of
a dead 'monster' at Loch Ness on the afternoon before
April Fool's Day, so in 1933 the rest of Fleet Street seemed
to sense something fishy about Mr Wetherall's hoof-prints.

Not even *The Times* could resist taking a swipe at the
affair, and on 22 December it published the following
parody of the *Mail* and the hapless Wetherall:

Owing largely to the encouragement of 'The Times'
an expedition has set out at once for Loch Ness under
the experienced leadership of Admiral Sir Chauncery
Foulenough, the big-game hunter. The expedition
will include speedboats, divers, film companies,
geologists, archaeologists, zoologists, palaeontologists, seaplanes, gillies, expert shots, fishermen, whale
hunters, cheese fanciers, bootboys and Stinkerbelle,
the well known fairy. The aim of the expedition is to
drain the loch, send down divers and then shoot
Wendy from seaplanes. Two geologists were bitten
yesterday, one by a diplodocus, and the other by
Seacale, the Admiral's borzoi.

The London *Evening Standard* began to publish the daily
adventures of their imaginary couple, Messrs Low and
Terry, aboard their trawler *The Finnan Haddock*. 'As you

see, we have fastened an iron ring to the stern of the boat. This we shall put through the creature's nose,' exclaimed Mr Low in one of the first instalments.

Even F.W. Memory, the *Mail*'s man appeared to have misgivings about the find and recorded a conversation with Mr Wetherall in which he pointed out that he had been phenomenally lucky to discover the spoor in only four days. The big-game hunter replied that it was not luck but the triumph of experience, gained after tracking big game over thousands of miles. It is perhaps cruel to point out that Mr Wetherall apparently failed to notice that both the prints had been made with the same foot – a right hind one.

Plaster casts were made with appropriate solemnity and publicity and dispatched to the British Museum (Natural History) for examination. (*The Times* reacted to this by reporting that its expedition had taken a plaster cast of a large ear-mark found on a fern by the roadside!) However, the world had to wait in suspense over the Christmas holiday, and many people tried to satisfy their curiosity by journeying to Loch Ness. The press reported that 'monster-hunting parties' suddenly became fashionable and filled all the local hotels. Inverness was floodlit for the first time in its history, and rail travellers were welcomed at the station by a special display of fairy lights. It was reported that on Boxing Day cars formed an almost continuous line from Inverness down to Fort Augustus and back into Inverness.

On 4 January 1934 the bubble began to show the first signs of its imminent disintegration when the Museum issued its report on the cast, compiled by Dr W.T. Calman, Keeper of Zoology, and M.A.C. Hinton, Deputy Keeper of Zoology. The learned gentlemen reported, somewhat sniffily:

> We are unable to find any significant difference between these impressions and those made by the foot of a hippopotamus. The closest agreement is with

43

the right hind foot of a mounted specimen, probably not quite full grown. By the courtesy of the Superintendent of the Zoological Gardens, it has been possible to take a cast of the impression made by the same foot of a living female.

In the general character this impression also agrees with the Loch Ness footprints, but the impressions left by the fleshy portions of the sole are much fuller and more rounded than in the case of the dried mounted specimen or of the Loch Ness footprints.

The report caused red faces and an embarrassed shuffling of feet in one Fleet Street office and howls of laughter from all their rivals. The prints had, in fact, been made by the stuffed foot of a hippopotamus which was part of an umbrella stand owned by a Loch Ness resident. It is not clear to this day whether Mr Wetherall actually conspired with the young sons of the foot's owner to bring about the hoax or whether he too had been taken in by it.

Although this was not the only hoax perpetrated at the time (others moored barrels in the loch and built makeshift models), it was the one which received the greatest publicity and had the most detrimental effect on the story's credibility. Through that facet of the human mind which retains comedy and humour more easily than hard fact, the hoaxes were remembered and the genuine sightings either forgotten or ignored. Scientists mopped their brows and breathed a 'Just as I thought' sigh and most newspapers adopted a steadily more cynical approach.

To make matters even worse, in the early hours of the morning of 5 January a man claimed he had seen one of the animals bounding across the new motor road (see Chapter 6). This really was too much, even for many sympathetic observers.

For the *Daily Mail* expedition this new development was rather well timed, since it shifted an uncomfortably hot spotlight away from them. Messrs Wetherall and Pauli transferred their attentions to the place where the witness claimed the animal had passed. Strangely, three-toed footmarks, a heap of bones and a dead goat were shortly discovered. What is even stranger is that none of these things had been present when the witness had privately examined the area with members of his family earlier in the morning.

On 15 January Mr Wetherall claimed he saw one of the animals himself from the deck of the motor cruiser *Penguin*, chartered by the expedition. Unfortunately, everybody else on the boat happened to be looking in the other direction at the time. However, what he saw convinced him that Loch Ness contained a large grey seal and nothing more. The *Daily Mail* reported this as its conclusion and the expedition slipped quietly away. The following year Mr Wetherall resigned his Fellowship of the Royal Geographical Society.

The story was beginning to die the death of all those that receive an excess of sudden publicity and which then do not live up to expectations. So far, despite the efforts of the world's press and many hundreds of enthusiastic visitors, all that existed was a very hazy still photograph and a few seconds of cine film showing a water disturbance. Hardly a very convincing performance by a 'Monster' with such a devoted public.

Hoax or no hoax, Loch Ness had now been established as the home of a 'Monster'. It is frequently suggested that the whole thing was an invention by the local Tourist Board. Ironically it was an hotel-owner, as we have seen, who sparked it off and began the modern phase of the saga. However, although local businessmen were quick to cash in on the mystery there are simply no grounds for suggesting that they created it in the first place.

In February 1934, Inverness Town Council reduced its grant to the Highlands Advertising Board by one third because they considered the 'Monster' in itself to be sufficient publicity for the region. A.F. MacKenzie, the Board's secretary, said: 'The district is hoping for a £10,000 summer season. It all depends on the Monster.' It appears they were not disappointed. At Easter the Royal Automobile Club reported that Loch Ness had outstripped the West Country in the number of requests for travel information and had become the most popular destination for motorists in Britain.

A new industry in souvenirs was created. Among the collection of Monster pincushions, tea-cosies and chocolate effigies was 'Sandy, the Loch Ness Monster – in three sizes – covered in green embossed velveteen and filled with Java kapok'. In London a famous restaurant served 'Le filet de sole Loch Ness'. In Massachusetts and Connecticut a new fashion in women's clothes was inspired by the animals. It was an ensemble called simply 'Loch Ness', consisting of a 'slender dark green wool frock with a hip length jacket of the same fabric with long front tails furred in grey fox.'

Of all the evidence which has accumulated over the past forty years there is one photograph that has attracted more publicity than any other. It has become known simply as 'the Surgeon's Photograph'.

The man who took the series of pictures which includes the famous photograph was Lieutenant Colonel Robert Kenneth Wilson, M.A., M.B., Ch.B.Camb., F.R.C.S., a gynaecologist who, when he took the photographs in April 1934, was practising in Queen Anne Street, just off Harley Street, London.

After the Second World War, during which he served in the Royal Artillery, Colonel Wilson and his family moved abroad and eventually settled in Australia, where he died in 1969.

His contribution to the saga was (unintentionally) great but for professional reasons he always shunned all connection with it.

Because of this desire to avoid publicity, the circumstances of the taking of the photographs have never been entirely clear. However, by piecing together original letters from Colonel Wilson, information from his wife, and contemporary press accounts, it is possible to describe the events surrounding the photography.

Colonel Wilson and a Maurice Chambers of Thornbury were the lessees of a wild-fowl shoot on the north shore of the Beauly Firth close to Inverness. Having a few days' leave in the spring of 1934, Colonel Wilson and a friend decided to travel north to visit the shoot and take some photographs of wild fowl and trains. Accordingly, he borrowed a quarter-plate camera fitted with a telephoto lens.

On the day in question, 19 April, they were driving northwards along the new motor road above Loch Ness. At about 7 or 7.30 a.m., Colonel Wilson stopped the car about two miles north of Invermoriston on a small promontory, well studded with trees and about 100 feet above water level, next to a small stream. Colonel Wilson continues in a letter:

> I had got over the dyke and was standing a few yards down the slope and looking towards the loch when I noticed a considerable commotion on the surface some distance out from the shore, perhaps two or three hundred yards out. I watched it for perhaps a minute or so and saw something break the surface. My friend shouted: 'My God, it's the Monster!'
>
> I ran the few yards to the car and got the camera and then went down and along the steep bank for about fifty yards to where my friend was and got the camera focused on something which was moving through the water. I could not say what this object was as I was far too busy managing the camera in my amateurish way.

Colonel Wilson made four exposures in a space of about two minutes, by which time the object had completely disappeared. 'I had no idea at the time whether I had got anything on the plates or not. I only thought I might have,' he said.

As soon as they arrived in Inverness, Colonel Wilson

took the four plates to Ogston's, a local chemist, where he gave them to George Morrison to be developed. As he handed them in Colonel Wilson asked for particular care to be taken with them, at which Mr Morrison remarked: 'You haven't got the Loch Ness Monster, have you?' Colonel Wilson replied that he thought he might have. The plates were ready the same day. The first two were blank; the third, the famous one, showed what appeared to be an animal's upraised head and neck, and the last one showed the head disappearing into the water. On Mr Morrison's advice, Colonel Wilson sold the copyright of the best photograph to the *Daily Mail*, which published it on 21 April 1934, thereby challenging the evasive ingenuity of the scientific community yet again.

Colonel Wilson refused to enlarge upon the bare facts of his story and would not try to estimate the size of the object. In fact, he never claimed that he had photographed the 'Monster', all he ever said was that he photographed an object moving in the waters of Loch Ness. He wrote: 'I am not able to describe what I saw. As I finished, the object moved a little and submerged.' However, his friend saw the animal clearly and described it in terms very similar to the appearances on the photographs.

The detached and objective approach of Colonel Wilson is interesting. He made no wild claims and, as one would expect from a professional medical man of standing, he merely reported what had happened as far as his recollection would allow him. Having done that he wished to have no part in the affair.

The general climate of zoological opinion was of bewildered bafflement. Dr Calman of the Natural History Museum said he could not hazard a guess as to what the object was. Others fell back on the 'tree root' theory.

The well-known photograph shows the characteristic long, graceful neck and small head, behind which is what may be part of the body just breaking the surface. For this new edition I have located – in the files of the *Illustrated London News* – a copy of the original print, showing what I believe is the entire negative area. The far shore is visible in the background. We get a much better idea of scale: the facts would appear to be as Colonel Wilson described them.

The second photograph, which is taken from a print which George Morrison kept from the original negative, shows the top of the neck and the head just before it submerged. Despite the hazy outline, one can clearly see the similarity between the two. The second picture proves that the object is not, as one scientist has continually suggested, the tail of an otter in the act of diving. If it had been, there would obviously have been no time for the photographer to have changed plates and taken a second photograph.

These are most valuable pictures. They have been rigorously scrutinised for any evidence of faking and no flaws have ever been found in them.

Three months after Colonel Wilson took his photographs the first serious investigation of any size to resolve the mystery was launched. Its sponsor was Sir Edward Mountain, Chairman of the Eagle Star and British Dominions Insurance Company. He had taken Beaufort Castle near Beauly for the summer of 1934 and was soon attracted by the events at Loch Ness. Being an enterprising businessman with a healthy curiosity he decided to finance a photographic expedition to the loch.

With the help of his firm's publicity manager and Captain James Fraser of Inverness, who was placed in overall charge of the expedition, twenty unemployed men were signed up from the Inverness labour exchange. On their insurance cards they all entered their occupations as 'Watchers for the Monster', which was duly registered by the Department of Health.

Each man was supplied with a pair of binoculars and a Kodak box camera. They were paid £2 a week, with a bonus of ten guineas for anyone who took a successful photograph. Two coaches were hired which, for the five weeks from 13 July, brought the men out from Inverness at

8 o'clock every morning. Fourteen men were positioned along the northern shore and six along the southern. They watched from their stations each day until 6 p.m., when they were taken back into Inverness to report to the press waiting at the Eagle Star offices.

During the course of the expedition a total of eleven reasonably clear sightings were made and several photographs were taken. One of the best sightings was made by Mr P. Grant at about 10.45 a.m. on 12 August from Abriachan Pier. In his daily report he wrote:

> I saw the object appear in the water about 120 yards from the shore. I had no glasses or camera but was able to make out clearly the monster's head which appeared to be like that of a goat. On top of the head were two stumps resembling a sheep's horns broken off. The neck was about 40 inches long and where neck and body met appeared considerable swelling which resembled a fowl with a full crop. The colour of the body was between nigger and dark brown and appeared to be lighter underneath. The skin appeared to be smooth, the markings were like that of a lizard. The animal appeared to have flippers on the fore part of the body and these were extended straight forward and were not being used. The eyes appeared to be mere slits like the eye of a darning needle. I watched the creature for about five minutes then it submerged. It was moving at a speed of about 8 m.p.h., and there was no wash or commotion in the water, but after it had disappeared air bubbles appeared at the front and the rear. Length of the body was 20ft.

Of the five photographs taken which showed anything, four show water disturbances which can clearly be attributed to passing boats. The fifth shows an isolated dark object with what appears to be spray being thrown up on one side of it. The picture quality is poor and the object is hazy, but it does at least suggest the presence of something large in the water.

The greatest success of the expedition was achieved by Captain Fraser himself. After five weeks the watchers were laid off and Captain Fraser, the first true 'Monster hunter', and one assistant kept up the watch. At about 7.15 a.m. on the morning of 15 September, Captain Fraser took up his position below the road above and just north of Urquhart Castle. This, in his own words, is what happened:

I was looking northwards when I noticed something in the water about three quarters of a mile away, just out of Urquhart Bay. I could not recollect a rock being there so raised my binoculars and studied it. There was a slight heat haze which did not make things very clear but I could see a dark object in the water. The only thing I could describe it as being like is an upturned, flat-bottomed boat. It must have been about 15 feet long and was dark in colour.

I thought I might as well shoot some film so put the cine camera to my eye, pressed the button and fortunately it started to operate. I filmed it for about two minutes and then something came up out of the water, there was a spume of spray and it disappeared.

The film was packed and dispatched to London by train, where members of the Kodak staff met it and developed it. The camera Captain Fraser had used was a 16mm Kodak cine with a six-inch telephoto lens. The film was soon viewed by zoologists who by now had apparently decided that strength would lie in unity since, with very few exceptions and for no apparent scientific reason, they stated that the object was a seal.

At a meeting of the Linnaean Society in London the seal theory was expounded with greater confidence, although one member suggested that it might be an otter. Commander Gould, who spoke at the meeting, repeated a remark

51

made to him during his own field inquiries that London scientists seemed to think that Highlanders were all half-witted and did not know a seal when they saw one. Actually, of course, many of them saw more seals in a month than most Londoners do in their whole lives. Sir Edward Mountain wrote after the meeting: 'The scientists would have been much wiser to say that they did not know what it was. To say, as some did, that it was a seal and that the head and neck (if seen!) belonged to something else was to say the least, a pity.'

Meanwhile, as the men of learning in London winced, Captain Fraser was continuing his vigil. When I met him by the lochside in the summer of 1973 he recounted some of the experiences of his watch, many of which are indicative of the general atmosphere and attitude to the mystery back in 1934. Among his many recollections he described how, at one time, there were nearly 200 cars drawn up on the road behind him, their occupants lined up, straining their eyes and following his every movement. 'I would turn to the right and they would all turn to the right. I would point to something and near pandemonium would break out – it was the funniest thing you could imagine!'

He went on to describe how one day two large cars drew up and a group of people descended into the field to meet him. Among them was an alderman from a large English city.

He asked me when it was going to come up and I replied: 'Any moment now.' He looked at his watch and said that they would wait for an hour. After the hour had passed and nothing had appeared he came up to me greatly agitated and said: 'You know I could have you imprisoned for getting people here under false pretences.'

Well, of course, at first I thought he must be joking, but he wasn't – he was deadly serious. I told him he didn't have to come and he became very indignant and stormed off.

52

I asked Captain Fraser whether he suffered much ridicule. He replied that he did, particularly from British visitors. 'They just looked upon it as the biggest joke of the century. There was far greater interest from foreigners, particularly Americans.' Two of his visitors, he recalled, had come all the way from Australia just to spend a few days at Loch Ness. 'On another occasion I met an American with a copy of a New York newspaper. In England at the time the big news was the launching of the *Queen Mary*. This was pictured in the American paper but, in comparison, there were four pages devoted to "Latest Loch Ness Monster Sightings".'

One person interested in the expedition was King George V. He twice made inquiries about the progress of Sir Edward's team, and members of the Royal Family visited the loch on several occasions.

At about this time a Paris newspaper reported that the 'Monster' was really a German airship which had fallen into the loch during the last war. (Four years later a party of Germans were to claim that they had captured the 'Monster' and spirited it secretly out of the country and that it was on display in Bavaria.) Mr John Young, a seventy-year-old gravedigger from Lewiston, used a telephone for the first time in his life in June 1934 to tell the press that he had seen one of the creatures. 'I always thought it was a bit of a joke, but now I am convinced that it is true,' he said. 'I was walking along the road beside Urquhart Castle when the beast came up. It had a long neck and a small head. It was very big.'

In November 1935 'Nessie' was blamed for giving Inverness a name for bad drinking habits. Ex-Provost Petrie said: 'The town has a bad reputation for strong drink, not through any fault of ours, but through the Loch Ness Monster, because any time it is alleged to have been seen people attribute it to strong drink!' In May 1934 a London opera correspondent reported in disgust about 'an audible murmur in the Covent Garden auditorium when the dragon came on to be slain in *Siegfried* last night. First of all, people began to whisper what sounded like "Loch Ness Monster", followed by disapproving sounds.' Later the same year a motion picture entitled *The Secret of the Loch* was shot on location starring Seymour Hicks.

Commander Rupert Gould's book, published in the summer of 1934, enjoyed a mixed reception. Among the more hostile critics some tried to cast doubts on his sanity and integrity. Dr W.T. Calman wrote in the *Spectator*:

> There is no need to question that all of them (fifty-eight witnesses who reported sightings between May 1933 and May 1934) saw something unusual in the familiar surroundings of the loch; but there is a possibility that neither they nor Commander Gould fully realise how easily and inevitably recollections of things seen become tinged and distorted by previous and even by subsequent impressions.

It is only fair to note that Commander Gould embarked on his inquiries fully aware of the shortcomings of the human power of recollection and with no anticipation that they 'would lead to any surprising conclusions.'

By the end of 1934 the mystery had more or less exhausted its potential as a subject for prolonged media coverage, although its visitor-pulling power was undiminished. Sightings continued, but unless they were of exceptional interest they would usually be ignored by all but the local press.

In August 1938 a private party of twenty adventurers announced that they were to set off to Loch Ness to kill and capture the 'Monster' with harpoons, guns, speedboats and nets. Fortunately their plans were dropped when the local police and the Fishery Board stepped in. This provoked a fresh demand for official legal protection for the animals. The case of Pelorus Jack, a huge grampus which for many years around the turn of the century used to pilot ships through Cook Strait, New Zealand, was quoted as a precedent; he had been protected by an Order in Council of the New Zealand Government. The British Government, however, refused to show similar sentiment, and no law or official order was passed. Nevertheless, the animals were not entirely ignored by the courts. During a case on whale oil in the Court of Appeal in 1938, when one of the judges was trying to discover whether whales are to be found in the Arctic, his colleague Lord Justice Greer offered the helpful advice 'You might find one in Loch Ness!'

The year 1938 also saw the attempted launching of another serious expedition. Captain D.J. Munro, R.N., proposed establishing a company, 'Loch Ness Monster Ltd', with blocks of one-shilling shares. He estimated it needed £1,500 to finance the scheme, which involved setting up three fixed camera stations on the loch shore, each manned by 'One naval officer in charge of trained observers. One marine (private) or blue-jacket and two others.' Captain Munro stated: 'No dividend can be expected. At the same time if good shots are obtained by the cameras the results may be most valuable.' Sadly the scheme never materialised, since only £90 was forthcoming. It was to be a quarter of a century before a similar scheme was operated at Loch Ness.

A few more photographs and films were taken in the years before the war. On 10 June 1934 a group of Morayshire holidaymakers had a sighting near Fort Augustus, and a photograph was taken showing a long, dark object on the surface. The woman who took the picture said:

We were always doubtful about the truth of any Monster existing in Loch Ness, but now I have no doubt that there is some living thing in the Loch which scientists have not yet been able to explain. I happened to gaze across the loch and I was amazed to see an object slowly come to the surface. It made very little commotion.

I cried: 'Look, it's the Monster,' and took a snap with my little camera. Then it swam for a few yards and disappeared. It was black, about 15 to 18 feet long and 200 yards or so away.

Mr Malcolm Irvine took another film on 22 September 1936 which he said showed one of the animals. He had been carrying on an intermittent search after taking his first film in December 1933, and although he had had several more brief sightings he had not had an opportunity to take any more film until he saw an unidentifiable object coming across the loch from Foyers. Describing the film he said: 'It shows the head and neck parallel with the surface and rising and falling with the movement of the huge body. The humps are also seen rising and falling gently as the flippers move beneath them. It was over 30ft long and almost black in colour.'

After seeing the film, Eric Foxon, a Fellow of the Linnaean Society which had displayed no enthusiasm for the subject two years earlier when shown Captain Fraser's film, said: 'The animal does not fall into any known category. The doubts of the sceptics are shattered. Henceforward everyone will require to admit that there is something in Loch Ness.'

His remark fell on deaf ears. The press and the Establishment had become rather indifferent to the 'Monster' and were unwilling to risk further contact with it. They were all rather more inclined towards the view of Mr Boulenger of the London Zoo Aquarium: 'The whole business is a stunt foisted on a credulous public and only excused by a certain element of low comedy' (*Observer*, 1 July 1934)

The world was now having to focus its attention on that other monster who had shared the headlines with Nessie in 1933. The people of Europe began to prepare themselves for the coming conflict and, as troops replaced tourists on the shores of Loch Ness, the trivialities of 'monster-hunting' were forgotten.

Chapter Four

'LOOK – THE LOCH NESS MONSTER!'

In countries throughout the world the verbal testimony of a witness is fundamental to the judicial procedure. There are several thousand people who believe they have seen an unknown animal in Loch Ness. Whatever proportion of these reports one can explain away in terms of dishonesty and genuine misinterpretation, there has always remained a substantial quantity, possibly only 15 to 20 per cent, which simply defy attempts to dismiss them in terms of known animals and objects, hoaxes or fraudulent witnesses.

It seems a puzzling reflection on our capacity to be fair and logical that the testimony of so many reliable witnesses, often offered under oath, should for so long have been considered inadmissible as proof that there is something unknown in Loch Ness. The puzzle approaches absurdity when one studies the quality of many of the reports and the qualifications of the witnesses. Included in this chapter are the accounts of monks, lawyers, the sister-in-law of a British Prime Minister, a Nobel Prize winner, a Knight Commander, a Count, policemen, professional men of repute and many people experienced in loch observation. And this chapter represents only a tiny fraction of the total eyewitness evidence available.

It is, of course, right that the standards of scientific acceptance should be most stringent, but equally they must surely be sufficiently flexible to give way when overwhelming pressure is placed on them. The reaction of the scientific community to the Loch Ness phenomenon has been sadly reminiscent of a remark made by Dr James Ritchie, Keeper of the Royal Scottish Museum's Natural

History Department, who, on hearing that an unusual carcase had been washed up at Stronsay in 1808, said: 'There is no need to depend on the obscure descriptions of the house painters and crofters of Orkney which set the scientific world a-jingling.'

Alex Campbell has already been mentioned in connection with his report of the Mackay sighting for the *Inverness Courier* in April 1933. During a lifetime spent in contact with Loch Ness, including forty-seven years as one of its water bailiffs, Mr Campbell encountered Nessie himself on a number of occasions. On 16 July 1958 he saw *two* animals near Borlum Bay. One large black hump was heading diagonally towards the far side of the loch, churning the surface around it, while the other black hump was lying comparatively quietly near St Benedict's Abbey.

A couple of years previously Mr Campbell came into uncomfortably close contact with a solid object in the loch. He described to me what happened:

It was a beautiful summer day in 1955 or 1956. I was out rowing my boat in the middle of the loch opposite the Horseshoe. Without any warning the boat started to heave underneath me. It was terrifying. My dog was with me in the boat – an Airedale terrier – and he leapt from where he was in the stern sheets to lie crouching and shivering under my seat. I was really scared – honest to goodness I was. It is the only time I have ever felt frightened on this loch in my whole life. I can't explain it – the boat just seemed to rise and then stagger back almost immediately. Believe me, I put my back into the oars to get away from the spot – I didn't even dare move to the stern to start the motor.

The reaction of fear on the part of the dog is interesting. Mr Campbell came across a similar animal display one day just before the last war when he visited a family of gypsies camped by the lochside near Point Clair. Earlier in the morning, he was told, the father of the family had been woken by the restlessness of a pony tethered nearby. He got up and was trying to quieten it when he looked out over the water and saw the cause of the animal's excitement. About forty yards from the shore was a creature with 'a huge black, swanlike neck raising and dipping into the water as it cruised slowly around.' Although it was several hours after the incident, Mr Campbell said the father was still visibly shaken by it.

On 17 June 1934 a group of members of the Inverness Scientific Society and Field Club saw one of the animals in mid-loch from near Abriachan. Amongst them were the ex-Provost of Inverness, David Petrie, Colonel E.G. Henderson, a member of Inverness Town Council, and Mr George MacBean, Registrar for the Burgh of Inverness. The coach in which they were travelling was pulled up when a big black object was noticed out in the water. At first they thought it might be a piece of debris, but this theory had to be discarded when they realised it was travelling against the wind and waves. Ex-Provost Petrie later said 'It appeared to be a huge living creature.'

The animals seemed to favour people in authority in 1934, for on 8 August Inverness-shire's Member of Parliament, Sir Murdoch Macdonald, K.C.M.G. (a distinguished engineer who was a consultant in the construction of the Aswan Dam), saw one of them:

> I set out with my son early from Inverness as I had an appointment with the Secretary of State in Portree at 10 a.m. There was not a ripple on the water. Between 6 a.m. and 7 a.m., as we reached a high point on the road about four miles short of Invermoriston, I saw something on the loch . . . we stopped and looked.
>
> What we saw were two hummocks about equal in length and separated by a space equal to this length,

the whole occupying about 15 feet, I should estimate. At first the creature was almost still but after a moment or two my son pointed out that it had a slow motion towards Fort Augustus. It caused no ripple and moved along about 100 yards in five minutes. We drove on until we were abreast of it; at this point a trailer was drawn up beside the road. We got out of the car and I banged on the door.

A man, a Yorkshireman judging by his accent, came out partly dressed and wondered what we wanted.

I said, 'Do you see that log on the water?' He turned round, hesitated, then threw up his arms in the greatest excitement, exclaiming, 'By Jove, the Monster!'

He then got out a small pair of binoculars. The colour of the animal was blackish grey and it was obviously not a tree-trunk or a boat. We saw no head nor tail. As a result of all this I was half an hour late for my appointment. Sir Godfrey said, 'Well, that's as good an excuse as any other.'

Going back a few months, we find that on 26 May 1934 Brother Richard Horan of St Benedict's Abbey, Fort Augustus, had a very clear sighting. He was working near the Abbey boathouse when he heard a noise in the water. At first he did not bother to look up, but when he did so a few moments later he found one of the animals looking at him from a distance of about thirty yards. A graceful neck with a broad white stripe down its front stood about three and a half feet high at an angle of forty-five degrees to the water. He could not see any features on the head, although its muzzle appeared to be rather blunt and similar to a seal's. It moved about slowly until it found a rowing boat in its path, at which point it stopped momentarily and then swung round, causing a commotion in the water. Finally it plunged below the surface, and a mark similar to a torpedo track continued for a distance up the loch.

This sighting was independently corroborated by three other people watching from a different position.

A somewhat similar sighting was reported on 22 December 1935 by a Miss Rena MacKenzie of Invermoriston:

It was about 3 p.m. when I saw it. Suddenly its head and neck rose from the calm surface of the loch and moved along quite near the shore. The head was small in comparison to the length and thickness of the creature's neck. What struck me most was that the under part of the neck was perfectly white. After about five minutes a passing steamer sounded its siren and the creature, after turning its head in an agitated manner, plunged out of sight.

The possibility of witness error or dishonesty and the hoary old 'mass hallucination' theory can surely be ruled out when a large group of unconnected people all testify to a sighting of one of the animals. This happened on the afternoon of 28 October 1936, when nearly fifty people from different cars and buses and from all walks of life stood on the roadside a mile and a half south of Urquhart Castle and watched a head, neck and two-hump display by one of the animals for nearly a quarter of an hour. The first person to see the animal was Duncan MacMillan, from the door of his cottage situated above the road at Lennie. He saw a head and neck rise out of the water about 500 yards out in the loch, which was quite calm. Visibility was excellent and despite the distance Mr MacMillan had a clear view of the slowly moving object. He called to his wife, who joined him together with three visitors, his father and his wife's sister. As they stood and watched, two cars pulled up, followed by two coachloads of people and the local A.A. patrolman.

Mrs MacMillan described what then happened: 'Slowly the monster moved along with its head and neck clearly visible. The head was small and appeared to be greyish in colour. Then two distinct humps appeared, one of them fairly close to the head and the other some distance behind.'

A number of travellers had telescopes and binoculars, and one witness described something to the rear of the second hump, just below the surface. This appeared to be moving from side to side and propelling the body. A few snapshots were taken but evidently with little success in view of the distance. However, nobody doubted that they were watching a large, living animal.

The following report is most unusual, since apart from enjoying a very clear view of one of the animals the witness also observed the creature apparently feeding. The report is taken from the 1 July 1938 issue of the *Inverness Courier*, a newspaper which has a consistent record for accurate reporting of sightings:

On Tuesday night Mr John MacLean, who belongs to Glen-Urquhart, saw the Loch Ness Monster from near the Halfway House Hotel, Invermoriston. Mr MacLean, who was standing at the shore near the mouth of the Altsigh Burn, watching to see whether any trout were rising, as he was contemplating fishing, said in an interview: 'In a moment I saw an extraordinary sight. It was the monster's head and neck less than twenty yards from me and it was without any doubt in the act of swallowing food. It opened and closed its mouth several times quickly and then kept tossing its head backwards in exactly the same manner as a cormorant does after it has devoured a fish.' What the monster had eaten Mr MacLean could not say, but at that particular spot the water teems with excellent trout.

But more interesting things were to follow. No sooner had the creature finished its meal than it dived below. Before it did so, however, two distinct humps and the entire length of the tail came to the surface. The animal then vanished head first but came up again a few yards further west, and there it lay for two to three minutes on top of the water, the tail again quite clear on the surface and both head and neck as well as two humps showing. In a moment or two it began to dive very slowly, and in doing so the head was submerged first, followed by the humps; but at this point the foremost hump became much larger and rose, in fact, almost twice as high out of the water as it had been at any time during its appearance. Summing up his description of the creature Mr MacLean said:

> I was petrified with astonishment, and if I had had a camera with me I was so excited that I would probably have spoiled the chance of a lifetime. The monster, I am sure, is eighteen to twenty feet long, the tail fully six feet, and the largest hump was about three feet high. The head is small and pointed, the skin very dark brown on the back and like that of a horse when wet and glistening. The neck is rather thin and several feet long, but I saw no flippers or fins.

Miss Janet Fraser, who ran the Halfway House Hotel, confirmed that when Mr MacLean returned to the house immediately after the episode he appeared almost too overcome to tell her what had happened.

Sceptics frequently point to the shortcomings of the average person's ability to observe and report accurately as one of the main reasons for what, to them, is a misconceived belief that a living animal is responsible for the sightings. They rightly point out that virtually no two witnesses to a crime or an accident will ever describe exactly the same facts. And yet it is these very discrepancies in points of detail which give weight and substance to the reports. However, when it comes to Loch Ness sightings discrepancies are often taken as a sign of weakness and even of fraudulence. It is natural that different witnesses should report things in different ways and notice their own unique features. The discrepancies between eyewitness accounts show that people do not just imitate what others have reported in the past.

However feeble most of us may be at judging distance, size and speed, and at knowing the difference between an oildrum and a 'monster', there are those who are trained to observe. One such group is the Royal Observer Corps, and during the Second World War members of the R.O.C. were stationed around Loch Ness. It is said that several members saw the animals but were forbidden to report the fact because of military discipline.

One member, however, did make his sighting known to a close friend. At 5.15 a.m. on 25 May 1943, Mr C.B. Farrel, while on duty at Fort Augustus, saw an unidentified object on the loch. When he looked through his binoculars (Zeiss x 6) he saw a creature twenty-five to thirty feet long about 250 yards away. In colour it appeared to be dark olive brown on top and lighter underneath. Its eyes seemed to be large, and the neck was described as being graceful and four to five feet in length. It was evidently feeding, since it kept depressing its head and neck until they were submerged and then it would quickly withdraw them from the water and shake its head vigorously. In the end the whole body slid out of sight without causing any disturbance.

The Deputy Lord Lieutenant of Inverness-shire is Mr William Mackay, D.L., O.B.E., F.S.A. He is also the Chieftain of the Glen Urquhart Games and used to be Dean of the Faculty of Lawyers in Inverness. Throughout his life he has led an active outdoor existence, which has included two sightings of the animals. At his home in the beautiful Strath Glass, near Loch Ness, he gave me this account:

The first time I saw the so-called Loch Ness Monster was in 1937. I was driving some boys back from Fort Augustus after a cricket match, and between Temple Pier and Abriachan ' said in fun: 'Ten shillings to the boy who sees the Monster first.' A few minutes later we came round a corner and all the boys suddenly shouted at once: 'The Monster.' And there it was – two dark humps about three feet high, stationary in the water. We all got out and another three or four cars stopped too. Unfortunately I had to hurry on into Inverness but some of the boys in another car who remained saw it put up a long neck with a small head.

The next time Mr Mackay saw it, he told me, was just before the end of the last war. He was driving home from Foyers one evening when, about six hundred yards away across the loch opposite Urquhart Bay, he saw the same two humps again. He went on:

Fortunately this time I had my deerstalking tele-scope with me and so I stopped and examined the 'monster' through my glass. It appeared to be about thirty feet long in all, with a long neck which it kept flat on the water. There were two humps which were dark elephant grey in colour. It looked as though there was hair over its back and body. The wind was from the west and the beast seemed to be trying to keep its head on to the wind, because every now and then I saw splashes and a long tail appeared to be sculling and two flippers to be paddling to change its position. Before I left, a Mr Deans, a plumber, drove up and told me that he too had been watching the animal.

A sighting which was to be of some significance was made on 4 April 1947. The witnesses were J.W. McKillop, C.B.E., County Clerk of Inverness-shire, his son Norman McKillop, an Edinburgh architect, an English friend,

65

Kenneth Cottier, and John C. Mackay, chief reporter on the *Inverness Courier*. J.W. McKillop gave his account of what happened:

We had left Inverness by motor car to go to Oban. After less than twenty minutes' driving, when we were about a mile north of Drumnadrochit, I saw a long wake on the water. I stopped the car and all the party rushed to the side of the loch and watched the wake growing larger. I then observed a very large moving object at the head of what I thought was foam. It was travelling at a very high speed and one of the party thought it might be a motorboat, but that idea was soon dispelled, for there was no sound at all. The large leading object continued to move quickly. I watched it very carefully for four or five minutes and my only regret was that I had not taken my binoculars with me. Only the head and part of a black body were visible and the rest apparently was covered by the water.

I had no doubt that there was something abnormal in the loch and that it must be the monster or some unusually big living object which was making one of its rare appearances. Soon the head disappeared, but the trail was visible for some time before it too disappeared.

When Mr Cottier was interviewed this was the account he gave:

I had heard much about the Loch Ness Monster and was delighted to learn that our motor journey was by way of Loch Ness, all the more because it was a bright and sunny day. To my surprise the great loch was as calm as a pond, not a ripple on its broad expanse, and the sun almost in summer mood. The car stopped suddenly at a rise at the side of the loch

66

and Mr McKillop shouted that there was something unusual in the loch.

We unmistakably sighted on the placid surface of the loch a fairly long slipstream which quickly developed in length, at the head of which were what seemed to be two shiny humps, close together, of which the first was the larger. The rapidity with which this exhaust-like stream in the wake of the two humps lenthened led me to believe that it might be a boat but for the fact that, it being a perfectly calm, clear day, any sound of a motorboat engine (for only a motorboat could have travelled at this speed) would be distinctly heard. Having such a clear view I observed that what was moving must be of considerable dimensions to make such a stir in the water.

The possibility of its being a motorboat was, as he added, entirely ruled out when the object and then the wake disappeared from the surface. Mr John Mackay said: 'The dark, high head was clearly seen. There can be no denial by even the most rabid scoffer – many of whom have never seen the loch – that in Loch Ness there is something abnormal – something larger than the usual species of marine animal.'

The sequel to this sighting was that at the next meeting of Inverness County Council the standing orders were suspended so that Mr McKillop could tell his colleagues about his 'glimpse of the most notorious inhabitant of the County'. One member remarked that 'Everybody knew that whatever the Chief Administrative Officer of the County said would be true. They would trust Mr McKillop's eyes better than their own.' The *Inverness Courier* reported the meeting as follows:

'I confess,' he (Mr McKillop) said, 'that I had certain doubts about it myself but these were largely removed by the fact that several men on whose word

67

I could place reliance had seen the object. But any doubts that remained were completely dispelled on the afternoon of Good Friday when I had the good fortune to witness what is regarded as the Loch Ness Monster.

'I am firmly convinced there is something quite abnormal in the depths of the loch. It is capable of quite extraordinary speed and is capable of creating a commotion, a disturbance in the water that would suggest it must be of immense proportions.'

The meeting's Convenor, Lochiel, said that they were indebted to Mr McKillop for his statement.

'I was a great sceptic myself,' declared Lochiel, 'until I heard that Mr McKillop had seen it. I am quite convinced now there is a monster in Loch Ness. There could be no more trustworthy witness than our County Clerk.' (Applause)

Rev. Mr Graham: 'Nobody would believe me.' (Laughter) 'They would not even believe me when I said I saw it from a tearoom and not from an hotel.' (Laughter) Mr F.W. Walker said the 'Monster' should be made an honorary member of the County Council. Lochiel replied, amid laughter, 'that there was no provision for that in the Local Government Act.'

On the warm spring afternoon of 19 April 1950 Lady Maud Baillie, C.B.E., Commander of the A.T.S. during the last war and sister-in-law of Harold Macmillan (later the British Prime Minister), was driving along the Dores to Foyers road with Lady Spring-Rice, wife of a former British Ambassador to the United States, and Lady Maud's grandsons, Angus and Jonathan Warr, and Lady Spring-Rice's grandson and granddaughter. Lady Maud described to me what happened:

I had just pointed out Urquhart Castle to the children when one of them asked 'Is that a rock out there?' I glanced across the water and saw something about one third of the way across the loch. I knew immediately that it could not be a rock that far out, so I pulled the car in to the side of the road. Just as I did so the 'rock' moved off at a very rapid pace in a northerly direction and after a few seconds it was concealed by the roadside vegetation. We all hurried down to the water's edge but the object had gone. But it had left a terrific wash which soon hit the shore with some violence and caused one of the children to run back in horror. What greatly impressed us all was the speed of the object and the great commotion it caused. Lady Spring-Rice said the wash was big enough to have been put up by a powerful speed-boat. Although none of us saw it for long enough to give any real details, we all saw two separate big dark humps in the water. There was no question that it was a very large living animal.

Lady Maud, who has lived very near to the loch since the 1930s, went on to tell me about an occasion when she was asked by an old lady at her club in Edinburgh whether she was the person who had seen the 'Monster':

I replied that yes, I was, and asked her if she had ever seen it. To my surprise she said that she had, three times in one afternoon. I asked her to tell me about it and she described how a friend had once offered her a motor tour of the Great Glen so long as she did not bore her with silly remarks about a mythical 'Monster'. She promised that she would never mention it and the two of them set off. They were approaching Drumnadrochit in the car when this old lady saw one of the animals appear in the water below, but she remained silent and just watched it keep pace with them for a little while until it submerged. A moment later it resurfaced and this time the driver, who was the sceptic, saw it and said 'Good heavens, there's the Monster,' at which the old lady said 'Oh yes, I saw it a moment ago but didn't tell you because you made me promise not to mention it.' The two of them apparently watched it surface once more and then disappear for good. She didn't give any details of its appearance, but they were both quite convinced that it was the 'Monster'.

Lady Maud also provided evidence that some of the old Highland superstition about the animals still lingers on. She told me how a few years earlier her son had noticed a disturbance in the loch whilst out looking for deer on the estate above their home: 'He studied the area with his spyglass but didn't see anything break the surface. He then handed his glass to the keeper who was with him and said that there was something queer going on down the loch. But the keeper looked at him and refused to take the glass. He just said: "Aye, there's many a queer thing in that loch," and walked on.'

On 8 October 1958 a party of twenty-seven passengers on a bus watched a twenty-five-foot-long dark hump on the loch surface. Several of the witnesses broadcast an account of what they saw on the BBC Home Service on 16 October. They were interviewed by a BBC journalist, Andy Cowan Martin, who added his own experience to the programme. This is his story as broadcast:

It was a day in the month of June, way back in 1939, and I was flying from Kirkwall to Inverness and, just for fun, the pilot said he would take us over Loch Ness and we might see the Monster. We flew down the loch as far as Fort Augustus and on the way back I actually saw the Monster for about half a

70

minute or so, but by the time I'd yelled to the other people in the plane to look where I was pointing and the pilot had brought the plane down nearer the surface of the loch, the Monster – the thing – giant eel or whatever it was, had submerged and all that the others could see was a swirl of foam. Frankly they didn't believe me when I said that for a few seconds I had a clear view of two very prominent sort of humps and a third one that was not so prominent and it looked something like the head of a seal.

Very few people carry either a camera or a pair of binoculars with them as they go about their daily business. This fact is one of several reasons why there are so few photographs of the objects which have been seen in the loch. The residents of Loch Ness are far more likely to carry a telescope than a camera. Mr William Mackay studied the animal he saw through a glass; so did Peter MacMillan, the head gamekeeper of the Glenmoriston estate, in August 1954. Mr MacMillan was working near the mouth of the River Moriston when a heavy wash hit the shore and made him look up. He saw two humps moving across the loch at speed and putting up waves 'like a speedboat'. He focused a powerful telescope on the humps and could see that they were part of a large animal. The skin was rough and similar to that of an elephant. The visible parts were about thirty feet in length.

On Sunday 16 June 1957 Mr D. Campbell, a native of Inverness and for thirty-two years the headmaster of Aldourie Public School, was walking across the low hills at the loch's northern end. He had sat down to read when he happened to look down at the loch and noticed what he took to be two boats which had suddenly appeared. They were about three quarters of a mile away and were travelling towards Urquhart Castle at a distance of about 150 yards from each other. Mr Campbell recollects that he wondered at the unusual course being taken by the 'boats' and also at the absence of any sign of people or oars. Then, quite suddenly, the left-hand object 'shot' across and stopped a little way to the right of the other one. Then they both sank out of sight. This account is valuable since it is one of the comparatively few which describe more than one animal on the surface at the same time.

In 1952 Dr Richard Synge was awarded the Nobel Prize for Chemistry. Fourteen years earlier, in the summer of 1938, he was staying at Fort Augustus with his parents and sisters when he saw one of the animals in Loch Ness. This is how he described what happened: 'It was about 8 o'clock one morning when I saw a dark hump-like object in the loch, which after a while started to move northwards close to the west bank of the loch. We all followed it by car for about three miles. It was going at a fair speed and leaving a slight wake, about a quarter of a mile from the shore. It then became stationary and then submerged.'

At about 4.20 p.m. on 2 February 1959 Automobile Association patrolman Hamish Mackintosh was making a routine road report call to his office from the AA box at Brackla. As he finished he turned and looked out across the water and saw 'something out of this world. It was as if a dinosaur had reared up out of the loch.' A few hundred yards out was a tall, thin neck and a 'broad and very big' humped body, moving slowly towards the Brackla shore. The head and neck, which seemed to be towering about eight feet above the water, were greyish in colour and were turning from side to side. Mr Mackintosh was joined by a man from a nearby house, and both of them watched its slow progress for about five minutes. A fire engine went past but although they tried to wave it down it did not stop. However, a moment later two lorries did pull over and three more men joined the group. One of the most astonishing things, Mr Mackintosh said, was the way in which the animal submerged – it just sank perpendicularly without any commotion. After the event Mr Mackintosh declared that he would never again venture out onto Loch Ness in a small boat.

However, in 1963 four people did go onto the loch in a small boat – to chase after one of the animals and make one of the most exciting of all sightings at Loch Ness.

At about 7.30 on a still August evening, Mr Hugh Ayton and his son Jim were working in a field on their Balachladaich Farm, situated on the lochside about two miles south of Dores. With them was another local farmer, Alastair Grant, and a holidaymaker from Stirling, Fred Gerrard, with his son Barry. As I've already described in Chapter One, Hugh Ayton is a quiet, undemonstrative man: having met him a number of times and come to know him I would suggest that there could be no more reliable witness. This is what he told me:

My son was working with me in a field overlooking the loch when he looked up and saw something moving south about halfway across the loch. He shouted and the others ran up, and all five of us watched this thing moving down the loch. It was big and black and I realised that after fifteen years of farming here, at last I was actually watching the 'Monster'. The loch was calm and everything was quiet; there wasn't a noise anywhere – just this thing moving steadily forward. It was eerie, it really was.

Anyway we decided that the best thing would be to get the boat out and try to intercept it. So we all ran down to the jetty and four of us got into a rowing boat and set off. At first we rowed a short distance but then we started the little outboard motor.

The thing was still coming down the loch and as we got closer we could see more details of it. There was a long neck coming about six feet out of the water and a head which reminded me rather of a horse, though bigger and flatter. The body was made up of three low humps – about thirty to forty feet long in all, and about four feet high. The colour was dark and the skin looked rough. We must have got to within fifty yards of it and then it rose up a little out

73

of the water and dived and put up an enormous disturbance which swirled the boat around. A moment later the head appeared for a second a little further on and then it was gone for good.

In all it must have travelled about a mile, going at a steady pace all the time. At no time did we see any paddles or flippers.

One of the animals exposed itself for an aristocratic inspection on 28 September 1966. Count Emmanuel de Lichtervelde of Belgium was being driven around the loch by Guy Senior, Chairman of Inverness Unionist Association, and his wife. A few miles south of Dores they spotted a large dark object moving slowly along the loch. Mr Senior, a former naval officer, said: 'We stopped the car and watched the object for about six minutes. There were two distinct humps travelling at about eight knots but not causing much disturbance. It was definitely an animal we saw and very big. It could not possibly have been a boat or a wake caused by any vessel in the water.'

Count Lichtervelde was reported as saying: 'It was the most wonderful thing that could ever have happened to me. Nobody will believe me when I return to Belgium and say I have seen the famous "Monster".'

The most convincing testimonies often come from those who previously doubted the existence of the animals. Until a mid-April day of 1967 Mrs Dorothy Fraser, who lives in a cottage high on the hillside overlooking the loch at Achnahannet, was such a person. This is her story, which, even in print, conveys much of the vivacity of its teller:

I was out in the garden and just thinking what a glorious day it was when all of a sudden I saw something come up gently out of the loch. It was a big, grey-black oval mass. I was so absolutely

74

flabbergasted that I went weak at the knees. The first thing that came to my mind was that it was a submarine. 'Russians,' I said to myself, and looked for the periscope. Then it began to move, the penny dropped and I felt even more weak at the knees. After all these years when I've pooh-poohed the idea to scores of visitors, it was 'Nessie' herself.

It moved out to the centre of the loch, gently at first, and then it gathered speed until it was going quite fast, and then, as suddenly as it came, it sank, just like a porpoise going down. All that was left was a wake, and you could have said it was from a paddle-steamer, the waves were so big.

Although I am high up here and it must have been about quarter of a mile down and away from me, I had an excellent grandstand view. It must have been very big to have been so clear at that distance. It reminded me of the back of a huge giant tortoise.

Now I'm a firm believer. There is a lot of ridicule, but all one can do is tell the truth and hope that in the end everyone will realise that it *is* the truth.

It may have been noticed from the foregoing that the majority of the sightings have taken place when the loch was calm. This characteristic runs through about ninety per cent of all known sightings and perhaps suggests that the animals favour calm water for their surface appearances. Alternatively, it may simply be that they are easier to see when the loch surface is not broken up by waves. For instance, the following appearance by one of the animals would have gone unnoticed had there not been a boat nearby.

On 16 March 1967 John Cameron, a lock-keeper employed on the Caledonian Canal at Fort Augustus, was out salmon-fishing in his boat opposite Glendoe pier. There was a stiff easterly wind and a three-foot wave on the loch. At about 3 p.m. Mr Cameron watched in astonishment as a large 'upturned boat' shaped object surged through the water, against the waves and wind, just twenty yards away from him and disappeared. It was about twelve feet in length, dark brown in colour, and had a crinkly surface. Mr Cameron told an *Inverness Courier* reporter: 'Believe me, it must be a very large animal as I saw only part of it, and a powerful animal at that. You should have seen the way it sliced through the waves, quite effortlessly.'

Until about 11.45 a.m. on 22 June 1971 William Dewar, a draughtsman from Lanarkshire, was among those who were sceptical about the existence of the 'Monster'. However, as he and his wife drove towards Fort Augustus on the A82, his doubts were shattered as his wife suddenly exclaimed 'Look, it's the Loch Ness Monster!' Three hundred yards away in the smooth water below them was a creature with a 'snake-like' head and neck moving quite rapidly in a southerly direction. About four feet behind the neck was a ten-foot long dark hump standing two to three feet out of the water. After about a minute the animal submerged, leaving a bewildered and very excited couple standing by the roadside.

On successive days in October 1971 the animals were seen by a number of people, including a police inspector, a police sergeant and a monk. On 13 October, Police Inspector Henry Henderson and Police Sergeant George Mackenzie, both from Inverness, were among a group of people who watched two humps move up the loch near Altsigh Youth Hostel. The total length was estimated at thirty to forty feet, the speed at ten to fifteen m.p.h. Inspector Henderson wrote in a report: 'It was obvious that the two objects were part of one large animate object.' The next morning, 14 October, Father Gregory Brusey of the Fort Augustus Abbey was walking by the lochside below the Abbey with a friend, Roger Pugh of London. 'Suddenly there was a terrific commotion in the waters of the bay. In the midst of this disturbance we saw

76

quite distinctly the neck of the beast standing out of the water to what we calculated later to be a height of about ten feet. It swam towards us at a slight angle and after about 20 seconds slowly disappeared.'

Many of Father Brusey's colleagues at the Abbey have seen the creatures at one time or another. Father Aloysius Carruth, M.A., who has followed the mystery closely since the 1930s, and has written a small booklet on the subject (published by the Abbey Press, Fort Augustus), saw a large dark object proceeding up the centre of the loch early one morning in 1965. His brother, the Very Reverend Msgr G.E. Carruth, had a good sighting of the head, neck and humps in 1940.

Every year the sightings continue. On the evening of 27 July 1973 five people stood in the drive of the Foyers Hotel and watched one of the animals swim across the loch at speed. One witness, Mr J. Shaw of London, wrote: 'It is said that "seeing is believing", and we are now of the opinion that something exists in that loch.' Another witness, Mr E.J.R. Moran of Yorkshire, said: 'I can assure you now that although I was a sceptic before, now I don't mind what anyone thinks – I am convinced that I have seen a creature of some kind in Loch Ness.'

On 8 February 1974, two Inverness County Council employees, Henry Wilson and Andy Call, saw 'what appeared to be a serpent with a horse's head' travelling through the water opposite Urquhart Castle. It left 'a wake like a submarine'.

On 23 June 1978 Bill Wright from Camelon, Falkirk was fishing from the shore below Urquhart Castle when an animal surfaced about 30 yards away from him. 'Not unlike an upturned boat: black in colour.' Moments later a head and neck appeared; 'the neck was twelve feet long: the head about the size of a football.' Mr Wright was very surprised and scrambled back up the bank. He said later that he'd fished the loch many times but never seen anything unusual before. 'After this,' he said, 'I have no doubt the creatures exist.'

And so it goes on – just as it has for the past fifty-odd years. Each time it happens somebody else shakes their head as a fantasy gives way to a living creature of flesh and blood. The rich and the poor, the proud and the humble – they stand and watch in self-effacing amazement as a legend comes to life before their eyes.

Loch Ness: aerial view looking north from above Fort Augustus

The ruins of Castle Urquhart

View south from Dores

STRANGE SPECTACLE ON LOCH NESS

What was it?

(FROM A CORRESPONDENT).

Loch Ness has for generations been credited with being the home of a fearsome-looking monster, but, somehow or other, the "water-kelpie," as this legendary creature is called, has always been regarded as a myth, if not a joke. Now, however, comes the news that the beast has been seen once more, for, on Friday of last week, a well-known business man, who lives near Inverness, and his wife (a University graduate), when motoring along the north shore of the loch, not far from Abriachan Pier, were startled to see a tremendous upheaval on the loch, which, previously, had been as calm as the proverbial mill-pond. The lady was the first to notice the disturbance, which occurred fully three-quarters of a mile from the shore, and it was her sudden cries to stop that drew her husband's attention to the water.

There, the creature disported itself, rolling and plunging for fully a minute, its body resembling that of a whale, and the water cascading and churning like a simmering cauldron. Soon, however, it disappeared in a boiling mass of foam. Both onlookers confessed that there was something uncanny about the whole thing, for they realised that here was no ordinary denizen of the depths, because, apart from its enormous size, the beast, in taking the final plunge, sent out waves that were big enough to have been caused by a passing steamer. The watchers waited for almost half-an-hour in the hope that the monster (if such it was) would come to the surface again; but they had seen the last of it. Questioned as to the length of the beast, the lady stated that, judging by the state of the water in the affected area, it seemed to be many feet long.

It will be remembered that a few years ago, a party of Inverness anglers reported that when crossing the loch in a rowing-boat, they encountered an unknown creature, whose bulk, movements, and the amount of water it displaced at once suggested that it was either a very large seal, a porpoise, or, indeed, the monster itself!

But the story, which duly appeared in the press, received scant attention and less credence. In fact, most of those people who aired their views on the matter did so in a manner that bespoke feelings of the utmost scepticism.

It should be mentioned that, so far as is known, neither seals or porpoises have ever been known to enter Loch Ness. Indeed, in the case of the latter, it would be utterly impossible for them to do so, and, as to the seals, it is a fact that though they have on rare occasions been seen in the River Ness, their presence in Loch Ness has never once been definitely established.

Left: Alex Campbell's report of the Mackay sighting in the *Inverness Courier:* the start of the 'Monster' saga
Above: Alex Campbell, water bailiff and *Courier* correspondent in Fort Augustus
Below: The new motor road which opened up the loch's northern shore in 1933

Hugh Gray's photograph: the first which claimed to show the 'Monster'

One of the first monster-hunters at the loch in the winter of 1933-4 rigging a flash camera triggered by a trip wire

M.A. Wetherall (*left*), the big-game hunter engaged in December 1933 by the *Daily Mail*, with his cameraman Gustave Pauli on Dores pier

Mr Wetherall examining the famous 'footprints' on the beach near Dores

A local policeman warning people not to do anything to harm any unknown animals in the loch

December 1933: a cage being prepared for shipment to Loch Ness in case one of the creatures should be caught

The famous photograph taken by Colonel R.K. Wilson, 'the Surgeon', on 19 April 1934 north of Invermoriston, which is said to show the neck and head of one of the animals protruding from the water·

Colonel R.K. Wilson: 'the Surgeon'

The final photograph taken by R.K. Wilson, showing the neck and head submerging

Lachlan Stuart's photograph, taken in July 1951, evidently of bales of hay covered with tarpaulin

P.A. Macnab

P.A. Macnab's photograph, taken in July 1955

Stills from Tim Dinsdale's film:

The hump shortly after it was first spotted

Range now 1600 yards: the hump has submerged but leaves large wash

It turns abruptly left and moves parallel to the far shore: speed 10 m.p.h.

A 14-foot boat with 5 h.p. outboard engine filmed as a comparison

Chapter Five

CURIOUSER AND CURIOUSER

The period from the Second World War to the late 1950s, when a new book on the subject appeared, was rather an uninspiring one for the Loch Ness mystery. It was always lurking in the background, and occasionally it would pop up in the news and create a fresh flutter of excitement. But no major progress was made. It became a classic 'hoary old chestnut' – dragged out every summer for a new feature article going over the old ground, cracking the old jokes and finishing with the usual question marks.

But the period had its highlights. The animals' fatal attraction for those in the information industry even reached as far as Josef Goebbels, Nazi Germany's Minister of Propaganda. In 1940 he devoted a double page in the *Hamburger Illustrierte* to 'Nessie', exposing her as a cunning invention by British tourist agencies. A year later Mussolini's paper *Popolo d'Italia* printed the news that bombing of Britain had been so intense and successful that the Loch Ness Monster had been killed by a direct hit. An Italian bomber pilot had apparently claimed to have 'straddled Nessie with a stick of bombs and left her lying on the surface'.

The creatures were, in fact, very far from such an ignominious demise. Eleven sightings were reported in 1941, despite the absence of tourists. In April 1944 Engineer-Commander R.A.R. Meiklem, R.N., and his wife watched the humped back of one of the animals cross the loch in front of their house in Fort Augustus. Mrs Meiklem remarked: 'It gave one a rather uncanny feeling, although I was delighted at having had such an excellent

79

view of it for several minutes.' Their account was reported in a news bulletin sent to prisoners of war in Europe.

In May of the following year, Lieutenant Colonel W.H. Lane, his wife and two neighbours watched a similar display from their home at Tigh-na-Bruach, just south of Invermoriston. One of them said 'It was a huge black object. Watching it closely, it remained about two minutes on the surface after which it suddenly disappeared leaving a big wake on the loch.' Colonel Lane, who studied the wake through binoculars, said 'There was a slight curve in the wake, which looked, as far as I can judge, as if a moving torpedo was in the water. There can be no doubt it was made by a large, fast-moving object.'

It is impossible to calculate the number of sightings made during the war. The areas to the west of the loch were all restricted and were used for military purposes. Soldiers were stationed around the loch but because of an embargo on reporting troop movements the press could not refer to any sightings by them. The loch itself was used for testing equipment. It is known that during the First World War two submarines passed through it. Whether or not they had any unusual encounters is not known. However, during the Second World War one vessel of Her Majesty's Royal Navy did, according to its commander, encounter one of the animals. It hit one.

In 1943 Francis Russell Flint was a Lieutenant Commander in charge of a motor launch on passage through the Caledonian Canal from Leith to Swansea. On board were twenty other officers and ratings. In 1969 Commander Russell Flint described what happened: 'It was a gorgeous sunny day. We were heading south from Inverness in the vicinity of Fort Augustus, travelling at our top speed of about twenty-five knots. We were taking things easy when there was the most terrific jolt. Everybody was knocked back. And then we looked for'ard. And there it was. There was a very large animal form which disappeared in a flurry of water. It was definitely a living creature – certainly not debris or anything like that.'

Commander Russell Flint immediately sent the following signal to the Admiralty: 'Regret to inform your Lordships, damage to starboard bow following collision with Loch Ness Monster. Proceeding at reduced speed to Fort Augustus.' Apparently their Lordships were not much impressed by this signal, and Commander Russell Flint received 'a bit of a blast' when he returned to base.

If true, this experience is unique. If it did happen as the Commander claims, the beast must either have been extremely drowsy (it was, as Commander Russell Flint states, 'a gorgeous sunny day') or perhaps unwell not to have been aware of the approaching launch. The animals usually seem hypersensitive to noise and dive immediately.

After the war, as life slowly returned to normal, visitors began to trickle back to the Highlands. A newspaper reported in August 1947: 'An attempt has been made to relaunch the Loch Ness Monster, fun-topic of 1933. Thirty people claimed they saw it yesterday – complete with two humps.'

Nessie's big newspaper splash in 1950 suggested that, despite Commander Russell Flint's claim, the Royal Navy was as scornful about the whole affair as the rest of the establishment. The *Daily Herald* of 8 November 1950 carried a provocative headline, 'The Secret of Loch Ness,' under which it was stated that 'The Navy knows the real truth about the Loch Ness Monster . . . hitherto the explanation has been a top secret known only to a few but now, after 32 years, the secrecy ban has been removed.'

Splendid sensationalist journalism – the *Daily Herald* must have sold well that day, as, no doubt, did newspapers all over the world which took up the story. Actually the shattering disclosure turned out to relate to a number of eight-foot diameter, four-horned uncharged mines that had been anchored in Loch Ness in August 1918, at depths of between '600 feet and one mile' (which is strange in itself since the greatest recorded depth is less than 1,000 feet). According to the *Daily Herald* H.M.S. *Welbeck* had found the loch to be seven miles deep.

81

Admiralty experts, it was reported, had been having a quiet chuckle about the 'Monster' since 1933 but had never previously divulged that its true identity was in fact a string of naval mines. Scottish newspapers immediately rallied to the animals' defence. 'Highlands Ablaze in Defence of "Nessie"', reported the *Aberdeen Press and Journal*; '"Nessie" Just Mines? Highlanders Howl', said the *Daily Record*; 'Daily Paper Successfully Spoofed', said the *Inverness Courier*. The truth was that in 1922 another vessel had been to Loch Ness and recovered all the mine anchors. The mines were not found, and since they were designed to have a life of only a few years they were obviously on the bottom. Hugh Gray, who fifteen years later was to photograph one of the animals, was on board H.M.S. *Welbeck* in 1918 when the mines were laid. He said: 'Some of the mines came to the surface shortly after they had been laid down but the terrific pressure had made them as flat as pancakes. From that day to this there is no record of anyone seeing a mine in the loch.'

The *Inverness Courier* remarked scornfully (10 November 1950) that the only thing which had gone bang was the *Daily Herald*'s story, which exploded in its own face!

The following year a man by the name of Lachlan Stuart took a photograph which has been widely accepted as authentic ever since. In fact it would now appear that Lachlan Stuart's photograph, of three angular 'humps' a short distance offshore, was a hoax: Mr Stuart's account of what happened, a fabrication. He evidently intended no great mischief, and was both surprised and amused that his picture – in reality of three partly submerged bales of hay covered in tarpaulin – should have been taken seriously.

Mr Stuart claimed to have looked out of the window of his croft at Whitefield, about five miles south of Dores, at 6.30 on the morning of 14 July 1951. He was, he said, preparing to step outside to milk his cow; instead, he claimed, he saw first one, and then two humps appear out in the loch. He and a friend, a Mr Taylor Hay, were then supposed to have dashed down to the water's edge with

82

Stuart's box camera, whereupon they snapped a portrait of the Monster's (by now) *three*-humped superstructure.

Word soon reached the Scottish *Daily Express* correspondent in Inverness, who caught up with Stuart over lunch and persuaded him to hand over the film. The picture has since been widely published; indeed, it has enjoyed a degree of credibility, thanks in part to Lachlan Stuart's evident plausibility when he was interviewed three days later by Mrs Constance Whyte, the wife of the Manager of the Caledonian Canal, who had begun an interest in the mystery which was to lead her to write her much-respected book *More Than a Legend* (of which more in a moment). Mrs Whyte was greatly impressed by Lachlan Stuart and said she put forward his photograph with confidence. It was, as it would now seem, a most uncharacteristic lapse in judgement.

Because, as certain newspapers would put it, I can now reveal that a couple of weeks later Lachlan Stuart took another Loch Ness resident, who is known to me and with whom I have confirmed the following details, on a stroll along the beach and showed him the bales of hay and sheets of tarpaulin which he'd used to manufacture his Monster. They were hidden in a clump of bushes. The man who was shown these props gave Lachlan Stuart a promise of silence and since, over subsequent years, he was never either interested or impressed by all the hoo-ha about Nessie, he never thought to break his promise and reveal the reality of the photograph as it had been shown to him. That he has now done, and I'm grateful: it is important that the record be clarified and corrected as much as possible.

At the time of its publication, the Stuart photograph prompted a new spasm of public interest and as a direct result the BBC decided it was time it made some contribution to the investigation, and preparations were begun for a special television inquiry. A ninety-minute programme was broadcast on 26 September 1951 and consisted of a courtroom trial of the 'Monster', with a counsel for fact, Mr 'Verity', and a counsel for legend advocating before a judge and jury. The entire script had been prepared beforehand, and although a number of eyewitnesses, including Alex Campbell, Lady Maud Baillie and Lachlan Stuart, made personal appearances, there was little attempt at an objective survey of the evidence. A critic in *The Listener* (11 October 1951) wrote: 'Rarely has so compelling a subject for the viewing majority been more fantastically maltreated.' The programme had included, for some reason, a survey of cattle ranching in Scotland and a parody of press activities at the loch in 1933.

The latter portrayed 'Denis Walters', a Fleet Street journalist, and 'Bill Briggs' his photographer, evidently at their wits' end to produce a story. Walters complains: 'Nobody's seen the monster for five days. I gave a kid ten bob today, but he wouldn't say he'd seen the damn thing. His mother gave me the money back. She said I was corrupting her bairn and she'd get the polis if I did it again.' So they build a model out of barrels and motor tyres which they plan to haul across the loch surface by an ingenious system of ropes, pulleys and drainpipes which lead up through the kitchen sink of a conveniently situated ruined croft. Their dastardly scheme is foiled by 'Donald the Deer-Stalker', who steals the model and hurries off to the pub, where he finds 'Dunfield', another reporter, brandishing a stuffed hippopotamus hoof which he has been stamping all over the neighbourhood. The sequence closed with a newspaper headline flashed across the screen: 'Loch Ness Sensation. Monster has Four Left Feet.'

The last witness called on the programme was Dr Maurice Burton, at the time a Deputy Keeper of Zoology at the British Museum (Natural History), who told the 'court' that although most of his colleagues did not believe in the animals, he had an open mind. As we shall see, Dr Burton's mind was later to oscillate from being one of the phenomenon's staunchest zoological supporters to being its arch critic. The final verdict of the programme was 'Not Proven'. To quote *The Listener*'s critic again: 'Writing about the Loch Ness Monster inquiry requires a restraint that is as hard to bear as the programme, television's biggest let-down for some time.'

However, 1951 produced several good sightings. The following is an account by J. Harper-Smith, O.B.E., Ll.B., Town Clerk of Lincoln. During June 1951 he spent several days in Inverness-shire on a fishing holiday with his son, an Army officer:

We went over to the village of Dores to inquire about hiring a boat. After arranging this we had a chat with the old lady who runs the Dores Inn. I asked her if the locals believed in the 'Monster'. She looked at me very seriously and said: 'It isn't a question of believing in it – most of us have seen it at one time or another and we *know* it is there.' Unfortunately (for me) I still remained sceptical.

The next afternoon we went out fishing but because it was wet when we set out I left my cine camera and binoculars behind. By about 9 p.m. the loch was like a mirror. We were just starting to take down our rods when my son pointed with his arm and said: 'Is that a periscope over there?'

I looked and realised something was coming up out of the water. Within a few seconds a black head was followed by a similar-coloured neck several feet long. While we were eagerly looking for the body the head and neck began moving forward at a very fast speed followed by a huge wash. As it came nearer we noticed some oscillations of the head and neck. We began to edge in nearer the shore but when it had come to within about 800 yards 'it' turned and went back up the centre of the loch and shortly afterwards submerged. We put the length of the neck at about five feet and the diameter at about a foot.

Mr Harper-Smith concluded by saying: 'I live in hope that I

may one day be fortunate enough to recapture what was the greatest thrill of my life.'

At about midday on 13 November 1951 Colonel Patrick Grant, at that time owner of Knockie Lodge, high up in the hills behind the 'Horseshoe' shore line, was driving north out of Fort Augustus.

> Quite suddenly I noticed a great disturbance in the water at about 150 yards from the shore . . . I saw a length, perhaps six feet, of some black object showing a foot or less out of the water and as I looked the object disappeared and reappeared a moment later at least a hundred yards away and nearer the shore. The speed of movement was very great. I am positive that what I saw was a living creature but not a porpoise or a whale or a big seal. (*Inverness Courier*, 16 November 1951)

Unknown to Colonel Grant this sighting was also witnessed by Mrs A.C. Kirton, wife of a Fort Augustus doctor, from a wooden bridge over the River Oich. She independently corroborated the disturbance and the appearance of the hump at the time and place reported by the Colonel.

In 1952 tragedy struck Loch Ness when it took the life of John Cobb as he became the fastest man to travel on water. With his 6,000 h.p. £15,000 speedboat *Crusader* he arrived at the loch on 26 August to try to add the world water speed record to the land speed record which he already held. Late on the morning of 29 September, he made one northerly run up the mirror-calm surface of the loch. Then he turned and commenced the run which was to take him to a record-breaking speed of 206 m.p.h. along the specially marked-out mile and which ended in the disintegration of *Crusader* and his death. The accident happened when *Crusader* hit a patch of turbulence. Inevitably there have been suggestions that the Monster caused the small disturbance which threw the boat into such violent vibration that it literally fell apart. However, it is now accepted that the ripples were the remnants of the reflected wake from the first run slowly settling on the surface.

John Cobb was recovered alive from the wreckage, wearing a special inflatable suit, and he was carried up the hill to Achnahannet where he died. A stone memorial now stands at the roadside, erected in memory of 'A Very Gallant Gentleman' by the people of Glen Urquhart.

In April 1957 Constance Whyte's book *More Than a Legend* was published (by Hamish Hamilton). It was the first attempt in the twenty-three years since the publication of Commander Gould's book to collate the evidence and present the 'Monster' as a serious subject worthy of scientific study. Mrs Whyte, a qualified doctor married to the Manager and Engineer of the Caledonian Canal, Frank Whyte, had moved to Inverness in 1937. Twelve years later she was asked to write an article on the 'Monster' for a privately circulated magazine, and what till then had been a casual interest in the mystery was changed to a fascination as she delved more deeply into the mine of reported information. Describing the reasons for writing the book Mrs Whyte, who never saw the animals herself despite living in Inverness for twenty-three years, wrote:

> A book had to be written. The search for truth is always worthwhile but in this instance it was the vindication of many people of integrity who had reported honestly what they had seen in Loch Ness which was my main motive. Friends of mine had been subjected to ridicule and contempt and I felt it was time to counteract the flippant and frivolous attitude of the Press and of the media generally.

The success of *More Than a Legend* was reflected in the volume of correspondence received by the author. Its publication was undoubtedly the first and very significant turning-point towards the modern campaign of serious investigation.

However, when the book was first published, Crompton Library Committee in Lancashire was one of several which refused to stock it. 'The Loch Ness Monster is a lot of tomfoolery,' said Councillor F.H. Sykes of Crompton. But after the Chairman had actually read the book they changed their minds.

It was perhaps a wise decision, since interest in the 'Monster' was undoubtedly increasing as more and more people visited the Highlands every year. As an example let us take a very ordinary sighting and see the extent to which it was publicised throughout the world. On 11 March 1957 Inspector John Grant of Inverness-shire police, Derek Fowles, a teacher at Fort Augustus Abbey School, and Ian Grant, a garage proprietor, all watched a two-humped object moving in the loch near Drumnadrochit. Thanks to the zeal and efficiency of the international press agencies, this story appeared in literally hundreds of newspapers all over the world. The *New York Post* headlined it 'A Sure Sign of Spring – The Loch Ness Monster'; the *Irish Press* wrote about its being 'the sure sign of the start of the silly season.' Elsewhere, the sighting was reported in, to name but a few, the *Mid-Ocean News,* Bermuda; the *Diamond Fields Advertiser*, Kimberley in Australia; *the Iraq Times,* Baghdad; the *Buenos Aires Herald*; and the *Otago Daily Times* of New Zealand.

In view of this worldwide interest it seems quite proper that on 15 March a toast to 'Nessie's' health was proposed in the House of Commons by John Rankin, Labour, during a debate on industry in the North of Scotland!

Two months later Hector Hughes, another Labour M.P., got up in the House and asked the Secretary of State for Scotland, John Maclay, whether he would be prepared to authorise the use of the latest underwater viewing and listening devices to locate the animals. Referring to *More Than a Legend* Mr Hughes said: 'Does not the Secretary of State realise that he owes an obligation to science in this matter and that recent learned works have indicated that such a survey might reveal the existence in Loch Ness of a prehistoric or unique monster, fish or reptile, of some kind, the discovery of which might add considerably to science?' The Secretary of State refused, and the debate closed with a suggestion by another member that Mr Hughes should literally 'go and jump into the lake' and look for the 'Monster' himself.

This debate prompted the *Washington Star* to write a leading article deploring any such attempt at finding the animals. 'The Loch Ness Monster', it wrote, 'is one of the world's nicest and most engaging personalities . . . Leave him alone. Hands off. Mind your own business, Mr Hughes.'

A very spirited display by one of the animals was put up in December 1957. Mr Raymond Bain, a Fort Augustus resident, was driving north along the lochside about three miles south of Urquhart Castle when his attention was attracted by the appearance of a large animal swimming swiftly in the loch about 150 yards out. He saw a long neck and head, swan-like in outline, and a thirty-foot long black body. However, the most impressive thing about the animal was its speed. 'I paced the beast with my car,' he said, 'but I could not keep up with it although I was travelling at 35 m.p.h. Sometimes it would slow down and I would catch up with it and then it would dash off again.' The animal eventually disappeared near Urquhart Castle. Mr Bain added 'Now there is no doubt in my mind that the loch holds a very strange, large, extraordinarily powerful animal.'

By the spring of 1958 several expeditions were in the planning stage. A team of fifty Scottish divers announced that they were to plumb the loch's depths, and Mr H.L. Cockrell, a fish hatchery owner from Dumfries, said that he was going to set out in an Eskimo kayak to look for the animals, armed with a camera and a commando knife. This news prompted Hector Hughes into yet more Parliamentary activity. He tabled a question asking what action the Scottish Secretary proposed to take to protect 'this valuable Scottish asset'. He also reiterated his earlier demand for a Government equipped expedition. His call was, predictably, ignored in Parliamentary circles.*

However, the Royal Navy was being linked with a new BBC programme on the phenomenon. In March the press got to hear about a scheme whereby the Navy would, as a training exercise, provide a vessel equipped with ASDIC and echo sounders to be used by the BBC to carry out sweeps of the loch. The leader columns immediately waxed indignant and the Admiralty had second thoughts and withdrew its support.

Nevertheless, the BBC persevered and *The Legend of the Loch* was broadcast to an audience of about eight million people on 15 May, just twenty-five years after it had all begun. It was an outside broadcast direct from the loch and involved producer John Buchan and his technical team of fifty engineers in the most complex transmission ever attempted till then. Judging from the massive press build-up and the subsequent reviews, it was a great success.

The presenter, Raymond Baxter, interviewed a number of eye-witnesses, including J. Harper Smith and Dr Richard Synge. A team of frogmen was shown operating underwater television cameras off Urquhart Castle, which admirably demonstrated the problems of working under-water in the gloom of Loch Ness. Although naturally there was no timely surface appearance by one of the animals to make the programme complete, one of them apparently had a tantalisingly brief encounter with the BBC's echo-sounding equipment about an hour before the programme went on the air.

The BBC's boat, the Clyde puffer *Kaffir*, was crossing Urquhart Bay, having picked up the engineering crew to take up station off the Castle. David Anderson, operator of the Marconi echo sounder aboard *Kaffir*, explained what happened: 'The object was picked up seventy-yards

* So too was a speech he made in Parliament in May about a giant alligator-like claw which a Loch Ness resident claimed to have found on the shore. Mr Hughes asked the question of Parliament: 'Do you not think it is stultifying in this scientific age not to take serious notice of the important discoveries which may be made there?'

north-east of Urquhart Castle. I cut the sensitivity back and the object reappeared – as a black heavy mark. I pointed it out to Mr. Baxter. The object was fairly large, maybe twenty feet long, and diving away from the vessel at between three and ten fathoms, causing considerable agitation of the water.'

Whatever it was, its echo was quite unlike that of either a single fish or a shoal. None of the Marconi technicians could suggest what it was. It had dived from a depth of twelve feet to sixty feet before it was lost.

The BBC was not the only part of the media anxious to make a star out of 'Nessie'. The British film industry decided in 1958 that it was time it produced its answer to Hollywood's monster from 20,000 fathoms, and the obvious candidate for such a part was 'Nessie'. The result was *The Giant Behemoth* in which the 'Monster' turns out to be a prehistoric radioactive Palaeosaurus over 200 feet long which abandons its tedious life in the Highlands, travels south and runs amuck in London, trampling over various famous landmarks.

The year also produced two still photographs. One of them was taken by Mr H.L. Cockrell, whose canoeing plans caused the Parliamentary question earlier in the year. During the late summer he spent several days at the loch paddling about its enigmatic waters with a specially rigged flash camera attached to his life-jacket. On his final night-operation he encountered something moving in the water which may have been one of the animals – or, as Mr Cockrell says, it may have been just a stick. This is his story as printed in the *Weekly Scotsman* (16 October 1958).

Just about dawn I had my first real test. A light breeze suddenly dropped and left me on a mirror surface about halfway between shores with Invermoriston almost abeam to starboard. Something appeared – or I noticed it for the first time – about 50 yards away on my port bow. It seemed to be swimming very steadily and converging on me. It looked like a very large flat head four or five feet long and wide. About three feet astern of this I noticed another thin line. All very low in the water just awash.

I was convinced it was the head and neck of a very large creature . . . I simply could not believe it. I was not a bit amused. With a considerable effort of will I swung in to intercept and to my horror it appeared to sheer towards me with ponderous power.

I hesitated. There was no-one anywhere near on that great sheet of water to witness a retreat but it was obviously too late to run. Curiously enough I found this a great relief. My heart began to beat normally and my muscles suddenly felt in good trim. I took a shot with my camera in case I got too close for my focus and went in . . . There was a light squall out of the glen behind Invermoriston and the object appeared to sink. When the squall cleared I could still see something on the surface. I closed in again cautiously. It remained motionless and I found it was a long stick about an inch thick.

I arrived home and really believed my particular 'Monster' was a stick until the films were developed.

The film showed quite a large affair which had a distinct wash. There was no reason for this wash as the picture also shows the water mirror calm . . . What caused the wash? Could it have been 'Nessie' after all? I just don't know.

A week after Mr Cockrell's story and picture appeared in the *Weekly Scotsman* the paper published another photograph, which had been sent in by an interested reader, Mr P.A. Macnab, a bank manager and County Councillor in Ayrshire. Mr Macnab had taken his photograph on the early afternoon of Friday 29 July 1955, but 'through diffidence and fear of ridicule I have kept it to myself until now.' His photograph, which like the Surgeon's, has become a Loch Ness classic, shows a long dark object of considerable size off Urquhart Castle tower. Here, for the first time, is the complete story of how he took it and one other photograph which he shortly afterwards destroyed:

I was returning from a holiday in the north with my son and pulled the car up on the road just above Urquhart Castle. It was a calm, warm hazy afternoon. I was all ready to take a shot of Urquhart Castle when my attention was held by a movement in the calm water over to the left. Naturally I thought of the 'Monster' and hurriedly changed over the standard lens of my Exacta (127) camera to a six-inch tele-photo. As I was doing so a quick glance showed that some black or dark enormous water creature was cruising on the surface.

Without a tripod and in a great hurry I took the shot. I also took a very quick shot with another camera, a fixed-focus Kodak, before the creature submerged.

My son was busy under the bonnet of the car at the time and when he looked in response to my shouts there were just ripples on the water. Several cars and a bus stopped but they could see nothing and listened to my description with patent disbelief.

Disbelief is what Mr Macnab also found after he had developed the photographs and shown them to friends. 'So great was the scepticism and the leg-pulling by friends to whom I showed the picture that in a spirit of exasperation I threw the second negative away and nearly got rid of the first as well.'

The object was travelling from left to right at about eight knots. The photograph has an added importance because size and scale can be deduced from the Castle tower in the corner, which is sixty-four feet high. Mr Macnab himself says he thinks there may be two creatures visible in the photograph, but even so the one hump is extremely large and would appear to be in the region of fifty feet in length.

*

And so we come to the end of twenty years of 'Monster' history. 1959 saw interest reviving even more. An Italian journalist claimed he had invented 'Nessie' back in 1933 when he had been short of a story one week; 'Beppo', a famous circus clown, went for a dive in the loch and was dragged out delirious, mumbling about 'unseen eyes' looking at him from slimy black depths; in November the fishing vessel *Guiding Star* picked up yet another inexplicable echo sounding of an object moving in the water column; and a diver from Hong Kong remarked after a fruitless search: 'I look hard down there, but I no see her!'

The phenomenon was about to be subjected to the period of most intense investigation in its history. However, before studying the excitement and achievements of the Loch Ness Investigation let us look first at what is perhaps the most extraordinary, indeed even incredible feature of the whole Loch Ness story: the strange habit which the animals apparently have of leaving the loch, and of coming ashore.

Chapter Six

THE MONSTER COMES ASHORE

Many visitors to Loch Ness arrive half expecting to see its 'Monster' gambolling in the water. Very few realise that if several witnesses are to be believed, they could encounter one of the animals on land. It is suggested that very occasionally these strange creatures leave their natural environment in the water and heave their massive bulks ashore.

For the earliest traceable land sighting we go back to the time of the First World War and join a teenage Fort Augustus girl playing on the shingly beach at Inchnacardoch Bay. The late Mrs Margaret Cameron was the young girl in question, and when I had the pleasure of meeting her in the summer of 1971 she described what happened late one Sunday afternoon in the month of September:

I was with my two brothers and my young sister Lizzie, who was in the pram. We were waiting for some friends and were passing the time by skimming stones across the water when we heard this awful crackling in the trees on the other side of the little bay.

It must have been something awfully big, we thought; and of course we had been warned not to go near the loch by our grandparents, as there were these wild horses in the loch, and we thought now this must be one of them!

So we sat for a wee while and this crackling seemed to be coming nearer and nearer, and then, suddenly, this big thing appeared out of the trees and started to move down the beach to the water. I couldn't tell you if it had a long neck or a short neck because it was pointing straight at us. It had a huge body and its movement as it came out of the trees was like a caterpillar. I would say it was a good twenty feet long – what we saw of it. Now, the colour of it – I hadn't seen an elephant in them days, but it's the colour of the elephant, and it seemed to have rather a shiny skin. Under it we saw two short, round feet at the front and it lurched to one side and put one foot into the water and then the other one. We didn't wait to see the end of it coming out – we got too big a fright. When we got home we were all sick and couldn't take our tea. So we had to explain what had happened and we told our mum and dad, and grandfather was there and I can see him banging the table and telling us not to tell anybody about it. Anyway, we were put to bed with a big dose of castor oil . . . It's still so very vivid in my mind – I'll never forget it.

Inchnacardoch Bay is about 150 yards wide, and although the children had only a comparatively short look at the animal emerging from the trees and bushes it was enough to tell them that it was quite unlike any other creature they had ever seen.

In contrast to the tranquillity of the setting of Mrs Cameron's experience, the next land sighting took place on a wet, blustery night in February 1919. The witnesses on this occasion were Jock Forbes, then a boy of twelve, and his father, a farmer in Foyers. They were returning late one night from the cattle sales in Inverness in their pony cart. Like Mrs Cameron's sighting above, the following details, as described to me by Jock Forbes himself, have not been published before:

It was a very dark, stormy night. My father and I had stopped off at my uncle's house at Scaniport and then continued on our journey. We were about two miles north of Inverfarigaig near the old ferry, where the bank isn't very steep, when the pony suddenly stopped and started backing away in fright. It very nearly backed us right off the road and down the bank.

Something large was crossing the road about twenty yards ahead of us – it came out of the trees above the road, moved slowly across the road and then down the bank and we heard a splash as, presumably, it went into the water.

It was too dark and I was too busy trying to control the pony to notice the details, but it was certainly a big beast, fully the width of the road.

My father, I remember, muttered something in Gaelic and after a moment or two we hurried on home and never really mentioned it again.

I asked Mr Forbes whether, as a boy, he had ever heard any stories of unusual animals having been seen on land. He replied that it was quite well known that a tinker lady at about the turn of the century had once come across a strange creature lying beside the Dores to Foyers road. The experience apparently so terrified her that henceforth she always made a long detour over the hills to avoid the spot.

Although both of these accounts refer to a large animal on land, neither really contains sufficient detail for us to be able to identify the animal with those seen in the water. Mrs Cameron could not see a neck but she did see two 'short, round feet' which, at the distance from which she was viewing, could have been flippers being used as legs in a seal-like manner. The next account confuses matters even more since the description is, in some respects, at variance with the picture of the animals we can build up from the majority of eyewitness reports.

At about 5 a.m. on an April morning in 1923, Alfred Cruickshank was driving his Model T Ford along the very hazardous road which preceded the A82 along the loch's northern shore. He was a chauffeur on his way from his home in Buckie to meet his employer on the train from Glasgow arriving at Speanbridge at 8 a.m. It was still dark, and Mr Cruickshank's route was being illuminated by the car's rather primitive head-lamps as he bumped and wound his way along the deserted road. About two miles north of Invermoriston he crested a small hill and his headlamps picked out a large object on the outside of a bend in the road about fifty yards ahead of him.

I could see something moving – it had a large humped body standing about six feet high with its belly trailing on the ground and about twelve feet long, to which was attached a long thick tail which was ten to twelve feet in length. It was moving slowly, sort of waddling away from the road on two legs which I could see on the near side.

I saw the outline of what appeared to be the head, which was big and pug-nosed and was set right on the body – in other words it didn't seem to have much of a neck.

I was slowing down to go round the corner so the lamps faded, but as I went round the corner I heard a grunting noise from where it was. I stopped the car once I was round the corner, but I couldn't turn the car round and I certainly wasn't going back on foot.

Mr Cruickshank described the colour as dark olive to khaki and lighter underneath, although obviously in the poor light it was difficult to determine colour clearly. The most discordant detail in Mr Cruickshank's story is the absence of the characteristic long, slender neck. When asked whether it was possible that the head was turned in his direction, thus giving the impression of a large head and no neck, he told me that he did not think this was so, neither did he feel that the head and neck could have been shielded from his view by bushes.

The most important consideration is that Mr Cruickshank is quite adamant that he saw a twenty- to twenty-five-foot-long animal moving by the side of the road. The fact that some of the details are inconsistent with our usual picture of the animals is perhaps understandable in view of the poor light and the brevity of his sighting. Such inconsistencies show, as has already been pointed out, that an individual witness is describing what he saw and is not adjusting his account to fall into line with others.

When Mr Cruickshank arrived at Speanbridge station and met his employer, the latter apparently asked him what was wrong, since he was looking very pale. 'He thought I must have had an accident,' recalled Mr Cruickshank, 'but I told him what had happened, and he said I must have been dreaming. A couple of other friends whom I told about the sighting said I must have been drunk. Apart from them I just told my wife and then kept quiet about it all.' Mr Cruickshank also recalled that towards the end of the 1920s he spoke to a girl working in a baker's shop in Fort Augustus who told him that she had once seen a large animal hauled up on to a beach near Fort Augustus. 'She said that she was coming down the hill east of the village on her bicycle when she saw a big animal lying on the beach below her. She was so frightened she jumped off her bicycle and ran the rest of the way home.'

The most famous land sighting of all was that witnessed by Mr and Mrs F.T.G. Spicer on 22 July 1933. George Spicer was a director of a firm of central London tailors, Messrs Todhouse, Reynard and Company. On the day in question they were returning home from a holiday in the North of Scotland. Before we proceed with their story it should be remembered that in July 1933 the 'Monster' was still a subject of relative obscurity; neither Mr nor Mrs Spicer had any idea that Loch Ness was supposed to harbour strange animals, which made their encounter with one even more stunning for them.

It was about 4 o'clock on a quiet summer afternoon. George Spicer was driving his Austin car south along the undulating Dores to Foyers road. They were about midway between the two villages and travelling at about twenty

99

m.p.h. Suddenly Mrs Spicer exclaimed: 'What on earth is that?'

About 200 yards ahead of them a horizontal trunk-like object was emerging from the bushes above the road. It was undulating into two or three arches and was held several feet above the road surface. Mr Spicer later likened it to a 'scenic railway'. The trunk was rapidly followed by a ponderous body. Mr Spicer takes up the story:*

It was horrible – an abomination. It did not move in the usual reptilian fashion but with these arches. The body shot across the road in jerks but because of the slope we could not see its lower parts and saw no limbs.

Although I accelerated towards it, it had vanished by the time we reached the spot. I got out of the car and could see where it had gone down through the bracken, but there was no sign of it in the water. The body was above five feet in height and filled the road. If it had stopped I should have done likewise as there was no room to turn the car round and it was quite big enough to have upset our car.

I estimated the length to be twenty-five to thirty feet. Its colour so far as the body is concerned could only be called a dark elephant grey. We saw no tail, nor did I notice any mouth on what I took to be the head of the creature. We later concluded that the tail must have been curled around alongside it since there was something protruding above its shoulder which gave the impression that it was carrying something on its back. My wife and I looked at each other in amazement. It had been a loathsome sight. To see that arched neck straggle across was something which still haunts us.

The Spicers continued on their way and met a cyclist. This

*This account is put together from letters from Mr Spicer and press accounts at the time.

100

was William McCulloch, a native of Foyers who, when he heard their story was, according to Mr Spicer, 'astounded – not frightened, just incredulous. He added that he was glad we had seen it because people were laughing at a busdriver friend of his in the village who had reported seeing it.' After the Spicers had driven on, Mr McCulloch cycled to the spot where they told him the animal had crossed, and he gave (previously unpublished) confirmation that the undergrowth was flattened, both above the road and below it down to the lochside. 'It was as if a steamroller had been through,' he said. When the Spicers reached Foyers Mr Spicer told several people what had happened but was either ignored or laughed at.

Although Mr Spicer wrote to the *Inverness Courier* in August, and the paper published his report, it was ignored until December, when the matter was given widespread coverage. In his letter to the *Courier* Mr Spicer appealed for information about this 'nearest approach to a dragon or prehistoric animal that I have ever seen in my life . . .' From the tone of his letter it is clear that he was totally unaware of the 'Loch Ness Monster'. He continued: 'Whatever it is and it may be a land and water animal, I think it should be destroyed as I am not sure whether had I been close to it I should have cared to have tackled it.'

On 7 December the Spicers' story appeared in the *Daily Sketch* and they at once found themselves besieged by reporters. The account was inevitably distorted, and the object seen at the animal's shoulder was interpreted as being 'a lamb in its mouth.' Mr Spicer stated that he was 'willing to take an oath and make an affidavit and so is my wife, that we saw this beast.' A few days later he described the sighting on the famous BBC radio programme *In Town Tonight*. He wrote (in a letter to the late F.W. Holiday dated 16 December 1936): 'I have been ridiculed a good bit but I believe most people think there is something there now, as it has been seen many times in the loch.'

Commander Rupert Gould visited the Spicers and recorded this observation: 'I became and remain convinced that their story was entirely bona fide; that they had undergone a most unusual experience which had left a lasting and rather unpleasant impression.'

Captain James Fraser, the leader of Sir Edward Mountain's expedition, also met George Spicer when the latter revisited the loch in 1934. He told me: 'I remember a man coming up to me and asking me how things were going. We talked for a few moments and then he told me who he was. He seemed a very quiet, retiring man and was only just recovering from the terrible ordeal of ridicule he and his wife had been through.'

In addition to the Spicer land sighting of 1933, one of the animals was also evidently seen on land in August by Mrs M.F. MacLennan of Drumnadrochit. She was walking along the road south of Dores when she saw a strange creature lying on the beach. She shouted to her husband, who was a short distance behind her, and the animal immediately plunged into the water. Mrs MacLennan described it as a dark grey mass about twenty to twenty-five feet long. She got an impression of a long neck twisted round towards its back, a humped body and four legs.

Mrs Reid, the wife of the postmaster at Inverfarigaig, claimed at Christmas 1933 that she was travelling along the road to Inverness when she saw an odd-looking animal lying in the bracken. It was only about ten feet in length and dark in colour. A William MacLean of Inverness claimed that he disturbed a large creature resting on the gravelly beach half a mile west of Dores. Apparently it slithered off into the loch and left a big wash. There is also a story that school-children in Drumnadrochit told their schoolmaster, some time in the early 1930s, that they had seen a most peculiar and horrifying animal in the over-grown marsh area at the delta of the rivers flowing into Urquhart Bay. Although it has not been possible to discover any further details of this last story, it is interesting because local legend states that years ago, the animals quite often used to crawl up the beds of the rivers flowing into Urquhart Bay.

The land sighting of January 1934 has already been mentioned in connection with the activities of that pair of big-game hunters, Messrs Wetherall and Pauli. The details of the sighting, which comes a close second to the Spicers' in terms of notoriety, are as follows.

Arthur Grant, a twenty-one-year-old veterinary student from Polmaily House, Glen Urquhart, was returning home from Inverness on his motorcycle at about 1 a.m. on Friday 5 January. 'Bobo' Mackay, Provost of Inverness, a life-long and at times extremely vociferous sceptic, confirms that Mr Grant was perfectly sober when he left Inverness at about 12.30 a.m. after making some final adjustments to his motorcycle. The night was brightly moonlit and as Mr Grant approached the Abriachan turn he noticed, some forty yards ahead of him, a dark object in the shadow of the bushes on the opposite side of the road:

> I was almost on it when it turned what I thought was a small head on a long neck in my direction. The creature apparently took fright and made two great bounds across the road and then went faster down to the loch, which it entered with a huge splash.
>
> I jumped off my cycle and followed it but from the disturbance on the surface it had evidently made away before I reached the shore. I had a splendid view of the object. In fact, I almost struck it with my motorcycle. The body was very hefty. I distinctly saw two front flippers and there seemed to be two other flippers which were behind and which it used to spring from.
>
> The tail would be from five to six feet long and very powerful; the curious thing about it was that the end was rounded off – it did not come to a point. The total length of the animal would be fifteen to twenty feet.

Mr Grant made a careful inspection of the path the animal had taken, marked the spot and went on home. When he arrived he woke his younger brother, told him what had happened and drew a sketch of what he had seen. When it was light Mr Grant returned to the scene with members of his family and they carried out another search for tracks or other remnants. None were found. The *Daily Mail* expedition (see Chapter 3) was then informed, and soon after they arrived, Messrs Wetherall and Pauli managed, as we have seen, to locate a pile of bones, a dead goat and some toe marks. It should be remembered that this was all happening the day after the Natural History Museum had identified Mr Wetherall's mysterious hoof-prints found near Dores as belonging to an umbrella stand. People were therefore in no mood to swallow a story of a land sighting, particularly after it had been dressed up with details of a half-eaten meal left at the roadside. Mr Grant found himself subjected to such violent ridicule that he was persuaded to tell some people that he had never seen the animal. The pressure on him became so unbearable that he had to miss a term at college.

The police took a special account of his experience, and Mr Grant made a statement to the Veterinary Society in Edinburgh. As a veterinary student he was, of course, in a rather better position than most as an observer. He said in a statement: 'Knowing something of natural history I can say that I have never seen anything in my life like the animal I saw. It looked like a hybrid . . . It had a head rather like a snake or an eel, flat at the top, with a large oval eye, longish neck and somewhat longer tail. The body was much thicker towards the tail than was the front portion. In colour it was black or dark brown and had a skin rather like that of a whale. The head must have been about six feet from the ground as it crossed the road.'

From a major highway we move to a deserted beach for the next land sighting. At about 6.30 on the Sunday morning of 3 June 1934, a young housemaid, Miss Margaret Munro, looked out of a window at her employer's house, Kilchumein Lodge, which is set about 300 yards back from

Borlum Bay, just east of Fort Augustus. She saw 'the largest living creature I have ever seen.' For the next twenty-five minutes she watched and studied through a pair of binoculars a large animal rolling on the shingly beach in the bright morning sunshine.

Most of the animal was clear of the water. It had 'a giraffe-like neck and an absurdly small head out of all proportion to the size of the body which was dark grey in colour. The under part of the chest was white and the skin was like an elephant's. Two very short forelegs or flippers were clearly seen. The animal kept turning itself in the sunshine, and it was able to arch its back into large humps. Finally it lowered its head and quietly entered the water and disappeared' (*The Scotsman*, 5 June 1934).

If true, this is one of the most significant of all the land accounts and is spoilt only by the lack of corroboration. Miss Munro had only recently joined the staff at the Lodge and no one else was up at that time on the Sunday morning. In view of the early hour and her new surroundings, she did not like to wake her employers, Mr and Mrs Arthur Pimley.

When Mr and Mrs Pimley did hear what Miss Munro had seen they were understandably rather irritated at having missed such an experience. At about 9 o'clock in the morning they walked down to the beach and found: 'On rather heavy shingle an impression which might have been caused by a huge body and in the centre of the indentation was a branch which appeared to have been pressed into the gravel' (*The Scotsman*, 5 June 1934).

With the exception of a land sighting claimed in July 1934 by Ian J. Matheson of Fort Augustus, who said he saw a large animal on the shore near Glendoe Sawmill, nobody appears to have seen any further terrestrial excursions by the animals until 1960.

Why this sudden shyness by the animals? The volume of disturbance caused by steadily increasing traffic could have something to do with it. After 1933 and 1934 the animals

105

had to adapt to a new and much noisier atmosphere, which might have dampened any instincts to come ashore. It is significant that when, in 1960, another animal was seen out of the water it was on the Horseshoe stretch of shoreline, where there is no road and no disturbance.

At about 3.30 on the afternoon of Sunday 28 February 1960, Torquil MacLeod, a dedicated 'monster-hunter' engaged on a private expedition sponsored by Sir Charles Dixon, was driving south about two and a half miles south of Invermoriston. He was glancing across the loch to the rugged, circular fall of scree which gives that area the name 'Horseshoe' when he saw something large and dark moving on the narrow beach. Having stopped the car and focused his binoculars on the object he found himself looking at a huge animal lying partly out of the water. A few hours later he wrote the following letter to Constance Whtye:

> Altourie,
> Blackfold
> Inverness.

> Sunday, February 28, 1960.

Dear Mrs Whyte

I have had my first hint of success today! I have seen the L.N.M. at a range of one mile through x 8 glasses in broad daylight (raining). It was half ashore and I had a clear view of it for nine minutes during which time its neck moved from side to side, the animal eventually turning itself suddenly to the left in a sort of U shape and flopping into deep water (which I deduced from the fact that it did not re-appear or leave any wake, only ripples where it went in.)

I am as excited as a schoolboy about it all and this sighting has abolished the last faint doubts I had that it may have been some cognate form of animal.

As it turned I had a clear view of its left fore flipper

106

which is grey in colour, spade-shaped and devoid of any markings which might indicate toes or claws, i.e., it is therefore a flipper and not a foot.

Most unfortunately the head is too small to show any details at such a distance and in any case, except for about one second as it turned, it was facing more or less directly away from me all the time . . .

I confess to being rather appalled at its size, somehow the descriptions have not quite sunk in, or perhaps I have become too familiar with them, but there is no doubt that the individual animal I saw this afternoon was of the order of 40/60 feet in length, and I did not at any time, alas, see its tail as the body was at no time completely clear of the water. It looked, as other witnesses have said, like elephant's skin but I got the impression that the back was more rounded than humped, looking at it end on from behind with the animal resting at an angle on the shore, i.e., with its forepart higher than its hindquarters. This may of course have been due to its posture or even an effect of light and shadows such as there was.

I had a colour cine camera with me but no telephoto lens, so I reserved what film I had loaded in case it approached. I gave it half an hour after its disappearance but saw no evidence of it or its wash and so came home.

It must be the most formidable sight at close quarters. As my glasses are graticulated and I took the most careful note of marks on the shore at each end of the animal I will be able to estimate a minimum length when I have worked out my graticulation tables . . .

Mr MacLeod described the animal's head and neck as being similar to an elephant's trunk which kept moving from side to side and up and down. A pair of large paddles were visible at the rear end and, as he describes in the letter, as the animal lurched around to enter the water one of its fore paddles came into view. The minimum length, he calculated from almanac tables, was fifty feet, excluding the tail, which he did not see.

The value of this account lies in the weight one can attach to the observations of a trained watcher and experienced naturalist such as Mr MacLeod. He had the animal clearly in view for nine minutes and studied it closely; his report reflects the care and accuracy of his observations. The one outstanding point of difference between this and all the other descriptions of creatures seen on land is the size. The animal Mr MacLeod saw and measured so carefully was huge – over sixty feet long if we include the tail. In contrast, all the estimates of size in the previous land accounts describe comparatively small or medium-sized animals. Mr Cruickshank described a twenty to twenty-five foot animal; the Spicers put the length at about twenty-five feet and Arthur Grant saw a fifteen to twenty foot animal. This perhaps suggests that it is the smaller and younger animals which are more inclined to come ashore.

One further semi-land sighting deserves mention here. On 6 June 1963 six expedition members of the Loch Ness Investigation Bureau (see Chapter 7) observed and studied through binoculars at a range of just over two miles a large object which moved through shallow water and eventually remained stationary on or just off the beach at a point on the south shore opposite Urquhart Castle. The eyewitnesses gained the impression of a long, slim appendage, and 16mm cine film was shot of it. This film was subsequently analysed by the Joint Air Reconnaissance Intelligence Centre of the Royal Air Force, which reported that the object was five feet in height and seventeen feet in length. The extreme range made further evaluation impossible.

We have about a dozen reports of the animals being seen on land over a sixty-year period. In view of our almost total ignorance about these creatures it is rather futile to try to speculate why they might come ashore. It has been suggested that it may be connected with their breeding habits, or that it is some hereditary instinct left over from previous generations which used to be truly amphibious.

One wonders whether there will ever again be a land sighting like the Spicers', when one of these lumbering anachronisms stumbles into twentieth-century man's environment and on to his machinery. It is, if nothing else, a stimulating consideration for the motorist at Loch Ness!

Chapter Seven

THE NET CLOSES

Early on the morning of Saturday 23 April 1960 an English aeronautical engineer named Tim Dinsdale set out for a drive along the shores of Loch Ness which was to change the course of his life. He was 'monster-hunting'; a harmless enough pursuit, indulged in by scores of people before him, which can be very enjoyable so long as it is not undertaken too strenuously.

However, Mr Dinsdale had been taking it very seriously. For months past he had researched the subject and for the previous five days of his private expedition he had been rising at dawn and setting out to patrol various sectors of the loch – so far without any success. On this particular morning he was accustoming himself to a common emotion among monster-hunters – disappointment, since this was the final day of his expedition. The next morning he had to return to his home in Berkshire and pick up once again the rather more humdrum routine of his profession.

At about 8.30 he decided to cut short his vigil opposite the Horseshoe and return to Foyers for breakfast. Half an hour later he was passing through Upper Foyers village and nearing his hotel. At this point the road is about 300 feet above the loch and set some distance back from it. Trees obscure the water for much of the way but there is the occasional break bringing Foyers Bay and the surrounding loch into view. It was while coasting past one of these gaps that Tim Dinsdale looked out across the loch and noticed something on the surface about 1,300 yards away. In his book *Loch Ness Monster* (page 100) he describes what then happened:

Unhurriedly I stopped the car and raising my binoculars, focused them carefully upon it. The object was perfectly clear and now quite large, and although when first I had seen it, it lay sideways on, during the few seconds I had taken with the binoculars it seemed to have turned away from me. It lay motionless on the water, a long oval shape, a distinct mahogany colour and on the left flank a huge dark blotch could be seen, like the dapple on a cow. For some reason it reminded me of the back of an African buffalo – it had fullness and girth and stood well above the water, and although I could see it from end to end there was no visible sign of a dorsal fin upon it; and then, abruptly, it began to move. I saw ripples break away from the further end and I knew at once I was looking at the extraordinary humped back of some huge living creature!

Mr Dinsdale turned to the 16mm Bolex cine camera standing on its tripod in the car next to him and began to film the animal. It swam away across the loch following an erratic course and throwing out an extensive V-shaped wake. It was slowly submerging, and 200 to 300 yards from the far shore it abruptly changed direction and started swimming south, parallel to the shore. By now it was almost beneath the surface and Mr Dinsdale decided on a desperate gamble. He was running short of film – so far he had been filming for four minutes – and needed to get closer to the shore in case the animal turned and headed back across the loch. He therefore stopped filming and drove madly on, down through Lower Foyers, across a field and to the water's edge. When he got there the loch surface was calm. The animal had returned to the depths.

It was this film, just fifty feet of celluloid, which

111

heralded a new phase in the saga of the 'Monster'. For the first time since the 1930s somebody had taken a film, and a good film, of one of the animals. Suddenly the star's wrinkles disappeared. 'Nessie' was firmly back in the news, and this was a comeback which was going to last.

Although at first Mr Dinsdale tried to keep the film a secret and hoped to show it to the scientific community in private, before long the press got to hear about it. On 13 June 1960 the *Daily Mail* published details and stills from it. That evening Mr Dinsdale appeared on BBC Television's *Panorama* and the film was shown. There was a large public response and Mr Dinsdale received mail from all over the country from people expressing their support for and belief in these animals. Some observed how similar the object in the film was to something they themselves had seen in the loch.

Coincidentally, at about the same time as the film was given its first public showing, preparations were being made for another serious expedition to the loch. Thanks originally to Constance Whyte's *More Than a Legend* and, more particularly, to the encouragement of the phenomenon's only faithful zoological champion at the time, Dr Denys W. Tucker, a Principal Scientific Officer at the British Museum (Natural History), a team of thirty graduates and undergraduates from the universities of Oxford and Cambridge embarked on 27 June for a month-long investigation. Their aim was to accomplish the first scientific survey of Loch Ness to determine whether it is ecologically capable of supporting a colony of large animals, and also to carry out photographic surveillance and echo-sounding sweeps.

Unfortunately, for reasons which will be outlined below, Dr Tucker was prevented from leading this expedition in person. However, under the organisation of Cambridge graduate Peter Baker, the party took to the field with their collection of cameras and a Marconi echo sounder. During the course of the search a brief sighting of a ten-foot-long hump was made on Sunday 10 July by

Bruce Ing off Achnahannet, and several unusual echo traces were recorded. Of these the most interesting occurred on 4 July, when an object was tracked as it dived at speed from the surface to sixty feet and back again.

The expedition made one important discovery; large shoals of char at a depth of about 100 feet, the existence of which had previously only been rumoured. The overall finding was that Loch Ness is quite capable of supporting a group of large predatory animals.*

We now come to one of the most sensitive topics in the Loch Ness story, that of Dr Denys Tucker and his dismissal from his post at the British Museum (Natural History) in June 1960. Suffice it to say here that, at the time, both the press and Dr Tucker suggested that his involvement in the Loch Ness investigation and his publicly expressed belief in the animals' existence were at least a contributory factor in the confused circumstances of his departure from the Museum.

Dr Tucker had held a Museum post for eleven years and is an internationally respected expert on eels. For several years before 1960 he had vigorously pursued the Loch Ness question and had lectured on it to leading societies and at universities, though not without attempts by some university authorities to prevent the lectures. He records in a letter dated 9 January 1960 the reception he received when giving a talk entitled 'Loch Ness – the Case for Investigation' to a distinguished zoological club in London. For obvious reasons, names are omitted:

> At the dinner prior to the meeting, several members made snide remarks: 'So you're going to tell us how to catch the Monster, hee, hee!' . . . in the half hour discussion which followed [the talk], there was only one hostile critic – who sneered at Gould and ridiculed almost all the evidence and said it was

* Full reports on the expedition findings appeared in *The Scotsman* of 12, 13 and 14 September 1960.

clearly a seal. To my great delight he was practically lynched by the rest of the audience and howled down. Professor — for example, was shouting: 'You shut your – mouth! What the – hell do you know about it?'

From which it would seem that interest and support were germinating even amongst the boffins. This did not, however, save Dr Tucker in June. *The Times* reported: 'Dr Tucker said that when he told the museum authorities that he was going to investigate the Loch Ness Monster as a holiday task, he was told not to do this. He replied that they could not stop him unless they dismissed him and if they did there would be a great fuss in the Press.' Questions were, in fact, asked in Parliament.*

On the afternoon of Sunday 7 August 1960 one of the animals was independently watched by a party of people on land and by a family aboard a yacht, who also took photographs of the disturbance it made as it passed them. The shore group included Torquil MacLeod (who six months earlier had had the land sighting at the Horseshoe), his wife and a Mr and Mrs Seddon-Smith from Australia. Aboard the forty-foot motor yacht *Finola* were company director R.H. Lowrie and his family from Newcastle upon Tyne. Their log reads:

4.15 p.m. Brian on watch. Family below for Sunday lunch. Brian enquired: 'What is this monster supposed to look like? There is something coming up astern.' All hands on deck witness a curious form coming up astern between six and ten knots looking like a couple of ducks, occasionally submerging, and a neck-like protrusion breaking surface. The Monster – nothing less. As it came abeam we were fascinated, so much so that it had passed to starboard before anyone remembered that we had an old camera

* See 'The Zoologist's Tale', p. 205.

aboard. After about ten minutes it swung away to starboard towards Aldourie Point and some photographs were then taken. It swam quickly causing considerable disturbance and showing a large area of green and brown, and proceeded on a collision reciprocal course to our own.

A hurried family conference unanimously decided that something sinister was approaching, and that we should alter course to avoid a close contact.

From the shore and through binoculars Mr MacLeod could see distinct rhythmic splashes as if made by paddle action. The object's speed was estimated at eight to nine knots. Although the photographs show only the long V-wake, the Lowrie family estimated the length of the object to have been similar to that of their boat, forty feet.

The year 1961 is notable for the inception of an organisation which, in its lifetime, was to be the subject of almost as much local controversy as that generated on a wider scale by its quarry. This was the Loch Ness Investigation Bureau.

In August 1960, as a result of the new spate of interest after Tim Dinsdale's film, two well-known naturalists decided to take up the cudgels in an attempt to see what practical help could be extracted from within the establishment's ambidextrous defences. Accordingly, the two naturalists, Sir Peter Scott, son of the great Antarctic explorer and eminent founder of the Wildfowl Trust, and Richard Fitter, Council Member of the Fauna Preservation Society, approached a Member of Parliament and requested him to try to get Government assistance for 'a flat-out attempt to find what exactly is in Loch Ness.'

The MP they chose was Highland laird David James, M.B.E., D.S.C., Antarctic traveller, author and famous wartime escaper. At first Mr James eschewed involvement in such a singular subject, but once he had read *More Than a Legend* his curiosity and crusading spirit were aroused. In his booklet *Loch Ness Investigation* he wrote: 'It seemed to me quite evident that a massive case was going by default simply because the already available evidence had not been sufficiently widely disseminated, particularly to those people who are best qualified to form a judgement, namely the professional zoologists.'

Although Mr James declined to raise the matter in Parliament as Hector Hughes had done several years before, he soon became one of the driving forces in the new campaign for recognition of the animals' existence.

One of the group's first acts was to convene a special meeting in London in April 1961 to discuss the Loch Ness phenomenon. It was attended by five leading scientists; they heard evidence from Mr and Mrs Lowrie, Torquil MacLeod, Peter Baker and the Rev. William Dobb (who had a good hump sighting in August 1960) and saw Peter Macnab's photograph and Tim Dinsdale's film. After much deliberation, the expert panel decided that there was a prima facie case for investigation and that it was a subject worthy of submission to the Royal Society for investigation and to the Royal Navy for any assistance it could provide. However, none of these resolutions produced any positive results, which is understandable when one considers what one very prominent scientist said about the evidence he had seen: 'Absurd as it may seem I am forced to believe that it is actually more likely that what was seen was some artificial body, perhaps some wirelessly controlled submersible model "monster" operated by some super "leg-puller" who has been playing his tricks for some ten years or more.'

This approaches the level of the lowest cartoon humour, which frequently depicts a team of kilted frogmen swimming in Loch Ness wearing a 'Monster' outfit rather like an aquatic pantomime horse.

Notwithstanding this lack of official support, the Bureau for Investigating the Loch Ness Phenomena Ltd (as it was originally called) was formally incorporated on 20 March 1962, with David James, Constance Whyte,

Peter Scott and Richard Fitter as its directors. It was a registered charity which proposed to act primarily as a clearing-house for information and secondly as an active research body. It was decided that any profits accruing at the end of its existence should be donated to the World Wildlife Fund and the Council for Nature.

The Bureau's first foray into the active role of 'monster-hunting' took place in October 1962, when, with the assistance of Associated Television, two ex-wartime Government searchlights, each with a range of six miles, were taken to the loch and played across its dark waters every night for two weeks. The team's hope was that the animals might be attracted by the beam. On the night of 19 October one of the searchlight operators, Michael Spear, observed a 'finger-like object' standing six to eight feet out of the water, caught in the beam. Earlier that afternoon seven of the twenty-four expedition members saw and filmed a 'long, dark shape', moving through the waters off Urquhart Bay at a range of about 200 yards, which was visibly disturbing fish. Subsequent analysis by the Royal Air Force's Central Reconnaissance Establishment verified the visible length to be about eight feet, and added: 'It is not wave effect, but has some solidity, is dark in tone and glistens.'

A committee which studied the expedition's findings in November of that year and which consisted of a barrister, a marine biologist, and two naturalists (none of whom was connected with the Bureau) found: 'That there is some unidentified animate object in Loch Ness which, if it be a mammal, amphibian, reptile, fish or mollusc of any known order, is of such size as to be worthy of careful scientific examination and identification.'

A twenty-minute ATV programme, *Report on the Loch Ness Monster*, broadcast the panel's findings but made little impact on either public or press, except the *Inverness Courier*, which headlined: 'There is a Monster in Loch Ness – Expedition's Findings Accepted by Experts – Highlanders Vindicated.' It is the sort of newspaper headline one dreams about but, as with so much of importance which occurred during this period, it slipped by unnoticed.

Apart from the Bureau, other teams were also in the field in 1962. Lieutenant-Colonel H.G. Hasler, D.S.O., O.B.E., (leader of the 'Cockleshell Heroes' who in 1942 carried out a daring canoe raid on German ships in Bordeaux harbour), and a team of forty volunteers maintained a two-month watch from the beginning of June from boats and from the shore. Hydrophones, the underwater listening device, were used, and several low-frequency tapping noises were recorded which seemed animal-like in nature. Two brief sightings were made, one of which was witnessed by Commander Sir Peter Ogilvy-Wedderburn, Bt, when three small humps appeared in Urquhart Bay at a range of about fifty feet.

In July, Dr Peter Baker led another team from Cambridge University which put in nearly five hundred hours of surface observation as well as undertaking another sonar search. Three sightings of unidentified objects were made. Four boats were equipped with very sensitive echo sounders and in the course of a number of sweeps along the loch three underwater contacts were picked up, one of which immediately preceded a surface sighting.

It would be both time-consuming and tedious to catalogue all of the many things which occurred at Loch Ness in the mid-1960s, a period of intense activity involving scores of expeditions, ranging in size from the lone camper with a snapshot camera to the progressively larger Bureau expeditions. A broad outline of the events will be given here.

In 1963 about fifty Bureau volunteers spent two weeks at the loch at the beginning of June, living in caravans and tents at Achnahannet. Ten camera stations were established at strategic positions around the loch and, with the assistance of local residents, were manned from 4 a.m. to 10 p.m. every day. On 13 June, the day before the expedition packed up, film was shot of what appears to have been one of the animals from a camera position at Urquhart Castle. By coincidence, a reporter and a photographer from the Aberdeen *Evening Express* were present during the sighting. The reporter, Jay Dawson, wrote:

When we arrived at the expedition site, everybody in the party was in a state of excitement peering towards the calm, misty loch through binoculars. At first I could see nothing. Then, about a quarter of the way out from the shore and half a mile from where I was standing I saw a dark object bobbing up and down in the water.

It was moving slightly and seemed to be playing around. I could scarcely believe my eyes. Unfortunately it was too far away from me to make out definite details but I'm certain it was not any normal-sized loch creature. I have never seen anything like it in the loch before and I am convinced it was the Monster.

When we had reached a better vantage point the Monster had disappeared below the surface, creating a disturbance. As I watched I overheard one of the expedition cameramen, who had rushed to the scene before us and got pictures, say that he had a 'head and neck in the can'. (*Evening Express*, 13 June 1963)

The cameraman's optimism was unfortunately misplaced; the film was largely ruined by a heavy heat haze which impaired clarity. However, when the expedition's findings were put to another panel of independent experts in London in the autumn of 1963 they stated: 'We are impressed by the fact that distinct progression along the surface can be observed in the film and was reported by observers. There was turbulence around the object and a streak behind it . . . If this was an animate cbject, it was an animal of a species wholly unknown to any of us.'

119

The 1964 expedition took a rather different form. Instead of concentrating a lot of watching into a two-week period, it was decided to keep two camera stations going from mid-May to October, manned by successive groups of volunteers. With the financial and physical assistance of Associated Television (its deputy chairman, the late Norman Collins, had recently joined the Bureau as its Chairman) two impressive long-range camera rigs were built, consisting of a 35mm cine camera fitted with a 36-inch lens with the magnifying power to pick out a nine-inch object at a range of up to two miles, and two ex-R.A.F. 'still' cameras with 20-inch lenses, all operated from one control. One of these rigs was mounted on a platform on the ramparts of Urquhart Castle and the other was placed on an observation tower erected on a beach on the southern shore almost opposite the Castle.

In fact neither of the Bureau rigs shot any film in 1964 but a visitor with a small 8mm cine camera did. In the latter part of May, Peter Hodge and his wife Pauline embarked on a private expedition inspired by Tim Dinsdale's film and book. At about 8.15 on the morning of 21 May, Mr Hodge clambered out of their tent, which was in the field at Achnahannet used the previous year by the Bureau. He described to me what happened:

I was going over to the car to get the cameras when I noticed a pole-like object sticking up out of the flat calm surface of the water, just above the tree line. It was just like a long pole. I couldn't make out any detail because I was looking into the sun. I called to Pauline and grabbed the cameras. Unfortunately I slammed the car door shut and the object immediately disappeared. A second later a wash started to track rapidly across the loch with a black dot at the head of it. I took several colour slides and Pauline started filming it with the cine camera.

It went right across the loch and then turned left and Pauline noticed that on the left hand side there

120

were splashes rather like a paddling effect . . . I would say that the neck must have been all of four feet tall when I first saw it. The speed as it travelled across the loch was about five to eight m.p.h.

The animal's progress was also watched by four students camped in the field who came piling out of their tent when Peter Hodge shouted to his wife.

Later that day they reported the event to the Bureau expedition at Urquhart Castle and were invited to join the organisation. Since then they have been amongst the most dedicated members of the 'monster-hunting' fraternity. Strangely enough, later that same evening they had another unusual experience. A Bureau member, Ivor Newby, another 'monster-hunter' of long standing and wide experience, had arrived at Achnahannet with a Sighting Report Form for the Hodges. Peter Hodge again describes what happened:

It was rather a dull evening but the loch was still calm. I was talking to Ivor and suddenly realised he wasn't paying the slightest attention to what I was saying but was staring at the loch. I followed his gaze and saw that there were two dark objects just under or touching the surface quite near to where I had seen the neck in the morning. They clearly couldn't be rocks because there aren't any there. It is about 200 yards out from the shore and the water is over 100 feet deep. Each object was about ten feet in length. Ivor grabbed his camera and hurdled over a fence to get down the hill. I followed but caught my foot and did an almost complete somersault in the air . . . we shot some film but it was now getting so gloomy that we eventually lost sight of them . . . Nothing came out on this film.

In 1965 the Bureau moved its headquarters to Achnahannet, where it was to remain until the end of 1972, when it was finally forced to close down. A new watching policy was adopted. A main camera rig at headquarters was, in theory, manned continuously throughout the hours of daylight of the summer-long annual expeditions. In addition, when the prevailing weather was suitable, camera-vans were despatched to vantage points along the loch's northern shore. Odd sequences of film were shot in both 1965 and 1966 but despite several thousand hours of watching through depressingly damp and windy summers, convincing close-up photography continued to evade the steadily expanding numbers of Bureau volunteers.

The major development of 1966 concerned Tim Dinsdale's 1960 film. Since taking it he had made many further trips in the hope of obtaining the final, definitive proof of the animals' existence, but he had had no further sightings. In 1961 he had given up his job: he was to devote the next 26 years to the investigation.

Encouraged by the Royal Air Force's Joint Air Reconnaissance Intelligence Centre's success at analysing their films,* David James gave them Mr Dinsdale's film for evaluation. J.A.R.I.C. is an internationally respected photographic and film analytical authority. Every frame of the original Dinsdale film was optically enlarged and examined, and in January 1966 the findings were reported. As an example of the degree of accuracy attained in such an analysis, J.A.R.I.C. estimated the length of the boat which Mr Dinsdale had filmed immediately after filming the animal (to provide a comparison with an object of known size and power) at 13·3 feet. In fact its length was 14 feet. Bearing in mind that they were working from the tiny area of a 16mm film negative and the range was over a mile, such accuracy is surely impressive and allows for no reasonable criticism of their findings.

The Intelligence Centre's experts stated in an official report later published by Her Majesty's Stationery Office

* In 1965 they studied a film showing two wakes moving at first together and then obliquely to each other.

122

that the object filmed was not a surface craft or a submarine, 'which leaves the conclusion that it *probably is an animate object*' (my italics).

It was, the report said, standing about three feet above the water when first sighted, and 'Even if the object is relatively flat bellied, the normal body "rounding" in nature would suggest that there is at least two feet under the water from which it may be deduced that a cross section through the object would be NOT LESS than six feet wide and five feet high.' It was also said that the original hump was between twelve and sixteen feet in length and was travelling at between seven and ten m.p.h. The report further stated that whereas the boat Mr Dinsdale filmed showed a distinguishable boat shape, the object had no such shape; therefore the possibility that it was a boat is completely ruled out.

In 1972 Mr Dinsdale's film was sent to the American computer-enhancement experts who worked on the *Apollo* moon photographs. Their computer scanner studied each frame of the film and found that, very briefly, two further parts of the body break the surface in addition to the main hump. This had been invisible under normal projection arrangements.

Dinsdale's film and its J.A.R.I.C. analysis remain one of the most impressive and important items of evidence. There have always been people who've suggested the object Dinsdale saw and filmed was merely a boat. There are two major points contradicting this. One, remember that first he studied it through binoculars (of seven times magnification) and it clearly was *not* a boat. Two, J.A.R.I.C., in its analysis, compares the object to the boat which Dinsdale filmed later. The two were quite different. J.A.R.I.C states the object was *not* a boat. The statements of the man who saw it and of the people who studied his film are clear, concise and unambiguous. It is right that any piece of evidence should be scrutinised and, if flawed, contradicted. In the case of the Dinsdale film I would submit that the probity of the man who took it and the skill of the men who examined it remain outstandingly more impressive than the arguments of those who doubt the film.

By 1967 American interest and involvement in the search had grown to such an extent that without it the Investigation Bureau would undoubtedly have collapsed. Professor Roy Mackal, a Professor of Biochemistry at the University of Chicago, had been appointed a Director of the Bureau and was gathering support in the U.S.A. Constance Whyte had, by this time, resigned from the organisation's board. In the spring, the Field Enterprises Educational Corporation of Chicago made a donation of $20,000 to the research fund, and the Highlands and Islands Development Board gave £1,000 in recognition of the Bureau's services to the local tourist trade. The donations made it possible to invest in more long-range cameras, which finally made contact with something during the 1967 expedition.

On 22 May, Bureau watcher Les Durkin filmed a disturbance and two low humps moving through the water near Invermoriston. J.A.R.I.C. reported: 'The length of the disturbed areas are 50 feet, 65 feet, 38 feet, and 45 feet. Their speed from left to right is approximately six knots, and they have portions raised some two feet above water level.'

On 13 June, another Bureau cameraman, Dick Raynor, watched and filmed an extensive V-shaped wake moving out of Dores Bay from his position near Abriachan. As he filmed it, the pleasure boat *Scott II* came into view and proceeded parallel with it for a short distance. J.A.R.I.C. reported on this, having optically enlarged it up to 38 times magnification: 'It is probable that the mean speed of the object is not less than five m.p.h., and a possible length for that part of the object which seems to break the surface is in the order of seven feet.'

Underwater Eyes

In 1968, while the Bureau carried on its surface lookout, a new group arrived to make their contribution to the investigation. In the spring Professor D.G. Tucker, Head of the Department of Electronic and Electrical Engineering at the University of Birmingham, with Dr Hugh Braithwaite and Dr D.J. Creasey, visited the loch and decided it would make an ideal testing ground for a new type of sonar apparatus they had designed. The team returned for two weeks in August and trials began. The sonar equipment was operated from Temple Pier, and a narrow beam was directed out under the waters of Urquhart Bay. A sonar pulse was transmitted every ten seconds, and a camera was aligned to photograph each resulting display on the oscillascope screen.

At about 4.30 p.m. on 28 August,* the sonar picked up an echo from 'a large object' dubbed 'A', estimated to be about twenty metres in length, rising from the loch floor at a range of 0·8 kilometres. For the next ten minutes this object moved in and out of the beam; it dived and rose at a rate of up to 120 feet per minute and accelerated to a speed of about nine knots. During this period it was joined by two other objects, 'B' and 'C'. Object B was almost certainly a shoal of fish; this was clear from its echo characteristics. Object C, however, behaved in a truly amazing fashion by normal animal standards. It reached a speed of fifteen knots and a diving velocity of 450 feet per minute. The scientists' report continues: 'Since objects A and C are clearly comprised of animals, is it possible they could be fish? The high rate of ascent and descent makes this seem very unlikely, and fishery biologists we have consulted cannot suggest what fish they might be.' Object C was long in the vertical plane and short horizontally, suggesting a streamlined object in the act of diving.

Although Professor Tucker made no claims about the identity of these strange objects, his results were ruthlessly

* As described in *New Scientist*, 19 December 1968.

attacked in the distinguished scientific journal *Nature* (Vol. 220, 28 December 1968), which stated that 'there is little reason to take seriously the claims of Dr Braithwaite and Professor Tucker to have found a monster.'

Once again one sees the scientific establishment trying to defend its territory from the possibility that something exists which it cannot understand. Professor Tucker is an eminent sonar engineer who clearly knew vastly more about his equipment than did the editors of *Nature*, who were not even able to get their basic facts correct in their criticism of the Birmingham results.

The Birmingham team carried out further work at the loch in both 1969 and 1970 but declined to publish any details of their findings.

Despite the scientific apathy shown in Britain towards the 1968 results, American scientists, who so often seem to have a healthier curiosity than some of their British counterparts, were taking a progressively greater interest in the investigation.

The summer of 1969 was a hectic one. Field Enterprises of America sponsored an unprecedentedly large Bureau expedition which involved a miniature submarine and a sonar search. The publicity which all this inevitably attracted was augmented by a special investigation by the Independent Television News *News at Ten* programme and the *Daily Mail* newspaper. The latter sent its veteran chief reporter, the late Vincent Mulchrone, to the loch.

Unfortunately there was another hoax. Even more unfortunately, just as in 1933, the *Daily Mail* was on the receiving end. Three English gentlemen produced a giant bone which they claimed to have stumbled across one day when they were fishing. Actually, it was a portion of the discarded jaw bone of a blue whale which had formed part of a garden rockery in the grounds of a Yorkshire museum. Sadly for the *Daily Mail*, this fact emerged only after it had splashed pictures of the bone all over its main news pages.

Centrepiece of the summer's activity was the miniature

yellow submarine *Viperfish*, designed, built and piloted by Dan Taylor from Atlanta, Georgia. Its purpose was to home-in on any targets picked up by the sonar, which was being operated by American electronics expert Robert Love from the chartered motor vessel *Rangitea*. In addition to *Viperfish* a Vickers Oceanics *Pisces* submersible was also at Loch Ness to carry out underwater diving trials, and to tow a five-ton dummy monster around the loch. This was one of the props in the film *The Private Life of Sherlock Holmes*, which was being shot at Urquhart Castle. The model, at much emotional and financial cost to the film-makers, sank on its first outing.

Pisces made a number of dives, one of which reached a depth of 820 feet, seventy feet deeper than the loch's official maximum depth. At 750 feet it encountered a strange whirlpool current, and elsewhere the crew noticed fish and eels with unusual colourings. Their most interesting experience from the 'monster hunting' point of view came on an occasion when the craft was hovering fifty feet off the bottom in the main channel of the loch about 300 yards north of Urquhart Castle. A sonar target was picked up at a range of 600 feet and the submersible began to home in on it. When it was 400 feet away the target moved and disappeared from the sonar screen and no further contact was made with it.

To add to the pandemonium, a film crew from the Walt Disney Film Company arrived, and under the direction of Ken Peterson what was intended to be a TV colour documentary was shot. Back in 1949, Walt Disney himself actively considered the Loch Ness Monster as a subject for one of his nature films but shelved the idea. Rather regrettably, the 1969 filming resulted in a half-hour semi-serious production, *Man, Mysteries and Monsters,* starring a multi-coloured, half-witted cartoon 'Monster' arguing indignantly with a doubtful commentator that he was not just the pink elephant of some over-lubricated Scotsman's dreams.

Meanwhile, the serious 'monster-hunt' was slowly getting

underway. Dan Taylor was having some difficulty in adapting his craft for the dangerous task he had undertaken, and *Viperfish* never really proved effective. It was too small for the vastness of Loch Ness, and gave its intrepid pilot some heart-stopping moments, as, for instance, when the pressure hatch was jolted partly open and water began to flood in, or when the whole two-ton craft was swirled right around by some unseen force whilst resting on the bottom.

Mounted on *Viperfish* was a biopsy dart fired by compressed air, with which it was hoped to recover a tiny portion of skin from one of the animals, allowing them to be identified. This dart had originally been introduced by Professor Roy Mackal several years previously, but when the press heard about it the result was a question in the House of Lords. Lord Kilmany asked Her Majesty's Government whether they were satisfied 'that any monsters that may chance to inhabit that loch will not be subjected to damage or assault?' The Joint Parliamentary Under-Secretary for Scotland, Lord Hughes, replied that he was satisfied, and went on to ignore a pointed question from Lord Hawke as to whether he would like to be 'potted' by an airgun to take samples of his tissue.

Extracts from this debate were broadcast to the *Apollo 11* astronauts on their pioneering journey to the moon.

For six weeks starting in September Bob Love and his team plodded up and down the loch at all hours of the day and night operating the specially adapted Honeywell sonar. Among a number of unusual contacts, one displayed all the characteristics of being caused by a very large animal when, on 10 October, an object was tracked for more than two minutes near Foyers.

It was unfortunate that this success did not occur a few weeks earlier when the ITN and *Daily Mail* expedition was presenting daily coverage of the investigation's progress. They had brought their own sonar team from the Plessey Company, which sat in the middle of the loch and piped 50 kilowatts of low-frequency 'pinging' into the water which reverberated along the loch's whole twenty-two-mile length. No contacts were made and the viewing and reading public was disappointed.

The following year, 1970, Tim Dinsdale took on the job of directing the Bureau's surface watching whilst Bob Love continued his sonar investigation. The summer also saw the debut of a new group of researchers who were later to play a very major role in the hunt: Dr Robert Rines and a small team from the Academy of Applied Science of Boston, Massachusetts, a private organisation set up in 1963 to look into unexplored areas of science and to foster cooperation between the applied sciences and other disciplines. Robert H. Rines was first attracted by the Loch Ness mystery in 1958, when on a visit to Inverness he read *More Than a Legend*. At that time he discussed the possibility of an expedition with scientific colleagues, but the project remained dormant until, in 1969, he heard a lecture on the subject at the Massachusetts Institute of Technology by Professor Roy Mackal and decided to offer the Academy's assistance to the search.

An autogyro was also used in the hunt for the first time in 1970. Its designer and pilot, Wing-Commander Ken Wallis, completed a month's flying over the loch, but without any success. Sonar chief Bob Love continued his underwater sweeps and also experimented with hydrophone equipment. Microphones were suspended in various localities from large oil drums containing the recording equipment. In total, four unusual sets of noises were picked up which appeared to be animate in origin. Amongst them were what Professor Mackal describes as 'clicks and knocks' which followed a regular rhythmic beat and which stopped every time a boat approached.

Bob Rines and his team, which included Dr Martin Klein, designer of the Klein Associates high-frequency side-scan sonar, arrived in September. Included in their equipment was a delightful collection of 'lures', consisting of a mixture of animal hormones which were fruitlessly trailed about the loch by the Academy team from Tim Dinsdale's boat *Water Horse*. However, their sonar was more successfui. On 21 September, the side-scan apparatus detected two large objects passing through its beam whilst it was lashed to the end of Temple Pier. A few moments later one of these objects passed back in the opposite direction, showing a reversed 'shape'. Two days later the side-scan transducer 'fish', which sends out and receives the sonar signal, was towed from *Water Horse* in the Horseshoe region and several more contacts with large, moving underwater objects were made.

This is, of necessity, a brief review of the many developments in the Loch Ness investigation during this period. So much happened during the late 1960s and early 1970s that it is impossible to dwell in any detail on individual events. But this review does, I hope, show that from 1968 onwards, expeditions consistently succeeded in tracking large underwater objects on sonar. The essence of the criteria of scientific acceptance is surely the ability to repeat a result under controlled conditions. Intriguing sonar contacts have been made at Loch Ness, again and again: yet official science has looked on impassively. It has given no encouragement. Alongside the serious side to this phase of the 'monster hunt,' the light-hearted and at times bizarre spin-offs from it continued as well. The presence of the Loch Ness Investigation Bureau's headquarters at Achnahannet, where an exhibition was open to visitors, attracted its share of the eccentric and the unusual. There was, for example, the man who claimed the loch was full of people from Venus and that the 'Monster' was a Venusian spaceship; or the character who believed it used to come out every night, fly around and eat human beings; or the annual bicycling visitor who would tell people he had found a 'Nessie-nest' and report this year's brood of eggs! The exhibition also attracted tens of thousands of other visitors. In 1971, for example,

50,000 people viewed the small display of photographs, maps and charts.

In 1961 it was reported that Pietro Annigoni had been commissioned to paint the Monster; the following year King Olav of Norway expressed special interest in the mystery when he visited Inverness.

In 1960 an Inverness councillor suggested offering a £5,000 reward for the first authentic photograph leading to positive zoological classification of the animals. The Common Good Committee threw the idea out since it was 'not competent' to do such a thing. At the same time an Isle of Wight zoo owner announced that he was training two dogs to 'sniff the monster out'.

In 1966 a Mr Barry Watson of Bingley, Yorkshire, attempted to swim the length of Loch Ness. He was evidently not impressed by the animals' record of good behaviour since he had an escort in boats armed with harpoon guns. Had anything appeared and had the date been 1971, they could perhaps have been £1 million the richer, for in that year a large Scotch whisky company offered this figure as a reward to anyone who captured the 'Monster' and delivered it to them in London. Obviously they turned a publicity-hungry blind eye to the legal restrictions on any such action, but nevertheless they took out an insurance policy with Lloyds. At first, they had great difficulty in obtaining cover, since nobody knew the correct category for 'Nessie' – livestock, marine or agricultural? After hesitating for three weeks a policy was issued and Lloyds upheld its tradition of offering insurance for every contingency.

In July 1970 a lecturer in visceral physiology at a London college, Douglas Drysdale, stated that any 'Monsters' in Loch Ness must have been killed by pollution. On the day he made his announcement two sightings were reported to the Loch Ness Investigation Bureau. During the British Week in Tokyo in 1969, Donald Harden of the 'London Museum at Kensington' gallantly

131

offered to deliver a lecture on any requested subject. Unfortunately for him the Japanese wanted to hear about 'Nessie', and the Board of Trade had to tell the inquisitive hosts that the 'Monster' was still regarded as a myth and not the sort of 'cultural subject Mr Harden felt capable of discussing.' He eventually gave his talk on the history of the Tower of London.

A peak in worldwide interest in the mystery seems to have been reached in 1969, no doubt as a result of all the lochside activity and publicity. At the end of the year, Encyclopaedia Britannica announced that Loch Ness was among the leaders in the table of ten subjects of greatest public interest, judged by the number of requests they received for information.

The serious expeditions were not the only ones to succeed in tracking the animals on sonar. In March 1964 the Stornoway fishing boat *Girl Norma* picked up a thirty-foot-long object at a depth of about 250 feet. In August 1966 the British Medical Association motor yacht *Pharma* tracked a moving object on the surface on its radar. One of those on board, Mike Amery, estimated it was about thirty feet long. In April 1969 the echo sounder of the trawler *Ha-Burn* detected a very large object over 700 feet down. Skipper James Runcie of Cullen said: 'There was definitely something unusual down there.' The following April the Fraserburgh trawler *Tea Rose* detected a large object rising through the water column at about seven knots. 'Never seen anything like it,' commented the skipper, Charles Duthy.

There were a number of good surface sightings as well, though none of them occurred in view of the Loch Ness Investigation Bureau's cameras, or if they did nobody was looking at the right moment.

One evening in July 1963 two Dores men, Dan McIntosh and James Cameron, were fishing from a small boat about 200 yards off Tor Point. At about 10 o'clock they realised that the boat was rocking on the flat calm water. Suddenly the head and neck of one of the animals reared four to five feet out of the water only twenty to thirty yards away from them. A short way behind the neck was a small hump. A moment later it sank vertically out of sight, causing a commotion in the water. The two men continued to fish but found that the area had suddenly become sterile. Mr McIntosh later described the appearance of the animal to F.W. Holiday. He said the head was wide and very ugly and was a continuation of the curve of the neck, that is, it was not distinctly separate from the neck. He saw no features on the head but said that there was a hairy mane hanging off its neck. Colour was brownish-black.

The following account is taken from a Loch Ness Investigation Bureau Sighting Report Form of 1965 and is one of the most interesting written accounts of the mental reaction of a person who quite unexpectedly comes across one of the animals. The author is Miss E.M.J. Keith, the headmistress of Rothienorman School:

My brother-in-law and I went out from Inverness to Dores on the beautiful evening of Tuesday, 30 March, with the intention of walking from Dores to Tor Point as I was interested in seeing the changing face of the countryside . . . There was a marvellous sunset with reflections of hills and red sky and the loch was as calm as a millpond . . . And then it happened! Paddling across the loch towards Dores and not very far out from the shore was this black creature. There was no commotion in the water. As it came in line with us the creature changed direction from crossing and proceeded down the middle of the loch. I was rooted to the spot for I had never seen anything like this before . . . That this was a living creature on the water there was no doubt, but of what species I had no idea. There was no lashing of the tail, though the big rings formed a large wake and continued to be visible throughout the entire sighting of the creature, which made good speed down the loch so easily, sometimes rising until some feet of black body could be seen. I felt that here was some unknown creature playing itself in Dores Bay . . . My brother-in-law began to talk of estimating distances but woman-like I was not interested. I was puzzled. I was almost shocked at what had happened to me. I kept repeating, 'What is it? It is black. It is big. It made a great speed leisurely. It must be – it can't be the Monster!' I was almost afraid to say the word aloud. Sightings are so rare that I had never expected that it would happen to me.

Miss Keith's brother-in-law, James Ballantyne, wrote:

The head was completely similar to that of a python and was held at right angles to the neck. The neck was very elongated and slim, thickening at a point some one foot above the water. The neck and head stood some four to six feet above the water . . . I saw no body but the speed at which it went through the water with its head held high and the distance travelled could only make one surmise that it had a huge body and a very strong method of propulsion . . . it was perfectly silhouetted against the setting sun and I can only say that I have never been so fascinated and thrilled although it is also a trifle frightening.

On the evening of 18 July 1970 one of the animals was watched for several minutes in Urquhart Bay by Mr and Mrs John Tyrrel from Kenya, and Wing-Commander and Mrs Basil Cary, who live in a cottage on the southern side of the Bay. Mr Tyrrel, a lecturer at Nairobi University, told how 'I observed the object through my binoculars and saw several distinct wakes as it moved and a narrow sleekish neck which tapered only towards the end. It did not move continuously but in two or three surges.'

They stopped a passing car containing five people, and

134

Wing-Commander and Mrs Cary came out of their house to see what the commotion was about. Mrs Cary takes up the story: 'By the time we got to the roadside there was just one hump visible, which looked dark brown except for where the light from the sunset was shining on it. After a moment it turned and went away towards the far shore and followed it for fifteen or perhaps twenty yards and then went down. But the nine of us stood and watched it, there was no question about it at all. The Tyrrels had had a marvellous view of the head and neck and body but the head and neck had gone down by the time we got there.'

In all, the Loch Ness Investigation Bureau accepted two hundred eye-witness accounts between 1963 and 1972. In most cases the witnesses were interviewed. Many reports were rejected because it was felt the people concerned had made a genuine mistake.

The Fakers
Since a basic purpose of this book is to set the Loch Ness record straight it unfortunately becomes necessary to deal with those who have produced, wittingly or unwittingly, photographs which when scrutinised critically leave many serious doubts as to their authenticity. In approaching this sensitive aspect of the story some people have suggested that one simply ignores these photographs. However, unless a clear distinction is drawn between reliable and unreliable evidence, the former can stand little chance of gaining credence and acceptance by the scientific community and the world at large. Fraudulent photographs infect genuine ones with the malignant reflux of suspicion; they confuse and degrade the real issue for which many people have been fighting for so long. It therefore seems correct to say a word about them since their continued production can only hinder scientific investigation of this subject.

On 2 October 1959 the *Sunday Express* reported that a

twenty-six-year-old Gateshead fireman, Peter O'Connor, was planning an expedition with sixty fellow members of the Northern Naturalists Association. The paper reported: 'The hunters will be armed with two Bren guns mounted on canoes, harpoon guns, underwater spearguns. "And," said Mr O'Connor, "we may use a bomb. I'll take a machete . . . if we are lucky we should only have one burst of firing." '

Mr O'Connor was speedily told by the authorities what he could do with his reported Bren guns and bomb, and the expedition was postponed. However, the following May, having appealed in vain to the Chancellors of the Universities of Oxford and Cambridge for help, Mr O'Connor went to the loch with one companion and camped near Foyers for a few days. At about 6.30 on the morning of 27 May, Mr O'Connor claims he took a photograph of one of the animals at a range of twenty-five yards whilst he was standing waist-deep in the water.

The photograph is truly amazing. It shows a large rounded body, sixteen feet long according to one of Mr O'Connor's estimates, and, to the front, a cylindrical object rising out of the water, which Mr O'Connor felt was the head and neck. In the *New Scientist* magazine of 23 January 1969, Dr Maurice Burton, who took a special interest in Mr O'Connor's photograph and had met him in 1959, wrote: 'On the shore (where Mr O'Connor claimed he had taken the picture a fortnight earlier) I found the remains of three large polythene bags, a ring of stones each about nine inches in diameter tied together with string and a stick that looked identical with the neck and head of O'Connor's monster. A photograph taken subsequently of an inflated polythene bag weighted with stones and with the stick wedged in front of it does not differ in any significant way from the O'Connor picture.'

Surprisingly, although it was two hours after dawn and the photograph was taken at water level, there is no background in the picture, just blackness. Mr O'Connor's stories, which together with his photograph have received quite wide publicity over the years, have contained so many contradictions that it would be unwise to accept this photograph as authentic.

In August 1969 a man called Frank Searle settled at Loch Ness intent upon remaining there until he solved its mystery. His home was a small tent by the water's edge near Dores. For the first two and a half years of his expedition, Mr Searle, a professional soldier for most of his life who before going north was the manager of a London greengrocery business, lived a hermit-like existence and maintained a constant and dedicated lochside vigil, enduring the many hardships, both mental and physical, of full-time 'monster-hunting'. During this time he had only a simple box camera, and although he claimed to have made over a dozen sightings he did not take any photographs showing tangible or easily discernible objects.

In the summer of 1972 Mr Searle was loaned sophisticated cine camera equipment and bought a 35mm reflex camera with a 200mm telephoto lens. Since then, Mr Searle has produced and disseminated a number of sets of photographs which he claims show the unknown animals which inhabit Loch Ness. Despite the availability of cine cameras, he has never been able to shoot any cine film to corroborate his still photographs.

Of all Mr Searle's photographs, perhaps the most remarkable is a series which he claims (see the booklet *Loch Ness and The Great Glen*) to have taken on the early evening of 21 October 1972. According to press reports (*Daily Record*, various editions, 1 November 1972), he was out in his dinghy when 'there was a tremendous splash and the monster appeared.' He took a series of three shots of an object lying on the surface of the water showing a strangely ungraceful and disproportioned head and neck with a wide open mouth. In all three shots Mr

Searle caught the 'animal' with its mouth open. The 'animal' then dived, according to Mr Searle, and reappeared a moment later on the other side of his dinghy, again about 250 yards away.

This time it was in a two-hump configuration – the smaller one purportedly being the head. The configuration does not change at all in the six further photographs he took. These photographs have been studied, and an unusually straight line has been observed on the back of the 'head' which, together with the sharp angle at the object's apex, gives it an appearance not unlike that of a floating oil-drum.

It is a regrettable fact which can be easily proved that these photographs have been tampered with. Mr Searle has also produced another series identical with the original shots in all respects except that an extra hump has been added to them by some process of superimposition or by rephotography.

Mr Searle also claims to have photographed the animals on 27 August 1972, 27 March and 1 August 1973, and 8 January 1974. All these pictures show curious shapes in the water very close to the beach. In all he claims to have over twenty photographs showing the animals.

Mr Searle's photographs have featured prominently in the popular British press and have been sold to newspapers, magazines and television companies throughout the world. Mr Searle has not, however, consented to the release of his pictures for serious study by photographic experts.

Because of the highly suspicious content of some of Mr Searle's photographs and the inconsistencies of the facts surrounding the taking of them, it is not possible to accept them as being authentic photographs of animate objects in Loch Ness. The true nature of the objects depicted in his photographs and the reasons for producing them are matters for speculation. A clue to the latter may lie in a remark made by Mr Searle when he was interviewed for an American television film (*Monsters – Mysteries or Myths?* broadcast by CBS in November 1974). He commented: 'I figure it would be worth a lot of money; the use of the pictures by the media all over the world would fetch something like £200,000 over the first six months. After that there would be lectures, personal appearances and so on.' Thankfully, Mr Searle has now left Loch Ness.

The 1972 Flipper Photographs
So far the story has progressed from the day St Columba apparently saw a 'water monster' in Loch Ness in A.D. 565, through the centuries of Highland strife and upheaval into the modern era and the start of the 'monster-hunt' in 1933. Ever since the first watchers went to Loch Ness in the autumn of that year, the ambition has been to obtain a close-up photograph of Nessie. Over the past fifty years, several hundred thousand man-hours must have been devoted to this objective – without success. In the years immediately before 1972, expeditions did succeed in tracking large underwater objects on sonar but never managed to place a camera near enough to one of them to take a photograph. These failures were about to be remedied.

In 1971, Dr Robert Rines and his Academy of Applied Science team brought an underwater electronic stroboscopic camera with them on their expedition. This equipment had been developed by Professor Harold Edgerton of the Massachusetts Institute of Technology – the famous 'Papa Flash' in Jacques Cousteau's adventures and inventor of the electronic flash-gun principle.

Although the strobe camera was operated without result over a two-week period in August 1971, earlier in that year Bob Rines did have the thrill of a surface sighting. Late in the long, light evening of 23 June he, with his wife Carol and Wing Commander and Mrs Basil Cary, observed a twenty-foot-long hump as it moved about two thirds of a mile away in Urquhart Bay. It was

139

examined through a telescope from the Cary's cottage overlooking Stone Point and compared in size to a fishing vessel anchored nearby. 'This', said Dr Rines, 'finally destroyed any last doubts I had that we are dealing with a very large living creature here at Loch Ness.'

The 1972 season opened with yet another hoax – perpetrated this time by those who should have known better: a team from a Yorkshire zoo. On the last day of March they publicly announced that they had found the body of a mysterious creature washed up near Foyers and that they had removed it and were taking it south for examination.

There are times when the establishment can act with amazing alacrity and this was one such occasion. Scotland's proprietary instincts were aroused, and police road-blocks were set up to foil this Sassenach plot to rob them of their 'Monster'. News-agency lines hummed, television news editors gasped, and Loch Ness residents sighed and remembered that tomorrow would be April Fool's Day. The hoax worked well until the police stopped the zoo men's van on the Forth road bridge, and the 'monster' was found to be a dead elephant-seal with its whiskers shorn off. The zoo 'scientists' did very nicely – a Sunday newspaper splashed their 'How we fooled everybody' story all over its front page the next day.

That was the light side to 1972, the one which grabbed most of the headlines. What follows is the other side, which occupied few of them.

At the beginning of August Bob Rines and a group from the Academy returned yet again with the underwater stroboscopic camera and Raytheon sonar equipment. In view of the important role which it was to play, a word here about the construction of the stroboscopic camera. It consists of two water-tight cylinders, one of which contains a very bright flashing light; the other holds a 16mm. camera which exposes one frame simultaneously with the light's illumination.

For several days a team consisting of the Academy

140

scientists and Investigation Bureau volunteers operated the sonar and the camera without any response from the loch's depths. The research was concentrated in Urquhart Bay; every night, when the loch was quiet and deserted, they set out in two small boats and deployed the equipment in such a way that the area being photographed by the camera was monitored by the sonar.

Late on the evening of 7 August, the crews took up their positions as normal on the northern side of Urquhart Bay. The sonar transducer (the box which sends out and receives the signal) was lowered to a depth of about thirty-five feet from the Bureau's boat *Narwhal*. About forty yards further out was the small motor cruiser *Nan*, from which the strobe camera was suspended at a depth of forty-five feet. The sonar beam was aligned to 'shine' in the direction of the underwater camera, which flashed and took a picture every fifteen seconds. Peter Davies of the Loch Ness Investigation Bureau, skipper of *Narwhal*, gave me this account of the night's events:

It had been quite choppy until about midnight, when the wind dropped and the water settled down to become jelly calm.

There were a lot of fish in the bay (salmon congregating for the autumn run up the river), which were appearing on the chart as tiny little dots about the size of a pin head . . .

It was about 1.45 a.m., Hilary Ross was watching the sonar screen and Dave Wiseman and myself were drowsing. Hilary suddenly said that she thought something odd was coming on. We both got up and joined her and noticed that the fish dots were becoming streaks, as if the fish were all moving rapidly away from the area.

Then it started – a big, black trace started to appear. To begin with we thought it must be two or three fish close together. But then it got bigger and blacker and thicker; we could hardly believe our eyes

141

– something huge was moving down there, very near to where the camera was. We watched it in silence for a moment – the size of it was so large in comparison with the fish. It appeared to be moving slowly but the trace kept on coming.

Peter then transferred from *Narwhal* into a smaller boat, *Fussy Hen,* tied up alongside, and started to paddle across to *Nan*, which held Bob Rines and the rest of the team.

I don't mind telling you that it was rather a strange feeling rowing across the pitch-black water knowing that there was a very large animal just thirty feet below. It was the sheer size of the echo-trace that was frightening. When I reached *Nan* I told Bob what was happening and he and Jan Willums (of the Academy) got into *Fussy Hen* and we rowed as quickly and as quietly as we could back across to *Narwhal*. When we got back on board the echo was still there, slowly being etched out on the paper. By now it was about the size of my thumb-nail. We were all excited but we just sat there, hardly daring to move, and watched in fascination as the trace got longer and longer.

By now there were no fish at all on the screen – just the trace of whatever was beneath the boats. Peter went on:

Then a slight breeze got up and *Narwhal* started to swing round and we lost it. The trace stopped. I got out on deck and tried to paddle *Narwhal* round again with an oar but it was no good. It had gone.

A few days later the Academy team flew back to the United States, taking with them the roll of 16mm film which had been recovered from the underwater camera, and the sonar chart. Many hopes rested on them: could it be, I

142

The search above water: one of the Loch Ness Investigation Bureau's camera vans above Urquhart Bay in the 60s ...

... and below water. The American scientist, Dr Robert Rines (*standing with hat*) positioning one of his camera rigs in Urquhart Bay

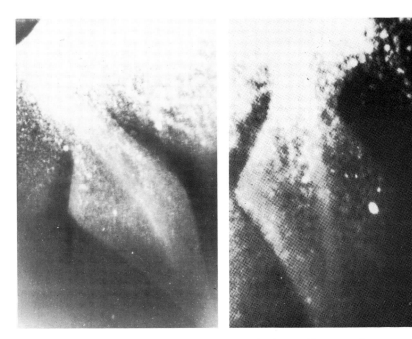

The 1972 underwater photographs of a flipper-like appendage, captured on film by Dr Robert Rines and his team

Sir Peter Scott's interpretation of what the 1972 underwater photographs show

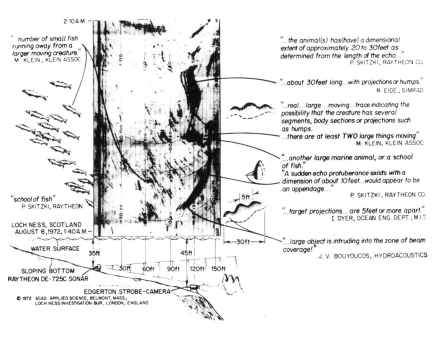

"...number of small fish running away from a larger moving creature."
M. KLEIN, KLEIN ASSOC.

"...the animal(s) has(have) a dimensional extent of approximately 20 to 30 feet as determined from the length of the echo..."
P. SKITZKI, RAYTHEON CO.

"...about 30 feet long...with projections or humps."
R. EIDE, SIMRAD

"...real...large...moving...trace indicating the possibility that the creature has several segments, body sections or projections such as humps.
...there are at least TWO large things moving"
M. KLEIN, KLEIN ASSOC.

"...another large marine animal, or a school of fish."
"A sudden echo protuberance exists with a dimension of about 10 feet...would appear to be an appendage..."
P. SKITZKI, RAYTHEON CO.

"school of fish"
P. SKITZKI, RAYTHEON

"...target projections...are 5 feet or more apart."
I. DYER, OCEAN ENG. DEPT., M.I.T.

LOCH NESS, SCOTLAND
AUGUST 8,1972, 1:40 A.M.

"...large object is intruding into the zone of beam coverage!"
J. V. BOUYOUCOS, HYDROACOUSTICS

WATER SURFACE

SLOPING BOTTOM
RAYTHEON DE-725C SONAR

EDGERTON STROBE-CAMERA
© 1972 ACAD. APPLIED SCIENCE, BELMONT, MASS.;
LOCH NESS INVESTIGATION BUR., LONDON, ENGLAND

The sonar chart from the night of 7/8 August 1972 when the underwater photographs were taken, showing the large intruder and the interpretations of sonar experts

Cryptocleidus, an 11-foot-long predator from the plesiosaur family, believed to have become extinct 70 million years ago

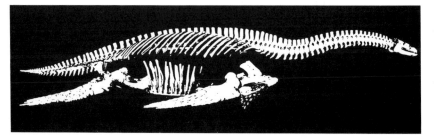

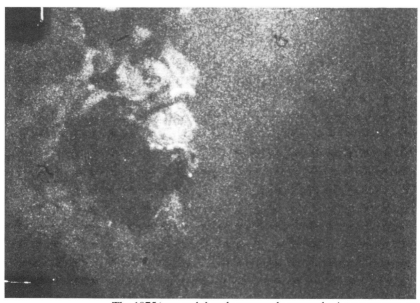

The 1975 'gargoyle' underwater photograph. A tree-stump, or something more mysterious?

The 1975 'neck and body' underwater photograph ... or part of the loch floor?

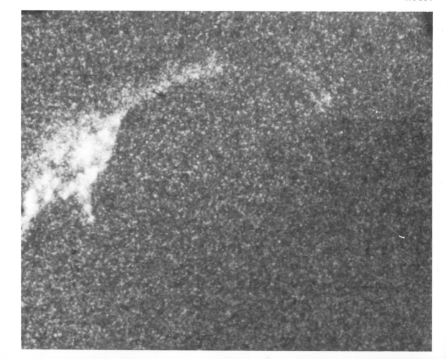

October 1987: the line of sonar boats of 'Operation Deepscan' moving up the loch

Adrian Shine *(left)*, Loch Ness researcher and leader of 'Operation Deepscan' with sonar chart

Inset: one of the unexplained sonar contacts obtained by the sonar sweeps

The wooden hut built by the author in a field above Urquhart Castle in the spring of 1972, from which he watched for many months

View from the author's camera hut towards Urquhart Castle

Hugh Ayton, the farmer who
followed one of the animals down
the loch in a boat in August 1963

Basil and Freddie Cary. Mrs Cary first saw
one of the animals in 1917; since then she's
had eighteen more sightings

Father Gregory Brusey of the Benedictine Abbey in Fort Augustus. He
and a colleague sighted one of the animals in October 1971

Constance Whyte, author of *More Than a Legend*. Mrs Whyte died in January 1982

David James, D.S.C., former M.P. and founder of the Loch Ness Investigation Bureau, who died in December 1986

Tim Dinsdale, 1924-1987. Champion of Loch Ness

remember wondering, that the camera had glimpsed whatever it was that had caused the sonar trace?

The films from the many nights of work in the bay were developed under bond at the head office of Eastman Kodak in the United States. Their staff signed statements that none of the films had been tampered with in any way whatsoever. The roll from the night of 7-8 August was located. And on it, at the time the sonar indicated there was a large underwater target in the vicinity of the camera, were several frames showing the hazy outlines of something solid. But the images were blurred and uncertain; the heavy suspension of peat particles in the water was like a fog, breaking up the beam of light and shielding the object which the camera was attempting to photograph.

To try to improve the definition the pictures were sent to the Jet Propulsion Laboratory (JPL) at the California Institute of Technology in Pasadena for computer enhancement. This is the process which has been used for many years by N.A.S.A. to sharpen up the space photographs; it is a technique which is also regularly used in the fields of astronomy, geology and forensic science. Inevitably, since a computer is involved, the process has aroused both curiosity and suspicion, culminating in 1984 in an article in a respected American science magazine which suggested that the pictures had been 're-touched' and, by implication, impugned the integrity of the Academy and the provenance of the pictures.

So before we go any further let me, in view of the significance of the 1972 underwater evidence, set down the facts about the computer enhancement process and its application to these pictures, so that retrospective attempts by those who were not there at the time but who have been only too eager lately to publish incomplete and prejudicial accounts of it all can be seen in a proper light.

I have met the scientist who carried out the computer enhancement. His name is Alan Gillespie. The 'enhancement' involves the computer in a number of scans of the image. In the case of a frame of 16mm film, which is just 8 x 10mm in size, the computer breaks the picture down into 800,000 microscopically small spots of light of different intensity. It then filters out the extraneous detail. It cannot put something there that was not there when the picture was taken: what it can do is remove some of the clutter which is obscuring the image and make it clearer and sharper. In the case of these pictures it filtered out the haziness caused by the peat in the water. As JPL has itself said in an emphatic statement: 'The process will not introduce objects resembling monsters into pictures which do not contain them.'

The computer did a number of different electronic scans. It produced several filtered versions which were then put together to form the published image. To quote Charles Wyckoff of the Academy: 'The composite was an entirely proper procedure that produced a picture containing all the original information of the original film with the edges of any solid objects emphasised as delineated by the computer scans.' It is disingenuous for critics to imply that the enhancement was some sleight of hand. It was not.

So what in fact do the pictures reveal? Two of them show a flipper-like object. Zoologists who studied them at the Academy's invitation concluded that the object was a right hind limb. The image appears in consecutive frames, in a slightly different configuration in each. A series of optical measurements have led the Academy to believe that the 'flipper' is between four and six feet in length. This calculation was done by Charles Wyckoff and by Professor Harold Edgerton, the camera's designer, himself. A third picture, which was taken a few minutes later, was also enhanced and it appears to show two separate, hazy images, but there is insufficient detail to suggest what they might be.

Perhaps more than anything it was the coincidence of the sonar and photographic data which offered new and persuasive evidence. The one cross-checked and seemed to corroborate the other. It was, after so many bleak years since the Dinsdale film in 1960, a development of considerable significance.

The material was seen by scientists at the British Museum (National History) at a private meeting in October attended by Bob Rines and Tim Dinsdale. In a statement they said there was no doubt that the photographs were genuine and that an object is visible in them, but added 'Information in the photographs is insufficient to enable identification.'

Zoologists at the Smithsonian Institution – the American equivalent of the British Museum – were rather less circumspect. Dr George Zug, the Curator of the Division of Reptiles and Amphibians, said the pictures showed 'a rhomboidal shape attached by a narrow base to a larger object. I interpret this as a flipper-like appendage protruding from the side of a robust body.' Henry Lyman, the Vice Chairman of the New England Aquarium in Boston, said: 'It does not appear mammalian. The general shape and form of the flipper does not fit anything known today.'

When the sonar experts studied the chart from the night of 7-8 August they found evidence to suggest that a second animal was in the vicinity when the photographs were taken. The length of the objects was estimated to be in the region of twenty to thirty feet. The experts' comments can be seen together with the relevant section of the sonar chart among the illustrations.

It seemed, in the autumn of 1972, that progress was being made at last. I was in my camera hut on the southern shore of Urquhart Bay on the night the photographs were taken. I well remember the boat crews' excitement early on the morning of 8 August when they came ashore with the sonar chart which showed the activity below them; then the wait while the Academy went home to examine the film and the sense of triumph when it was learned that there *were* photographs which showed something. Surely, we thought, this would stir the scientific establishment.

But when the pictures and sonar evidence were published on 1 November 1972 the response was disappointing. I travelled north from university in Leeds to be at the Investigation Bureau's headquarters on the lochside. The pictures were being presented by Bob Rines at a lecture to the Institute of Electrical and Electronics Engineers in Boston; they were thereafter put on display at the Boston Museum of Science. But in Britain little attention was paid to them; indeed newspapers were far more preoccupied by a dramatic (and entirely fraudulent) series of pictures of Nessie which were produced 48 hours ahead of Bob Rines' lecture by the eccentric Frank Searle, the lone monster-hunter in his tent near Dores. He'd got wind of the Academy's results and was determined that no one was going to steal his thunder. So he got busy with a couple of oil drums (and what looked like an old pair of bedroom slippers) and of course the results were far more along the lines of what Fleet Street imagined a Nessie story should be. The rather murky photographs and complicated sonar readings of the Academy seemed tedious by comparison. It was an easy victory for Mr Searle's monster!

The following year the Academy returned with a new underwater camera rig, linked to a sonar triggering device. It was placed about thirty feet down off the southern shore of Urquhart Bay, below my camera hut. For three months I looked after it, every few days lugging about a dozen twelve-volt car batteries up and down the hillside and out to the yacht which was positioned above the rig. Equipment aboard the boat would indicate if the cameras had been triggered, whereupon an American diver who was working for the Academy would go down and bring the cameras to the surface. Sadly, but to no one's great surprise, nothing seemed to work terribly well and although there was evidence of several sonar intrusions, no film was shot. My most vivid memory of that summer was of wiring up the car batteries wrongly. The short-circuit which resulted – and the cloud of acrid smoke which accompanied it – very nearly deposited me in the silt next to the camera rig.

The summer of 1973 also provided the electrifying

spectacle of the first Japanese attempt to locate Nessie. In September a team from Tokyo arrived, and the newsmen followed. Audiences were led to believe that Japanese technology and ingenuity were to be applied to the mystery. Not so. The expedition leader was a Mr Yoshio Kou who was an impresario; his 'principal sonar expert' was a lady who evidently made her living singing in a nightclub in Tokyo. She was, she told me, absolutely convinced that Nessie existed, though a little dismayed to find that Loch Ness was so big. They had fun; enjoyed the attention paid to them by their own and other countries' news media; posed energetically and then slipped home after a couple of months spent touring the Highlands. When he got back to Tokyo, Mr Kou declared that he was considering which of the world's other 'great adventures' to explore next.

The Loch Ness investigation had reached a turning point. The Investigation Bureau was forced to close down at the end of 1972 through lack of funds and the absence of the necessary planning approval from Inverness-shire Council to continue its stay at its headquarters site at Achnahannet. The Bureau had failed to prove that the loch contained an unidentified species, despite the thousands of hours of effort of its members. It had acted as the focal point of the inquiry, gathering and collating eyewitness evidence and lobbying gently through people such as David James and Peter Scott on Nessie's behalf. From now on the search would revert to smaller individual teams and individuals, and as the seventies slipped away and became the eighties the character of the investigation was to change once more.

Chapter Eight

MONSTER PHILOSOPHY

After taking his film in 1960, Tim Dinsdale spent many thousands of hours at Loch Ness searching for the answer to its mystery until his death at the end of 1987. Although he had brief head and neck sightings in both 1970 and 1971 he never shot any more film of any significance. Such is the nature of this battle – for the time being success depends entirely on luck. He gave up his job in 1961 to devote himself more fully to the investigation and he undertook more than fifty expeditions, exploring the loch both from the land and from the water. Some years ago I asked him what kept him going: this is the reply he gave:

Firstly because we are fighting for a matter of principle at Loch Ness – the truth, which is an absolute justification for the research in itself.

Also, of course, I am intrigued by the mystery of it and by the fact that it acts as a sort of mirror which reflects human behaviour. Our attitude to this sort of thing repeats itself again and again. The scientific community, in particular, has behaved towards this just as it has always behaved towards things which are not readily explainable or understandable.

There are so many examples of science rejecting subjects which it cannot understand or categorise. As a distinguished modern scientist, Professor Peter Medawar, wrote: 'Scientists tend not to ask themselves questions until they can see the rudiments of an answer in their minds. Embarrassing questions tend to remain unasked and, if asked, to be answered rudely.'

The Loch Ness phenomenon has been something of an irritation to zoologists for the past fifty years. Instead of facing up to it they have tended to turn their backs on the problem and in some instances have tried to camouflage their inability to comment authoritatively with confused statements which ignore the facts.

Philip Stalker, the first professional journalist to report on the 'Monster' way back in October 1933, and always one of the wisest journalistic writers on the subject, wrote in the *Weekly Scotsman* on 30 March 1957: 'If medical science had shown as little enterprise and as little courage, in its various fields, as marine zoologists have shown in regard to the Loch Ness animal, the Gold Coast would still be the White Man's Grave, appendicitis would still be a fatal illness and tuberculosis would be killing millions every year in Britain.'

The British Museum (Natural History) offered these observations on the affair in a booklet, *Scientific Research*, in 1956:

> The most famous case of the unsubmitted specimen is that of the 'Loch Ness Monster', in which the ingenuity of suggestion as to the nature of the animal concerned has been equalled only by the powers of imagination of some observers. The only scientific evidence to which the Museum can point in explanation of this phenomenon is the report, published in the *Glasgow Sunday Post* of 27 July, 1952, of some observations made by a theodolite by Mr Andrew McAfee. At a distance of 300 yards, he saw the three dark humps which characterise the description of the 'Monster'. With his theodolite, however, he was able to observe that the humps were shadows, and that they remained stationary while the ripples and wash of the water moved past them and gave the humps the appearance of movement.
>
> The phenomenon would therefore appear to be one of waves and water currents.

This statement does rather typify the shallowness of the establishment's sense of inquiry. Because the Museum could prove that one apparent sighting was a mistake it felt justified in concluding that it represented the validity of all sightings. This same rather obsessive instinct to deal only with the material which can be explained away has also been demonstrated by Dr Maurice Burton, formerly of the Natural History Museum. In his book *The Elusive Monster* (Rupert Hart Davis, 1961), written after a week-long visit to the loch in 1960 which convinced him that the animals do not exist,* he tends to select those accounts which are doubtful and proceeds to pull them to pieces. When he comes to the Spicer land sighting he merely says: 'I found it difficult to believe this story also', and goes on to suggest that they saw a family of otters crossing the road. The otter is also, in Dr Burton's view, responsible for both the Surgeon's Photograph and Hugh Gray's, and is what Arthur Grant saw bounding across the road in front of him.

Bearing in mind that otters are only three or four feet in length such suggestions seem rather absurd. Furthermore, it should be remembered that until the end of 1959 Dr Burton was arguing an opposite view. In the *Illustrated London News* of 20 February 1960 he wrote about the Surgeon's picture: 'If this photograph is genuine, as I am now convinced beyond all doubt it is, then there is no argument about the reality of the Loch Ness Monster, nor any doubt of its being a large animate body.' And in a letter dated 29 October 1959 he said: 'I have come to the conclusion that it is probably a plesiosaur-type animal.'

Perhaps a clue to Dr Burton's recent attitude lies in a remark he made in a letter dated 30 April 1962: 'I am now very resentful of those who, wittingly or unwittingly, have misled us and have caused me to spend so much time and effort needlessly, and made me look ridiculous.'

*Dr Burton described his inquiry as 'the biggest organised attempt to gather information on the problem of the Loch Ness Monster since the late Sir Edward Mountain took his team of observers north' (*Illustrated London News*, 16 July 1960).

150

Another of his assertions is that Tim Dinsdale's film shows a boat, even though J.A.R.I.C., who actually studied the film, categorically state that it is no such thing. Despite repeated requests for a statement on the validity of the 1972 results Dr Burton has said nothing.

I hope that by now this book may have established the case that Loch Ness could contain some species of unidentified creatures. From the hundreds of reliable eyewitness accounts an image emerges of a creature with a long, slender neck, small, 'snake-like' head, reasonably heavy body, a long, powerful tail and four apparently diamond-shaped paddles. Different witnesses have reported varying numbers of humps, from the one-humped 'upturned-boat' appearance to a two- or three-humped back.

Size seems to range from about fifteen to twenty feet to a maximum of perhaps fifty or so feet. The presence of a herd of the animals could reasonably account for most of the differences in size, colour and even overall shape reported by different witnesses. Little can be said about the structure of features on the head. Few observers have reported eyes or mouth. However, on several occasions what have appeared to be snail-like stalks on the top of the head have been seen. Two witnesses who reported this were Mrs Greta Finlay and her son Harry, who in August 1952 said they were within about twenty yards of one of the animals near Aldourie Pier. Mrs Finlay described 'two six-inch-long projections from the top of the head, each with a blob on the end.'

One of the most interesting sightings as far as head-detail is concerned took place in November 1973. The witness was Richard Jenkyns, a retired farmer who lived with his wife in a house close to the water near Invermoriston. This is the account he gave me:

The date was Saturday, 10 November, and the time 11.45 a.m. The weather was stormy with a strong north-westerly wind and two-foot waves on the loch

. . . I was on the bank about ten yards from the shore and twenty feet above it.

I had just started a tractor with a loud bang when almost immediately I heard a very large splash, as if someone had gone in from the high board very flat . . . I got off the tractor and went to look at the loch but could see nothing. A few moments later I glanced out again and there, nicely framed by a curved overhanging bough, about ten to fifteen yards out was a fish-like object (at first) starting to appear quite slowly and steadily until it was about eighteen inches above the water surface and then, a moment later, came up about another two feet. It then seemed to stay quite motionless for a short time and then moved slowly forward and slowly sank. It had travelled about forty yards.

Now, for the first time I realised that I had seen the beastie and I became rather bewildered. I could literally feel the hair on the back of my neck tingling.

Its colour was black or browny grey, texture neither rough nor smooth or shiny; matt is the best word I can think of. Diameter about nine inches, no fins or gills. There appeared to be very large scales on the head, but this was only an impression. There was a great gash of a mouth at least nine inches long and tight shut, and above the centre of the mouth what may have been a small, black eye or a blow hole . . . the general appearance was that of a tube, slightly rounded at the top with the head profile rather like that of a snake.

How did any unidentified creatures in Loch Ness get there in the first place? There are two possibilities: either the species has been trapped in it for several thousand years or it has entered more recently. When the last Ice Age ended, about 10,000 years ago, the ice melted and the level of the sea was raised, flooding many coastal valleys until the land, freed of the weight of ice, slowly rose and separated the sea from the inland waters. J.B. Sissons in *The Evolution of Scotland's Scenery* (Oliver and Boyd, 1967) explains it thus: 'The sea overtook the slowly rising land and invaded the coastal areas of much of Scotland, extending far inland along the major valleys.'

It is possible that during this period when Loch Ness was linked to the sea, a group of these animals swam into its sheltered waters and settled there. Eventually they found their return route to the sea blocked as the land rose and Loch Ness became an enclosed lake. Slowly the water lost its saline content, and the animals adapted to their new freshwater existence – a change which has been accomplished successfully by many other species; there are sharks in freshwater lakes in parts of Africa which were once connected to the sea.

The only alternative is that a family has entered the loch at some time since its isolation from the sea. Since Loch Ness is fifty-two feet above sea level the possibility of an underground tunnel can be ruled out. The only other potential entrance is via the River Ness, running from the loch's northern end into the sea at Inverness. However, this river is usually quite shallow, and it seems unlikely that a family of even young animals would attempt to ascend it from the sea.

The fact that the loch is about fifty feet above sea level would also seem to rule out any possible links with other Highland lochs. That this species exists in other lakes, notably Loch Morar (where many similar sightings have been reported and which was investigated recently by the Loch Morar Survey Group), seems possible but it is not possible that the animals commute from one home to another.

And so just what is this 'modern phoenix', as Constance Whyte put it? Mammal, reptile, amphibian, mollusc, fish or something which does not fit into any of these categories?

One must first consider what we know of their breathing

habits. The scarcity of surface appearances suggests that they are not mammalian, since if they were they would need to come to the surface to breathe. It is, however, just possible that they have nostrils set high on the head so that they need expose only this part of the body when breathing. In August 1934 Count Bentick, his wife and their daughter from Holland (his sister was lady-in-waiting to the Dutch Queen) were at the Halfway House, Atsigh, when they saw the top of the animal's head just protruding above the surface. From its mouth, Count Bentick noticed, 'a kind of steam came forth, but was blown back by a slight cold breeze.'

Of all the candidates for the identity of the 'Monster', the most widely canvassed is undoubtedly a Plesiosaur – a marine, fish-eating reptile thought to have been extinct for about seventy million years. This is a theory which was put forward by Dr Denys Tucker, the former British Museum expert mentioned in Chapter 7. If this is correct it would undoubtedly make the discovery the greatest zoological find of recent centuries. And indeed it must rate as a distinct possibility, since one of the Plesiosaur family, the Cryptocleidus was, as far as can be judged from skeletal remains, virtually identical in appearance to the animals in Loch Ness. It had the same long, slender neck, small head, long tail and four flippers and it is known originally to have existed in the area of the British Isles.*

The discovery of an animal which was thought to have been extinct for millions of years has a precedent. In 1938 a coelacanth, a five-foot-long, steel-blue coloured fish thought to have died out sixty to seventy million years ago, was caught by a fishing boat near Madagascar. By the time it was examined by Professor J.L.B. Smith of Rhodes University, the carcass had almost rotted away. However, enough remained to convince him that this was a coelacanth, an animal which he believed to be a missing link in the development of fish and amphibian reptiles.

* See 'The Zoologist's Tale', p. 205.

Another specimen was not caught for fourteen years, not until December 1952 when a native on the Comoro Islands landed one on a fishing line. Professor Smith was vindicated and his doubtful colleagues were forced to gape in astonishment. He wrote at the time: 'Why is this discovery so important? It is a stern warning to scientists not to be too dogmatic . . . '

It is a hard lesson to teach; it is one that was not absorbed after the discovery of other zoological 'impossibilities' such as the giant squid at the end of the nineteenth century and which has still not been learnt today.

Fish, apart from the eel, seem a very unlikely contender in view of the animals' distinct neck and the fact that they apparently exceed the maximum theoretical size of any gilled creature. Lastly, the invertebrate theory rather falls down when the land sightings are considered, since a creature of this bulk would appear to need a backbone and skeleton in order to transport its body on land. The only other possibility is that Loch Ness harbours something entirely unknown – a species not related to any of the known orders of animal. Whatever they are, they must have their ancestry in the sea, which naturally leads to some form of link with the legendary sea-serpent.

Throughout this book I have referred to 'animals' in Loch Ness. This is contrary to the wide-spread belief that if there is a 'Monster' it must be one solitary, superannuated and probably rather senile individual. This has never been seriously suggested as a possibility. Several sightings of two creatures have already been described here, and there are more which could be listed.

For instance, on 13 July 1950 a party of eight people watched three of the animals swimming about 300 yards out in the loch. One of the witnesses was Mr R.R. Gourlay. He described to the *Daily Express* what happened: 'In the centre were two black, shiny humps, five feet long and protruding two feet out of the water. On either side was a smaller monster, one of which made a great splashing noise as it disappeared towards the opposite

155

shore. The largest monster and the small one travelled together towards Urquhart Castle.'

In 1972 an American scientific journal, *Limnology and Oceanography* (Vol. 17, No.5), published a short article entitled 'The Population Density of Monsters in Loch Ness', by R.W. Sheldon of the Fisheries Research Board of Canada and S.R. Kerr of the Bedford Institute of Oceanography. Working on theoretical figures for the standing stock of the fish population and 'logarithmic size intervals' they concluded: 'A viable population could be quite small but probably would not be less than ten . . . It seems therefore that Loch Ness must contain a small number of large monsters. These could weigh as much as 1,500 kg. with a population of 10 to 20 individuals. A 1,500 kg. monster could be about 8 m. long (approx. 22 feet), a size that agrees well with observational data.'

Are these creatures dangerous? Evidence indicates that they are basically timid, but their very size and bulk require that they be respected. The reader may recall Alex Campbell's experience of having his boat heave under him as if something was surfacing from below. And, as many witnesses will testify, it is a very shocking, if not rather frightening experience to see one of these animals. The reason is quite simple; at Loch Ness one is dealing with the unknown, with an animal which, because of its size and mystique, has an inherent ability to inspire awe and wonder.

There are two locally quite well known stories of men actually being overcome by the sight of the animals. One day during the First World War, James Cameron, head gamekeeper at a local estate, went into the Drumna-drochit Inn, his face as white as paper, and asked for brandy. He refused to say what had happened, but later he did tell a friend, Kenneth Mackay, of how he had been out fishing in Urquhart Bay when an 'enormous animal' had surfaced close to the craft. The next thing he remembered was coming round, lying in the bottom of the boat.

On another occasion, this time going back to the year 1889, a Mr H.J. Craig and his brother were fishing from a boat near Urquhart Castle. Suddenly 'a huge form reared itself out of the water and went off at great speed.' In a letter to the *Inverness Courier* of 27 September 1947, Mr Craig wrote that he and his brother rowed for the shore in a state bordering on hysteria. When their father heard their story he instructed them never to tell anyone or refer to the incident again.

Fish have several times been seen to react to the presence of one of these animals. Mrs Winifred Cary, who had her first sighting in 1917 when she was a child, describes how in July 1954 she saw a big hump coming across the loch, '. . . and as it came nearer I saw salmon leaping out of its path and the thing seemed to turn and follow the fish.' And on one Sunday morning in June 1969, when the loch was very calm, ' . . . suddenly, in a strip about thirty or so yards long by about fifteen to twenty yards wide I saw fish moving everywhere and rising and jumping right out of the water, and yet they weren't rising anywhere else on the loch. And then through the middle of the fish I saw a wash going along towards Temple Pier, and a moment later a hump appeared at the head of the wash.'

Of the habits of the animals we know little. The only thing that can be said with certainty is that they are not primarily surface dwellers and they are certainly not inquisitive – if they were, they would have been located many years ago. The sonar research done by Bob Love in 1969 and 1970, consisting of numerous end-to-end sweeps of the loch, covering about 55 per cent of the water area, suggested that the animals are bottom- and side-dwelling. More than that it is impossible, at the moment, to say.

It is, of course, their almost total elusiveness which accounts for the lack of photographic proof of their existence. Despite the tens of thousands of hours of surface observation by hundreds of 'monster-hunters' the

157

results have been depressingly meagre.* It is hard fully to appreciate the problems of the investigation without having visited Loch Ness and experienced the frustration of weeks or months of watching without any result. Large as these animals are, they have an enormous area in which to hide and very little inclination to expose themselves to the groups of aspiring photographers. When one is seen, unless the viewer has a powerful camera and the presence of mind to use it, it can usually escape without giving anything away. Once one chance has gone it could be months or years before another opportunity arises.

People frequently ask why, if the animals exist, are no carcasses ever washed up? The answer is, as the local saying goes, that 'the loch never gives up its dead', because of its great depth and very low temperature. When a body expires it just settles on the bottom and is slowly covered by mud and silt. Given time and resources, it ought to be possible either to dredge the bottom or inspect it by submarine to try to locate the remains of one of the animals.

It is sometimes suggested that people who look for 'Monsters' in Loch Ness are a community of romantic drop-outs – a peculiar by-product of the irreverent and ungodly twentieth century, who are sustained by an addictive need to worship the bizarre. Certainly, many of those who have taken part in the investigation have been inspired by a quixotic enthusiasm and a renegade desire to give the scientific establishment a sharp kick in the pants but, in every case I can think of, such emotions have always been tempered by a rational and carefully conceived belief in the reality of the animals. Above all, it has

* There are, however, said to be two cine films of the animals in Loch Ness which have never been seen because they are locked up in a bank vault. Both were taken in the 1930s, one reputedly by a Dr MacRae and the other by a London banker, Mr James Currie. Mr Currie's film is said to be legally locked away 'until such time as the public takes such matters seriously'.

been the certain knowledge that one day they must be proved right that has kept successive generations of monster-hunters going; the belief that tomorrow, next month or next year the shred of final evidence must be forthcoming and all the immeasurable effort thereby justified.

It is a belief that has remained undiminished as summers have closed every year for more than half a century.

Chapter Nine

THE 1975 PHOTOGRAPHS

For some years it's been possible to have a flutter on Nessie. A firm of bookmakers which has branches in most parts of Britain offers odds of one hundred to one against the discovery of anything measuring up to a monsterish size or shape in Loch Ness. Nessie has thus taken her place alongside the finalists in the Miss World contest and the produce of the nation's bloodstock industry as an object of interest to the gambling fraternity.

Normally the money which rides on Nessie's existence is insignificant: the bet is intended mainly as an amusement for tourists. But in the late autumn and early winter of 1975 something very strange happened.

Betting shops in different parts of Scotland and England found that unusual amounts of money were being wagered on the Loch Ness Monster finally being discovered and officially recognised. On 12 November, newspapers reported a typical example of what was happening. A Scotsman had gone into a Ladbroke's betting shop in Oxford and placed a £50 bet at the odds of 100/1 that Nessie would soon be found to exist. When questioned, he muttered about his granny having had a premonition in her tea leaves.

Four days later, on 16 November, the Ladbroke's office in the Berkshire town of Reading found a queue of punters anxious to place bets on the Monster. In the next couple of days, the betting spread along the Thames Valley and into London.

Ladbroke's – shrewd people – realised something must be up. By the end of the week they stood to lose a quarter of a million pounds: the odds on Nessie's existence were slashed virtually overnight from 100/1 to 6/1. Britain's bookies were taking the Monster more seriously than its scientists ever had. At the same time, in newspaper offices, the hounds were unleashed: reporters were told to go and find out what on earth was going on.

On Friday 21 November the Glasgow *Daily Record* started to get to grips with the story. 'Nessie Plays the Lead in Top Boffin Show' read the headline. 'The Loch Ness Monster DOES exist . . . and that seems to be official', reported the first line of the story.

It went on to describe how a symposium was being planned under the auspices of the Royal Society of Edinburgh on 9 and 10 of December at which more than a hundred distinguished scientists from Britain, America, Canada and Europe would study 'new, top-secret under-water photographs and sonar charts of Nessie'. The *Daily Record* had obtained a copy of the symposium's programme which stated that the purpose of the meeting was to show the assembled experts the latest evidence 'concerning the large animals in Loch Ness and to invite them to express opinions about what kind of animal they could be.'

The weeks which followed were, I think, the most extraordinary – at first exciting but ultimately frustrating – of the entire Loch Ness story. I was caught in the middle of it: the first paperback edition of this book contained an exclusive description of this new material and was being printed with as much secrecy as possible by a company in Reading. But word started to leak out: the rush to the betting shops began and before long plans which had been months in their preparation started to collapse.

The symposium in Edinburgh never took place: the Royal Society backed out. But in its place a meeting was arranged in the Grand Committee Room of the Houses of Parliament in London. They were to this day, perhaps, Nessie's finest few hours, when distinguished men from the world of science and an assortment of Lords and MPs gathered at Westminster to listen at last: to hear the experiences of men like Tim Dinsdale and David James and of Dr Robert Rines and his colleagues from the Academy of Applied Science in the United States. The main items of evidence from more than forty years of searching were described.

Ironically enough, it now appears that the material Bob Rines gathered in 1975 – the material which prompted the Westminster meeting – was specious. I believe a genuine mistake was made: results were misinterpreted, not through any desire to mislead, but through error which, because the story of the 1975 underwater photographs got so hideously out of control, it was impossible at the time either to see or to correct. It is now time to do that.

After the success of 1972 with the flipper photographs, Bob Rines and his indefatigable colleague, Charles Wyckoff of Applied Photo Sciences in Boston, had experimented with automatic camera rigs linked to sonar triggering devices. Each summer Bob had returned with the new equipment: the cameras, electronic circuitry and accompanying paraphernalia which he, Charlie and their associates had spent long winter evenings designing, building and then testing in aquarium tanks and in the sea off the Massachusetts coast.

Early in June 1975 the team arrived with an array which, as usual, left me looking on with that kind of expression with which a moped rider would view an amphibious four-wheel-drive Jaguar. I know something about photography, but nothing about sonar or the 'computer-controlled' machinery which was supposed to kick-start the camera rig if Nessie came by.

A few days later it was all laid out in pieces in a shed at Bob's cottage high on the northern flank of Urquhart Bay. He and Charlie Wyckoff were checking the underwater housings and laying out the cables. At Bob's invitation a man with an interesting story to tell had joined us.

He was a crofter who owned a small farm further up

Glen Urquhart. Bob and Charlie started to describe how the underwater cameras worked. The crofter listened; then the inevitable question. And yes, he told us, his father had seen it, round about the turn of the century. One night when he'd been out doing some poaching 'the big beast' had raced by, creating a disturbance which had nearly capsized him.

The crofter told this story very quietly. In an instant, his reminiscence had taken us back some seventy-five years. And yet it was an undeniable fact that we knew virtually nothing more about the loch's mystery than had his father all those years before.

But perhaps this summer would yield more: a chance perhaps to reach out and grasp more than the murky shots of the flipper of three years before. Around us in the shed were the means: the sonar sets whose screens, staring out lifelessly from their packing cases, would shortly offer Bob and his engineers the chance to penetrate the underwater gloom of the loch; and the cameras, designed under the guidance of Jacques Cousteau's camera consultant, Dr Harold Edgerton at the Massachusetts Institute of Technology, which would try to put a proper shape and perhaps even some detail to any targets detected by the sonar.

A few days later the camera rig was lowered into Urquhart Bay. It stood about 85 feet down, not far from the spot where the 1972 pictures had been taken. It was a complex piece of equipment, but still little more than a pea-shooter in the vastness of the loch. After all, here were a couple of cameras with a range which could be measured in feet in a loch which was more than 20 miles long, a mile in width and in which London's tallest buildings could be stood upright and still be invisible.

Above the main camera rig Bob decided to place the old Doc Edgerton camera which had taken the 1972 flipper photos: it was hoped that the rhythmic flashing of the strobe light might be a lure; so once again the familiar bright yellow cylinders, one containing the camera, the

163

other the light, were made ready. Unlike the big rig which could function for several days without attention, the Edgerton camera had to be raised daily to have the film and batteries changed.

At about 4.30 on the afternoon of 19 June, Bob and Tim Dinsdale lowered the Edgerton rig from the small Academy boat *Hunter* as usual. It was suspended on a rope line: below it was the main rig on the loch floor. The Edgerton camera had been set to take a picture every 75 seconds.

In the course of the next 24 hours, flashing away unseen in the blackness of the bay, the Edgerton camera captured the images which were to cause such a stir in the nation's betting shops five months later, and which were also to bring spasms of discomfort and dyspepsia to the board-rooms of the British Museum (Natural History) and the Royal Society in Edinburgh.

I heard about the pictures at the end of August. Bob phoned from Boston one evening and explained that the latest batch of film from the Edgerton camera which had been processed as usual by Eastman Kodak had been viewed and found to contain some striking images. He told me that one shot was what he took to be the head of an animal: in another, part of what he believed might be a body and long neck could be seen.

It sounded, shall we say, promising. A few days later I flew to the United States to have a look at the pictures and gather details about them for publication in the first paperback edition of this book which was already in preparation.

It was the first time I had been to America. At Boston Airport I remember an immigration official asked me the reason for my visit. A perfectly truthful reply would have been that I had come to see a photograph which I had been told was the first close-up, full-face portrait of the Loch Ness Monster. But immigration officials, as I dis-covered later when I was travelling for BBC Television News, seem to take a delight in staring at you as though you are an empty space of low intelligence. So it was probably sensible that I kept quiet.

Later that evening, Bob and his wife Carol welcomed me to their apartment overlooking Boston Harbour. In due course their living room was darkened; a white window blind was lowered to act as a screen and Bob pulled a small paper packet of slides from his pocket.

The first picture he projected was recognisable enough. It was the underside of the hull of the Academy boat *Hunter*, silhouetted against the light. Somehow the rig had become tilted so that it was photographing up towards the surface.

The second image on the screen was darker: this time the camera and strobe light were photographing through the heavy gloom of the water, strongly stained with the peat brought down into the loch by the mountain streams. It was like a green fog in which the individual particles of this liquid suspension were almost large enough to see. And along one edge of the frame – through this haze – was a shape. It arched across the side of the picture and to the bottom it fattened into something which was rounder and from which protruded two other shapes. It was indistinct and towards the limit of the range of the flash, but there was one enticing interpretation which the image – the slender, arched shape joined to the bulkier form – did nothing to discourage. Might this be one of the animals with outstretched neck gliding along through the gloom, momentarily caught by the flash of the camera?

I had stood up and moved closer to the screen to examine the picture and an enlargement of the interesting portion more closely. I was still standing by the screen when Bob flicked the projector to the next slide.

I remember staring. For this was what they believed was the head. The head of the Loch Ness Monster from a range of about five feet.

For some moments the shapes were a hopeless jumble which seemed to have no coherence. I really had had no idea what to expect, except that if this photograph really was what they believed it to be then it was probably the most remarkable wildlife photograph ever taken. Bob and Carol deliberately stayed silent as first I narrowed my eyes and then tried to de-focus slightly on the image, tilting my head from one side to the other. Clearly there was no obvious interpretation of it, except that it certainly was not a handsome shape. But after a few moments I started to see some of the points which were exciting them: most significantly, there seemed to be a symmetry about it, an appearance which did seem to have facial characteristics. In colour it was a dark reddy-brown, and in the centre of the shape was . . . what? An open mouth perhaps, above which was a ridge and on either side of which appeared to be two symmetrical marks. Enough to turn it into a head? I wondered. But Bob told me that several eminent scientists, including Dr George Zug, the Curator of the Division of Reptiles and Amphibians at the Smithsonian Institution who'd flown up from Washington the previous day, had been impressed. And if a man such as that thought it might be the head of a living creature then who was I – a young university law student – to disagree?

The next day I went to see Charlie Wyckoff at the small laboratory in Needham Heights in Boston where he ran his company, Applied Photo Sciences. It had been Charlie who'd carried out the first examination of the films, laboriously going through literally thousands of frames one by one looking for anything unusual. He explained that the picture of what they thought could be an animal gliding towards the camera had been taken at about 4.30 on the morning of 20 June. The next 343 frames were blank: then, at frame number 1069 the image of the underside of the hull of *Hunter* had appeared. And two frames after that the picture of the 'head' had appeared on the screen. 'Holy crow, that looks like a cabbage,' was how Charlie recalled his own first reaction to what he found himself looking at. This 'head' photograph had been taken at about 11.45 on the morning of 20 June.

166

There were a number of obvious questions. First, how had the camera rig come to be pointing UP, towards the surface, just two frames before the 'head' picture was snapped? Again, the most enticing answer was that something, attracted perhaps by the regular flashing of the strobe light, had been playing with the rig (or even attacking it), and tilting it one way and another.

An intriguing proposition, undoubtedly. But before we take it or anything else about the 1975 photographs any further, there is one consideration which is central to any judgement about whether the objects they show are indeed animate intruders into the camera's field of view, or whether they aren't in fact inanimate artefacts which just happen to have ambiguous appearances.

The consideration is this. On the roll of film shot by the Edgerton camera during the 24-hour period from 19 to 20 June there are several other images. And it is now beyond doubt that these other images are of the floor of the loch. As the winds changed, *Hunter* had evidently drifted on its mooring, and it's clear that from time to time it must have moved into shallower water so that the camera rig was no longer swinging freely in Urquhart Bay, but was touching or even lying on the bottom, photographing the area around it.

At the time, in the autumn of 1975, I now believe as I've said, that we made a mistake and we invested an importance in the underwater pictures taken on 20 June which they do not deserve. I suppose that after the success of the flipper pictures in 1972 and with the longing which there was to come up with something clearer and better, critical judgements were not as sharp as they should have been. There was a desire, which should have been resisted, to see what we wanted to see in those two ambiguous scraps of 16mm celluloid film. Running alongside that wish was a failure to step back and consider all the implications of a roll of film which elsewhere showed quite clearly that the camera was photographing the

167

bottom of the loch. This fact in itself should have ruled out any images which were so obtained, let alone pictures as unclear as the two which excited us then.

So what is the so-called 1975 'head' or 'gargoyle' as it was soon dubbed? I think it may be a tree stump which was located and re-photographed twelve years later by a diver and former member of the Loch Ness Investigation Bureau, Dick Raynor. On Sunday 11 October 1987 I watched with fascination and some dismay from the cabin of a boat as he took an underwater closed-circuit television camera down and made a number of passes over and around the tree stump. On the television monitor aboard the boat there were moments, when the camera was at certain angles to the tree stump and the lighting was in a particular plane, when it seemed quite possible that this was the object which had been photographed back in 1975. We cannot be sure, and no-one has been able to reproduce the 'neck and body' shot. However it would be foolish to cling to the pictures in the face of such obvious uncertainties. Bob Rines, I think, now agrees. Indeed at various times since they were taken he has discussed with others the possibility that the 'head' shot might not be what it had initially seemed: on other pictures taken in the 19/20 June sequence he retains a mind which is open to any caveats which further study may produce.

But while the 1975 underwater photographs may no longer, ipso facto, deserve an unambiguous place in the evidential scales, they did serve a valuable purpose in concentrating scientific minds which had never until then applied themselves with any seriousness to Loch Ness. It is indeed an irony that the mass of evidence in the years up to 1975 – good evidence which remains completely credible – failed to do for Nessie what pictures which we no longer regard as reliable did achieve.

As I've already described, the news of the existence of the 1975 photographs started to leak out at the end of that

November. By then, at the instigation of Sir Peter Scott, the Royal Society of Edinburgh had been approached and had agreed to associate itself with a symposium which was planned to take place in Scotland's capital city on 9 and 10 December. The universities of Edinburgh and Heriot Watt had also agreed to participate. On the first day it was intended that scientists should discuss the Loch Ness phenomenon and try to reach a consensus about the most probable identity of any creatures which are in the lake. On the second day there would have been a news conference at which the outcome of the scientific deliberations would have been made public.

But when the press started to preview the symposium nearly three weeks before it was due to take place and publish detailed stories about the so-called new evidence, the situation very quickly became a nightmare. Instead of there being a controlled, rational discussion there was an angry, confused argument.

First off his stool and into the centre of the ring was Sir Frank Claringbull, the Director of the British Museum (Natural History) who issued a statement on 24 November saying that the object in the underwater photographs was 'a piece of tree'. An uncommonly accurate blow, or so it would now appear; but Sir Frank went on to tell the newspapers, who were wriggling uncomfortably at the thought of Nessie turning from a favourite fun character into a page one science sensation, that 'an element of hoax' could not be excluded from the pictures. Dr G.B. Corbet, the Deputy Keeper of Zoology, was reported as saying that it would have been possible 'to drop some object in the loch and tow it in front of the camera.' Some of Dr Corbet's colleagues at the Museum were even more tetchy: one senior scientist there unburdened himself to a journalist about 'wretched Americans', 'wretched photographs' and even 'wretched books'.

By 2 December the Royal Society and the two universities decided they had had enough: they withdrew their support for the Edinburgh symposium. There was, they said, a need to guard academic reputations and anyway, they added, there was now no chance of conducting a clinical debate in the full view of worldwide publicity. They were absolutely correct.

Three days later Bob Rines flew to London to join Sir Peter Scott in talks at the British Museum (Natural History). At the same time the Conservative MP, David James, founder of the Loch Ness Investigation Bureau, arranged for a special meeting to take place in the Grand Committee Room at the Houses of Parliament on the evening of 10 December. At first the five members of the British Museum team set up to deal with the matter said they wouldn't come, but after more talks with Bob and Sir Peter they decided that, after all, they would attend.

The Academy of Applied Science gathered its team. Harold Edgerton flew to London from Greece where he'd been working on Jacques Cousteau's research vessel *Calypso*; George Zug arrived from the Smithsonian Institution in Washington; the sonar expert Marty Klein and Charlie Wyckoff came from Massachusetts.

Nessie's big day, 10 December, began with the publication of an article by Bob Rines and Sir Peter Scott in the leading scientific journal *Nature* which suggested a formal name for the animals so that they could be added to the schedule of protected wildlife of the 1975 Conservation of Wild Creatures Act. The official name proposed was *Nessiteras rhombopteryx* which, translated from the Greek, means 'the wonder of Ness with the diamond fin', a reference to the flipper in the 1972 underwater photographs. The article went on to suggest as the common name for the animals, 'the Nessie' or 'the Loch Ness Monster', which was original.

And then, at 7.30 that evening, nearly two hundred scientists, journalists and members of both Houses of Parliament gathered in the Grand Committee Room in the Palace of Westminster. At no stage, either before or since, has Nessie been given a hearing in front of such an audience and in such surroundings.

The presentation opened with a few remarks from Lord Craighton, the chairman of the all-party committee on wildlife conservation. David James spoke on the work of the Investigation Bureau and Tim Dinsdale on his 1960 film, its subsequent 'probably animate' verdict from the R.A.F. and his other experiences at the loch. The next topic was the work of Bob Rines and the Academy of Applied Science.

Marty Klein described his sonar search at the loch in 1970 when on several occasions his side-scan apparatus had picked up traces of large moving objects; Harold Edgerton spoke about the underwater strobe camera and its various applications; Charlie Wyckoff demonstrated the problems of underwater photography in the peat-clogged waters of the loch.

And then it was Bob Rines' turn. He is an accomplished and confident speaker. He'd learnt the business of lecturing as a professor at Harvard University many years before, and the skills of advocacy as one of the United States' most respected patent attorneys in the years that followed. Sceptical judges, hostile witnesses, arrogant students: he had, in his different careers as scientist and lawyer, been faced with them all. On this occasion, in the Palace of Westminster, he was speaking up on behalf of a 'client' who officially did not exist to a 'jury' from the British Museum (Natural History) which, at best, seemed disdainful, at worst rather resentful of this man who had arrived with such fanciful ideas and eccentric colleagues.

First of all Bob described his first visit to the loch, way back in 1959: how he'd read Constance Whyte's book *More Than A Legend* and how even then he'd gone back to the United States and pondered, with scientific colleagues, the idea of mounting an expedition. But it was not until 1970 that he'd returned to the loch and begun a modest series of sonar experiments, sufficient, through the side-scan results of Marty Klein, to suggest that there were indeed large targets in the loch. He described the occasion, on 23 June 1971, when he and his wife Carol and Wing Commander and Mrs Basil Cary had watched a twenty-foot-long hump move through the waters of Urquhart Bay from the Carys' cottage at Strone. He told his audience that this experience had banished any doubts from his mind that in Loch Ness there are large, unidentified creatures and he had decided then to continue his search, using, as much as his resources would permit, the tools of underwater technology to try to push the animals' veil to one side and discover what they are.

He talked at length about the 1972 underwater photographs: he showed the two flipper pictures in both their unenhanced and enhanced states and another hazy picture, also taken on the night of 8/9 August 1972, which seemed to show two distant outlines in the water. It had been taken at a time when the sonar had indicated the presence of two separate echoes in the vicinity of the camera.

From 1972 he moved to the 1975 results. The photographs were projected onto a large screen. Whatever may now be thought of them, in that darkened room that night they brought gasps from the audience. The MP who was sitting next to me – who was, admittedly, drunk – dropped his cigarette on the carpet and sat with his mouth open.

Once the visual presentation was over, the scientists who'd been approached by the Academy and asked to make a study of the subject were invited to deliver their conclusions. Dr George Zug, the expert on reptiles from the U.S. National Museum of Natural History at the Smithsonian Institution in Washington said he felt the evidence on the existence of a population of large animals in Loch Ness should serve to encourage research at the loch: 'and remove the stigma of crackpot' from any scientist or group of scientists who wish to start an investigation there.

172

Dr Christopher McGowan, the Associate Curator in the Department of Vertebrate Palaeontology in the Royal Ontario Museum in Toronto, a recognised authority on extinct reptiles who'd carried out a thorough assessment of ALL the evidence including, to his great credit, making a private visit to the loch to speak to a number of eyewitnesses, said:

'I am satisfied that there is sufficient weight of evidence to support the proposition that there is an unexplained phenomenon of considerable interest in Loch Ness: the evidence suggests the presence of large aquatic animals. The Loch Ness phenomenon should be the subject of a consolidated inter-disciplinary effort.'

Professor A.W. Crompton, the Director of the Museum of Comparative Zoology at Harvard University said he found the Academy's evidence ' . . . sufficiently suggestive of a large aquatic animal to both urge and recommend that, in the future, more intensive investigations be undertaken.'

Professor Roy Mackal of the Division of Biological Sciences at the University of Chicago expressed his belief that ' . . . some of the (Academy's) pictures corroborate earlier evidence and substantiate the existence of large aquatic animals in Loch Ness.'

And Sir Peter Scott, a man of many eminent positions in the world of nature, told the meeting that in his view the totality of evidence amassed over more than forty years left ' . . . no further doubt in my mind that large animals exist in Loch Ness.'

The only statement offered to the meeting which was in total conflict with those above was the one from Dr J. Gordon Sheals, the Keeper of Zoology at the British Museum (Natural History). On behalf of the five Museum scientists who'd examined the material he said first that they were ' . . . entirely satisfied with the integrity and sincerity of the investigating team and the authenticity of the photographs.' But, he went on, the photographs 'do not constitute acceptable evidence of the existence of a large living animal.'

Dr Sheals added, with some apparent feeling, that he found it 'most regrettable' that Sir Peter Scott and Dr Rines had seen fit to try to award the animals the formal scientific title of *Nessiteras rhombopteryx*, since he felt this would give the general public a 'false impression' of the creatures' reality. Sir Peter replied that he found Dr Sheals' whole attitude to the subject 'most regrettable'.

The meeting closed. Dr Sheals and most of the British Museum team trouped out but, intriguingly, there were murmurings from at least one of them that they were not ALL happy with the statements about the phenomenon which were being made in their collective names. Sir Russell Johnston, the Liberal MP for Inverness-shire and previously a declared sceptic, said: 'This has been a very convincing and impressive presentation. It would appear there is something to explain.' And the Scottish Office Minister, Hugh Brown MP, said he would be passing the evidence on to government scientists for further study.

On the other hand the Conservative member for Edin-burgh South, Michael Clark Hutchison, said he thought it was all rubbish: 'I have never seen such rubbish in all my life,' he said. And the Conservative MP for Perthshire, Nicholas Fairbairn, agreed. But Mr Fairbairn hadn't been to the meeting.

In the following days the public debate continued. And the newspapers reported with some glee that an anagram of *Nessiteras rhombopteryx* is 'Monster hoax by Sir Peter S', a strange coincidence which attracted extensive com-ment: it was thought to be a discovery of considerable importance. The press failed, however, either to notice or, when told, to report that another anagram is: 'Yes both pix are monsters – R', (R for Rines).

*

174

I have tried in this chapter to describe what happened in 1975, and what we now know or suspect about the 1975 underwater photographs, as fully and as fairly as possible. If a mistake was made in their interpretation, it was an honest mistake, but nevertheless it is to be deeply regretted. But I hope that writing openly about it now underlines the determination to serve the standards which are of paramount importance at Loch Ness: namely, the search for accuracy and truth and the need to keep an open and unprejudiced mind about what happens there.

In that vein, and with the writer's permission, I offer the following observations from a letter sent to *The Scotsman* newspaper and published on 12 December 1975, as the publicity about the Westminster meeting was at its height and press and scientific opinion divided. It was written by Michael Scott-Moncrieff of Innerleithen, Peebleshire. It was an analysis of the contrasting attitudes of Bob Rines and the Academy on the one hand and Gordon Sheals and the British Museum on the other. Mr Scott-Moncrieff wrote as follows:

'On behalf of the thousands of ordinary sentient people who have sighted the strange creature – and, in particular, the thirty or forty in buses and cars who stopped behind our own car in June of 1957 to watch the creature (or creatures) sporting at power-boat speeds for at least five minutes, I would like to take this opportunity to thumb my nose at those extraordinary, fusty and incurious gentlemen from the Museum. How refreshing, on the other hand, is the enthusiasm of the gentlemen from Boston – and our own Sir Peter Scott. Hope, curiosity and humility are their inspiration – as they are with all true scientists. Hope in such evidence as there is. Sufficient curiosity to explore and examine it in detail. And a humble appreciation of the limitations of the knowledge of man.'

Whatever the rights or wrongs of the evidence published in 1975 it surely does no harm, at the conclusion of this chapter about it, to be reminded of the evidence which originates not from a piece of underwater machinery, but from one of the many eyewitnesses who've stood on the banks of Loch Ness and gazed out at its surface in astonishment.

Chapter Ten

THE UNENDING QUEST

It is conceivable that the century will end without there being a conclusion to this story. Already more than fifty years have passed since that day in April 1933 when Alex Campbell sent his story to the *Inverness Courier* and – apocryphal a moment though it may have been – Evan Barron uttered the word 'Monster' and committed it to print. The mystery defied those early expeditions; avoided the gaze of the watchers led by Captain James Fraser; survived the abusage of the big-game hunter Wetherall; has been immune to all the huffing and puffing down the years of the Museums and the cynicism of some newspaper correspondents. Not even the ravings of Josef Goebbels nor the improbable accuracy of one of Mussolini's bombers could put paid to the story. Nothing has been able to stop Nessie.

It is now more than thirty years since Constance Whyte set down the details in a distinguished book, *More Than A Legend*; more than a quarter of a century since Tim Dinsdale travelled to the lochside and took his film; almost as long since David James MP set up the Loch Ness Investigation Bureau.

They wrote, filmed and watched, and inspired many others to join them in this quest. Today, as we stand on the threshold of the 1990s, the mystery which became a fascination to them and a compelling force in their lives is still with us. Sadly though, Constance Whyte, Tim Dinsdale and David James are not.

Constance Whyte it was who encouraged me to write the first edition of this book in 1973. I was nineteen; I had

177

caught the fascination several years before and set off to the loch to seek out the eyewitnesses and gather information. She wrote to me after I'd organised a small exhibition for the national Schools' Association of Natural History Societies which every autumn was allowed to use the facilities at the British Museum (Natural History) to hold its annual meeting. I set up my stall about Nessie in one of the Museum's conference halls and stood beside it beaming at anyone who looked as though he might have emerged from under a layer of dust in one of the building's back rooms. And having an inordinate amount of cheek in those days I wrote to the *Inverness Courier* to tell them what I'd done: the *Courier* published a story.

Constance Whyte's letter arrived a few days later, expressing delight at this minor subversion of an institution which had been the source of such scorn. The 'sweep-it-under-the-carpet-quick attitude' of the Museum had been quite incredible, she wrote, and she recalled that those members of Museum staff who had shown signs of interest 'had been silenced'. She wrote those words in October 1970. In the years that followed she opened up her archives of thirty years of private research at the lochside to me: this book was the result. She died in January 1982. Of all that has been written on this subject, it was her book *More Than A Legend* which was the first in the post-war period to ask that honest people who had seen something unusual should at least be given the courtesy of a hearing, and to suggest that it was time a proper inquiry was begun.

No men took up that challenge with greater vigour in the sixties and seventies than David James and Tim Dinsdale. David it was who cajoled his naval and exploring chums to join his fledgling Investigation Bureau and spend their summer holidays keeping watch on the surface of the loch. It was slightly eccentric and extremely British: an adventure which was shared by baronets in their country tweeds who'd once done wartime watches with David aboard Royal Navy motor torpedo boats, and young people who were only too eager in the sixties to rub up against the accepted wisdoms of the day and, if possible, to stick a large pin in them. Loch Ness was a lark, but with a serious purpose, spearheaded by a resourceful group of enthusiasts for whom half the fun was conjuring up experiments with a minimum of equipment. At their head was David James: a man who'd marched out of a German prison camp in a celebrated wartime escape, who'd explored some of the least-welcoming corners of the globe on foot and by sailing ship and when those adventures had run out had gone into Parliament and in search of a legend. David died in December 1986 at his beloved home, Torosay Castle on the Isle of Mull. I saw him there a few months before his death: he had set his heart on one more visit to the lochside where he had spent so many hours. But the cancer which was killing him was to make such a trip impossible. He faced his illness in the same way as he had faced everything in his life: with immense courage.

If David's energy was the moving force behind much of the investigation, its unquenchable spirit was without question Tim Dinsdale. Even now his film, taken in April 1960, remains one of the most important items of evidence. Fifty-six times Tim returned to the loch in the years that followed: each expedition was of weeks or, often, months in duration. His ambition was to improve upon his original film. To that end he spent many hundreds of days and nights afloat on the loch in his tiny motor cruiser *Water Horse*. It was a gruelling, frequently dreadfully uncomfortable and downright dangerous mission, facing the loch's many moods at all hours and in all weather in such a small craft. Tim saw one of the animals twice more but he never got the chance to shoot another foot of film of any significance; in nearly thirty years of searching he was unable to better the sequence he obtained on the sixth day of his very first visit to the loch.

Tim died suddenly in December 1987. He was 63. His death took from the Loch Ness investigation the man who embodied the single-minded and often solitary quest of the amateur. Convinced by personal experience and contact

179

with eyewitnesses of the existence of the animals, he set out to try to prove it. He was given a glimpse and he spent twenty-seven years in pursuit: he will be remembered always at Loch Ness for the integrity which he brought to the search. For Tim there was only one way to do it, and that was the right and true way. A few days before he suffered the first of the heart attacks which were to prove fatal, he sent me a Christmas card explaining his plans for the following summer . . . for yet another expedition. For Tim, as he wrote at the conclusion of one of his books, the passage of time was immaterial to the final outcome: 'For where truth is involved,' he said, 'the facts stand up; as indeed do the people who recognise them.'

His words are an epitaph to him, to Constance Whyte, to David James and to others who have been principal players in this story and who are now dead: people such as F.W. 'Ted' Holiday, author of *The Great Orm of Loch Ness* who died in February 1979; Alex Campbell, the Fort Augustus water bailiff and local correspondent of the *Inverness Courier*; Norman Collins, Chairman of the Investigation Bureau and Deputy Chairman of Associated Television, one of the pioneers of television in Britain; Wing Commander Basil Cary, whose home overlooking Urquhart Castle was one of the favourite haunts of Nessie-hunters who came to share the humour and enjoy the hospitality of Basil and his wife Freddie, and listen to her account of sightings which date back to 1917; and Lionel Leslie, a cousin of Sir Winston Churchill and friend of David James. Lionel's life of adventure began in the 1920s when he walked through the Himalayas, across the north-east of Burma and on into China, becoming one of the first Westerners to explore that country. He and his wife Barbara had made their home on the island of Mull, a few miles from David James; Lionel died one month after David, in January 1987. A generation of noble-hearted adventurers who had responded to the Loch Ness enigma with a will to investigate had gone. And with their passing the loch has been left the poorer.

*

Out From The Barricades

The fiftieth anniversary of the start of the search came and went quietly in 1983. A few newspapers wrote about it; I remember I reported on it for BBC News. Now another decade is almost over; before long it will be the year 2,000. In this century we have found answers to so many things which have puzzled us; we have explored the five continents; our collective curiosity has taken man beyond our own heavens. But although at Loch Ness people have continued to report strange sights *on* the loch and expeditions have continued to make contact with unusual echoes *in* it, we still do not have an answer to the question which was first posed in 1933.

Aha, say the sceptics, the only thing we don't have is *your* sort of answer: the affirmation of the presence in the loch of an unknown species. And the very failure to produce such a coup is itself an answer: it is, they say, proof that there is nothing there; proof that the eyewitnesses and the researchers whose stories have been described in the preceding pages were mistaken after all. This story, the sceptics say, is much more a testament to the fallibility of the amateur than an indictment of the professional, in this case the zoologist.

And yet, despite hesitations at different times since the seventies, I do not believe such a verdict can be reconciled with the facts. I cannot say with certainty that there is an unidentified species in Loch Ness because I have never seen any sign of such a thing myself. But I have spoken to too many eyewitnesses who have impressed me and been shown too many inexplicable charted sonar echoes to walk away from Loch Ness with a dismissive shrug of the shoulders. The mystery deserves more than that: what is more, considering the prospect of what might be discovered there, it *demands* more than that.

There are signs, faint perhaps but nonetheless encouraging, that we have now reached a point in the saga where the two sides are showing a greater degree of understanding of each other. The moment is overdue: the stand-off between

181

the investigators and the establishment has lasted too long. It is time the barricades came down.

In comparison to the sixties and early seventies the approach now *is* calmer. Some of the sense of theatre has gone; the arguments from those on the lochside are less shrill. At the same time, the ice-cold douches of doubt from scientific establishments have, by and large, been less frequent.

The transition to this new period began, I think, after the episode of the 1975 Rines underwater photographs. It is as though the confrontation and the subsequent reflection upon it by both sides had a cathartic effect. For more than two hours, in the Grand Committee Room in the Houses of Parliament, the two sides faced each other: hackles rose, tempers boiled, but in the heat there was some sort of fusion. From that high point of emotion in the closing weeks of 1975 everybody learnt something and went away a little wiser.

In due course, as doubts about the 1975 photographs were raised, the Nessie-hunters came to understand that some of the caution of the scientists was entirely justified. On the other hand, within the laboratories and the museums, some of the scientists were doing some revision of their own: the body of evidence which had accumulated over the years was being quietly studied and some of the caution was seen to be excessive.

By tradition, as we have already noticed, the centre which has understandably been the most careful in its pronouncements about Loch Ness has been the British Museum of Natural History; the centre which must, in the end, be the arbiter on any matter of zoological importance within the United Kingdom.

The first public sign that opinions within the Museum were changing came in the summer of 1976, with one sentence from Dr Alan Charig, the Curator of Fossil Reptiles. It had become apparent, at the time of the Westminster meeting in December 1975, that privately Dr Charig was out of sympathy with the dismissive statements which were being published by the Museum in the joint name of the five scientists, of whom he was one, who'd been studying the subject. After the Westminster meeting was over, Dr Charig joined Bob Rines and the American scientists who'd gathered in London for private discussions. But the situation was still tense: feelings within the Natural History Museum hierarchy were, to say the least, very brittle and Dr Charig felt it was politic to keep his counsel.

But the following June, BBC Television transmitted a documentary about Loch Ness: the first full-length treatment of the subject by network British television for many years. And it provided the confirmation that there was a split within the Museum's ranks.

Alan Charig had decided to speak publicly for the first time. He told the programme he was angry that the Museum scientists were all depicted as reactionary old fuddy-duddies. They were not like that at all, he said. Then he disclosed that there were *different* opinions about Loch Ness among the scientists there; the first such acknowledgement. He went on to say that it was very difficult to explain away the hard core of eyewitness evidence: 'from earnest, sincere people' as he put it. 'So,' he concluded in his to-camera statement, 'if I had to give a casting vote I would cast it *in favour* of the Loch Ness Monster' (my emphasis).

Although Dr Charig, the Museum's leading expert on prehistoric reptiles, was quickly followed by the Keeper of Zoology, Dr J. Gordon Sheals (whose speciality was the study of spiders and mites) who referred to Nessie as 'this wretched Monster' and dismissed it as an amalgam of tree trunks and gas bubbles, the fact that a British Museum scientist had spoken as he had – even in such careful terms – was significant. If Dr Charig could be convinced by a study of the evidence, it was surely reasonable to conclude that the evidence could not be as deficient in merit as many other experts had suggested; the scientific basis for a species having survived undetected in the loch for many generations was a theory capable of being scientific fact

183

rather than forever remaining an invention of science fiction. It was an encouraging sign.

There was another indication of the changing climate on the lochside itself in 1976. Dr Christopher McGowan, the Associate Curator in the Department of Vertebrate Palaeontology at the Royal Ontario Museum in Toronto had joined Bob Rines' new expedition with the official blessing of his Museum authorities. Chris McGowan was British by birth and upbringing: he'd qualified at London University seven years earlier and then moved to Canada. The previous autumn he'd been one of the zoologists consulted by the Academy: he'd made a thorough study of the subject and had travelled to the loch to meet a number of eyewitnesses before preparing his affirmative statement for the Westminster meeting. Now he had become the first Museum zoologist of international standing to participate in a Monster-hunt with the backing of his establishment.

The Academy expedition in 1976 brought another underwater camera rig to the loch, and the attention of two major forces from the American news media: *The New York Times* and NBC Television, who had provided sponsorship. In return they not unnaturally required a beat on their rivals to any results which the Academy might obtain. It was an uncomfortable summer; the remainder of the press corps was indignant at the conditions which *The New York Times* and NBC tried to impose.

Temple Pier, the base from which Bob and his team were operating, was declared out of bounds. Nobody other than accredited members of the expedition and their media minders was supposed to be allowed out to the camera rig or aboard the Academy boat *Malaran*. It was most out of character with everything that had gone before; and the generally sour note was exacerbated by rows within the NBC team (three different Directors came and went within the space of two months) and a smouldering rivalry between the man from *The New York Times* and his opposite number from the *Boston Globe*, both of whom felt a proprietorial right to the Academy. In addition, there

184

was a problem with the Academy's American diver, who took one dip in the loch and decided he didn't care for the place at all. And as if that wasn't enough, a team from the *National Geographic* magazine arrived ostensibly to write a colour piece about the Highlands. The fact that they had several crate-loads of underwater cameras, a trawler, two underwater photographers and a sonar expert from the Woods Hole Oceanographic Institute by the name of Dr Robert Ballard* with them was one of those inconsistencies one was supposed not to notice.

In the event, Nessie avoided any clear contact with either team. The Academy did obtain several interesting sonar traces, but nothing ventured near the camera rig. On 24 June there were three separate contacts, then again on 25 and 28 June. At 10.44 p.m. on 30 June the sonar detected a large target 120 yards from the camera rig. It moved closer, to about 80 yards and remained there for about a minute. Then it moved away into deeper water. At 5.00 a.m. on 1 July a target was picked up in the sonar beam about 100 yards from the cameras, but it too moved off.

For Bob Rines it was an unhappy time. The team he'd assembled on the lochside that summer was the largest the Academy had put into the field but it went home disappointed by the lack of success and disillusioned by the tensions within the team and with the sponsoring organisations, who'd kept up the pressure for a spectacular result.

But it simply isn't going to happen like that: the process of persuading the scientific community in this country will be a slow one. Such was the prediction in that summer of 1976 by Chris McGowan, the British palaeontologist from the Royal Ontario Museum. He had left Britain, he told me one evening as we headed up the loch in *Malaran*, partly because he found the zoological establishment here unwilling to let scientists follow unorthodox instincts. Across the Atlantic there was less paranoia about becoming tangled up with a 'fringe' subject such as Loch Ness.

*This was the same Robert Ballard who some years later went in search of the wreck of the liner *Titanic*, and discovered it.

'Mind you,' he said, 'Britain suffered the Piltdown Man hoax – and you can understand how that has made the Museums *very* cautious.'

And so the Academy left, and though Bob Rines has returned to the lochside every summer since then to spend a few weeks in his cottage overlooking Urquhart Bay, its research programme has tailed off. From time to time, work has been done; there have been more sonar contacts and one notable plan to reverse the odds a little and adopt a more active form of underwater search. This was in 1979 when Bob and his colleagues drew up a plan to bring two dolphins to the loch. They would have had small automatic cameras strapped to them, and been let loose in the loch in the hope that their naturally inquisitive and gregarious instincts, coupled with their remarkable built-in sonic sensing ability, would have led them to a rendezvous with any large animals in the depths.

But when news of the plan leaked out there was an outcry from animal welfare groups who felt the dolphins would have been at risk. In fact, the plan was thwarted not by protests here in Britain, but by the death of one of the dolphins shortly before it was due to be shipped from Miami to Scotland. The dolphin trainer felt it would have been cruel and probably pointless to continue the project with only one animal, so the plan was shelved. New legislation in this country which requires that the movement of dolphins must have a government licence means that no such plan is likely to be given official sanction in the future. Nessie may not exist officially; but no Secretary of State for Scotland, the Environment or even Agriculture and Fisheries (Whitehall has never yet made up its mind where the bureaucratic buck for Loch Ness stops) is going to risk becoming embroiled in assignations, however improbable, involving dolphins and taking place in the depths of this particular body of water!

Into the Eighties
Since the start of the eighties the main thrust of the

investigation at Loch Ness has been carried out by a man whose ambition it is to prove that there is NOT a 'monster' there.

His name is Adrian Shine. He's an Englishman from London; an amateur naturalist whose boyhood interest in birds and butterflies and other creatures in his back garden was transformed into something more ambitious after he'd read some of the books about Loch Ness published in the sixties.

On the lochside today, at the age of forty, Adrian is a striking sight. The gentle, cultivated eccentricities of Tim Dinsdale and David James have been superseded by something more down to earth and forceful. On an overcast night on the loch, had you not steeled yourself beforehand, the sight of Adrian might give you rather a start, because the most visible feature about him is a very large bristling beard: it's one of those shaggy extravagances which seem de rigueur for men who are drawn to the study of our flora and fauna.

He it is who's taken on the mantle of the earlier generations of searchers, and he stands four-square with them in his sincerity of purpose and single-mindedness. But there is a subtle difference between Adrian Shine's purpose and that of his predecessors. And the difference is an important element in the changed atmosphere at the loch and in the receptiveness of members of the scientific community to the subject.

Every year since 1980 Adrian has headed an expedition to Loch Ness. Since the spring of 1988 he's lived on the lochside a few miles north of Drumnadrochit with his wife Jane, having given up a small printing business which he'd set up and helped to run in south London.

His scientific knowledge is self-taught but, like many who've missed the formal academic applications of university or college, it is broad and practical, taking in the skills which are necessary to the study of a large freshwater environment. That means understanding sonar, being particular about its shortcomings and ambiguities and having a curiosity about every aspect of the loch's biology, from organisms so small that they can only be seen with a microscope, to the size and variety of the fish population, the behaviour of underwater temperature gradients, its wave patterns and much more.

And if, in the course of this overall study of the habitat, something large and unexpected should come along, well, says Adrian, that would of course be fascinating. He is being a little disingenuous when he tells people that, because there is only one reason why he has pressed on with his experiments at Loch Ness for the past nine years (and why, for seven years before that, he mounted similar expeditions at Loch Morar). The reason is his desire to get to the bottom of the mystery and, if possible, to identify whatever it is that has been responsible for so many believeable sightings by eyewitnesses.

But Adrian has been sensible. He took stock of the situation at the end of the seventies and realised that the approach of the Investigation Bureau in the sixties and of many since then (with the notable exception of some of Bob Rines' work) had been making little progress; he reasoned that it had therefore failed and should be discarded. Put simply, much of the investigation which had characterised the sixties and seventies had been both too passive and too passionate. It was time, he felt, for a more active and a more objective approach. And central to it would be a research programme into many aspects of the loch's natural habitat with which professional scientists would feel an affinity. This programme would be of intrinsic value in providing information about a basin of water which, ironically, has been the scene of very little systematic exploration since the Bathymetrical Survey . . . of 1911!

'I want,' Adrian told me, 'to strip Loch Ness bare, layer by layer. And in finding answers to many seemingly "mundane" scientific puzzles, we hope to provide an answer to the one which fascinates the world.'

In so far as Nessie is concerned, the Shine philosophy seems to be to try to outflank the British Museum and the rest of the so-called zoological 'establishment', creeping up on them stage by stage with lots of carefully prepared scientific data, rather than marching in to confront a panel of Five Wise Men with the results of one experiment, as Bob Rines had done in 1975.

There is one more aspect to Adrian Shine's approach which marks him out from his predecessors. It is his public equivocation about whether or not Nessie actually exists or, to be more precise, over a definition of what would constitute a 'monster'. There is, he insists, no such thing in the loch.

'I am not,' he is fond of declaring, 'here in search of a Jurassic Reptile.' That is Shine-speak for 'phooey to plesiosaurs': in layman's language, it means that his programme does not expect to find creatures in Loch Ness which would give palpitations to Doctors Alan Charig and Chris McGowan, the palaeontologists mentioned earlier in this chapter whose specialities are the study of creatures supposed to have been extinct for millions of years.

But he does believe there is something: perhaps something rather smaller than the identikit Nessie: possibly something which is a variant or large version of an animal with which we are already familiar. And on many of the occasions when Adrian and his teams of young scientists and volunteers have set out in search of more clues, they have come back with them.

He began his work at Loch Ness in 1980, under canvas on Hugh Ayton's farm south of Dores with a group which included students from the Royal Holloway College of the University of London. Many of them had been with Adrian while he experimented at Loch Morar. He'd earned their respect in a hard and dangerous way by designing and building his own tiny submersible observation chamber called *Machan*. It was a fibreglass sphere, three foot six in diameter, more or less watertight and linked to the surface by a garden hose. Adrian sat in *Machan* 50 feet down in Morar, observing what went by while air was pumped down the hose pipe to him with an improvised pair of bellows. His team worried a little for his sanity, a lot for his safety; but on neither account need they have concerned themselves: Morar was merely the prologue to the bigger challenge of Loch Ness.

The first two years that they worked from the beach on Hugh Ayton's Balacladaich Farm saw comparatively brief expeditions: the team's main task was to familiarise itself with the new setting and the technical problems which it presented. There was little equipment and less money. But, as is his habit, Adrian improvised as best as he could. He designed a 40 foot long rubber boat which was built to his specifications and then used as a floating platform for the sonar with which the team was experimenting. They drifted the loch aboard the rubber boat: there were unusual midwater contacts. 'But at that stage,' says Adrian, 'we were still learning about sonar and how it behaved in a narrow basin like Loch Ness.' The contacts weren't clear enough to be regarded as evidence of anything unusual in the loch.

It was a different story in 1982. The 'Project', as Adrian has always insisted it be called rather than 'Investigation', again had the use of a Furuno 106A sonar set, which was supplemented by a second, Simrad SY scanning sonar. In the course of approximately 1,500 hours of sonar operation in May, June, August and September, forty unusual contacts were made. The Furuno sonar was operated from a 50-foot barge in the area of loch between Foyers and Urquhart Bay; the Simrad was mounted on the motor cruiser *New Atlantis*.

Twelve of the contacts were made with the Furuno sonar, which sent out a beam 9 degrees in width which could then be rotated and tilted to track targets. Some of the contacts were held in the beam for more than a minute: they ranged in depth from 14 to 130 metres (i.e. from 45 to 425 feet), and although some of them could conceivably have been caused by large fish, others seemed too strong. In Adrian's opinion, there were among the traces obtained by the two sonars that summer, 'contacts which were apparently stronger than one would expect from the loch's known inhabitants.'

In 1983 the Project conducted hours of experiments on the effects of thermal currents and side echoes on sonar: they plotted what fish looked like and investigated as many of the commonplace causes of large echoes as they could think of. Once again the resources were terribly limited; nevertheless the Project operated in relays from the beginning of June through to the autumn. They did extensive work with an echo sounder, a crude form of sonar, with which they investigated the loch's bottom profile off Achnahannet. In the course of this work they made one intriguing contact. It was obtained between 0630 and 0752 on the morning of 4 September when the echo sounder picked up a strong target, first at 141 metres depth (462 feet), then at 203 metres (666 feet), at 150 metres (492 feet) and finally at 194 metres (636 feet).

The programme was changed slightly the following year. Instead of operating a mobile sonar station, drifting or motoring along the loch, Adrian decided to tether the big inflatable in mid-loch off the Horseshoe scree on the remote southern shore in six hundred feet of water. That in itself was no small feat; the raft was then manned day and night for two months with the Furuno sonar sweeping the immediate vicinity.

Results were disappointing. There were scores of 'moderate-sized' contacts which Adrian decided to classify as fish echoes; none was of the size or strength of those obtained two years earlier in 1982. The Project was perplexed: from mobile patrols they obtained strong contacts on a fairly regular basis: moor the sonar in a fixed position and the contacts were much smaller. There was no obvious explanation.

1985 was a quiet year. Adrian had got married late in 1984: domestic considerations intervened. Nessie was left largely in peace, though other aspects of the Project's work continued as normal.

On every expedition the biology of the loch was becoming better understood. Under the supervision of David Martin, a graduate in marine biology from the University of Wales in Bangor, and Dr Anne Duncan from the Department of Zoology at the Royal Holloway College in London, all kinds of specimens and samples had been collected, some from the upper layers of the loch – many from the bottom, hundreds of feet below. A picture of the loch's hidden life was being built up.

The biological survey continued in 1986. Meanwhile, in the autumn of that year the Project began to prepare for its most spectacular single shot at the hidden life in the loch which excites commercial sponsors. An American sonar engineer called Darrell Lowrance, who runs a company which manufactures fish-finding sonar equipment, had become interested: Loch Ness represents a technical challenge to the electronic discipline of which he is a specialist. He and Adrian discussed the possibilities and decided to join forces for a search which was dubbed 'Operation Deepscan'. Darrell Lowrance and his company would provide the equipment and much of the sponsorship, Adrian would provide the people and local expertise, and Nessie would ensure that Lowrance Electronics of Tulsa, Oklahoma would receive the publicity which, in truth, was the main purpose of the whole exercise.

In October 1986 the operation was rehearsed. Ten motor cruisers were fitted with Lowrance X16 echo sounders. For several days they tried to get the hang of 'sweeping' the loch in line abreast. But the weather was atrocious, with winds blowing up to force six: the boat crews couldn't hold the line; the sonar operators found that each echo sounder interfered with its neighbours; they ended up with reams of largely meaningless readings. But it was decided the technical problems could be overcome. 'Operation Deepscan' would resume work in earnest in twelve months' time.

*

Operation Deepscan

'A Sonar Exploration of Loch Ness' . . . an operation which would, in the words of its own publicity, 'sweep the unfathomable depths of Loch Ness from shore to shore and end to end with a curtain through which nothing can escape.' There's nothing to beat the hyperbole of the professional publicist in full cry and this event was a gift. The pre-operation blurb was full of references to 'biggest' this and 'most comprehensive' that. It invoked the names of Macbeth and his Cawdor Castle, of Bonnie Prince Charlie and his flight from the English Redcoats, and conjured the image of snow-cloaked mountains, of the raw magnificence of the Highland landscape against which could be witnessed this unprecedented example of man's duel with the unknown. Small wonder that nearly three hundred members of the print and electronic news media, from all over the world, took a breather from weightier matters that autumn week and made a beeline for the loch where many of them spent a thoroughly enjoyable long weekend experiencing large measures of Highland hospitality.

There is no denying that it was an impressive spectacle: the sonar search, that is. The line-up of nineteen motor cruisers was fortunate that the weather for the two main days of the search, 9th and 10th October, was good; there was no repetition of the storm-force winds which had made the rehearsal so difficult. But in order to ensure that the echo-sounders could function, the sensitivity on each set had had to be turned down almost to minimum, otherwise the intended 'curtain' of sound and echoes would have been as indecipherable as it had been during the preparatory work the previous year. It meant some targets might not be picked up, but it was the only way the sonar line could be made to work.

The flotilla got ready for its first public sweep on the morning of 9th October. Just before the boats left the small harbour beneath the New Clansman Hotel where the expedition was based, Adrian addressed the crews through a megaphone.

One would have to say that the TV crews, especially the foreign ones, loved the moment. There is something pretty whacky about a big, bearded English naturalist with a battered old yachting cap jammed down over his ears, arms waving, doing what sounded like an imitation of Monty before a big battle, and urging his chaps to go out there (the loch) and do it (find a Monster): 'For all the maligned eyewitnesses who look to you for vindication.' No wonder the PR man went off for a stiff one to celebrate.

The important point, though, is that 'Operation Deepscan', thanks to the professionalism of Adrian and his loyal band, did get some interesting results: they did not, as he had warned, drag that 'Jurassic Reptile' kicking and snorting out of the water, but the sonar charts yielded yet more evidence that Loch Ness is capable of producing midwater targets which simply should NOT be there.

On that first day there were three such contacts, ranging in depth from 78 to nearly 180 metres (256 to 590 feet). One was of particular interest. It was detected when the line of boats was off Whitefield, the farm midway between Inverfarigaig and Dores, opposite Urquhart Bay. The target entered the sonar curtain at a depth of 174 metres (570 feet) and was held in tracking range for 140 seconds before it was lost. Other boats behind the main line, including *New Atlantis*, the cruiser fitted with the Simrad scanning sonar, tried to re-establish contact but without success. *New Atlantis* then took a precise fix of the position with Decca navigational equipment. The next day Adrian sent a group of five boats back to the spot to see if they could find the target again. If it had shown up a second time it could, in all probability, have been written off as a piece of submerged debris. But despite criss-crossing the spot, there was no sign of anything.

The three contacts made on the first day of the search were presented to the waiting media at a news conference in the New Clansman Hotel that night. David Steensland of Lowrance Electronics said that one of them, at 78 metres depth (256 feet), might have been caused by a 'very large (known) fish', though at that depth it was unlikely. The other two contacts he described as 'very strange'. In both cases he said the signals were larger than those he'd picked up many times from sharks off the coast of Florida.

Darrell Lowrance characterised the signals as being from a target: 'larger than a shark but smaller than a whale'. And Adrian said that in his opinion all three signals were unlike those which could be expected from the loch's known inhabitants, the salmon, eels and shoals of char. 'They are,' he told the newsmen, 'deep, midwater contacts of considerable strength.' But he would not be drawn into speculation about what might have caused them.

The next morning, in the loch north of Fort Augustus, the sonar line re-formed: the boats 150 feet apart, the skippers holding their positions by aligning with flags being flown at intervals along the line. Behind them, three more vessels including *New Atlantis*, ready to move up to try to track any targets which entered the sound curtain.

The line headed north at about three knots, buzzed periodically by a helicopter carrying television cameramen and under the merry scrutiny of the reporters, many of whom were aboard a pleasure steamer which had been specially chartered for the exercise and which carried media amenities (a press officer and bar). Others had hired their own boats which scurried about the line; the remainder kept pace from cars on the shore. Everybody seemed to be having a thoroughly good time: some of the cynics were even venturing the thought that maybe there might be something in it after all.

Weather conditions were good: a moderate south-westerly wind, the loch's surface was gentle; the line was coping well. There was every expectation that more contacts would be made. Every so often the radio chatter increased as a boat reported something unusual: some-times the line would slow, the support boats would move forward and shine their own more powerful sound waves in the direction of a possible intrusion.

But although there were a couple of indistinct contacts,

nothing was detected to match the targets of the previous day. An estimated sixty per cent of the loch's total area was swept, from just north of Fort Augustus to a point opposite Abriachan. True enough, the line left wide gaps at either side between the wing boats and the shore, and the sonar screen, with its sensitivity turned right down to exclude interference, was a fairly crude one. But all the same it was an anti-climax after the hopes which had been built up the day before. Undaunted, Adrian reported that the group of five boats which had re-examined the scene of the previous day's strongest contact had found that whatever it was had gone. A sign, at least, that all was not entirely still in the depths of the loch.

That evening the newsmen gathered in the bar of the New Clansman to hear Adrian's final report; unfortunately when he finally arrived it turned into rather a scratchy affair. The reporters were hungry to hear about more, big contacts. Adrian told them there hadn't been any. What could this imply? Deadlines demanded instant conclusions.

It was not the moment to start uttering ambiguous statements. Here were scores of reporters from all over the world, ready to pounce; every bit as happy to seize upon a story that Nessie had been proved not to exist as they were to write the reverse.

What they got from Adrian was, frankly, a very cumbersome dissertation about his investigations into the 1975 Rines underwater photographs which, of course, sounded very negative; a statement that he had never set out in the first place to discover a beast which he described as the 'media monster', followed by the declaration that: 'the Nessie that everybody imagines, does not exist'; to which he added, just for good measure: 'nobody really believed in that, anyway, did they?' Now, I understand what he meant and so, after reading all of this, may you: he was on his soapbox again about there not being one of those prehistoric sorts of monsters in the loch.

But the reporters were a mite perplexed; they looked at

each other, some asked for a translation, then they caught the line about 'Nessie does not exist' and decided on second thoughts not to bother, and by and large the subtleties of it all got lost in transmission. To the world outside it seemed that the 'biggest-ever', one-million-pound Monster hunt was ending with a definitive thumbs down for Nessie, which wasn't the case at all.

In fact, Adrian regarded the overall result as good: a large part of the loch had been surveyed, albeit rather crudely, and several inexplicable contacts had been gathered. The marks were there on the sonar charts: three more contacts to add to the scores which had been made in previous years. 'Operation Deepscan' may not have added to our knowledge, but it would seem to have played its part in confirming it.

Reflections on the Water
Stand at one end of the loch; keep a firm hold on reality but permit, if you will, the imagination to take in the scene that stretches away to the horizon. Twenty-two and a half miles of water and, beneath the surface, hidden from our view, a valley which is deep enough along most of its length to swallow the very tallest of Britain's skyscrapers. You could line them up along the floor of the loch and from the surface they would be quite invisible.

Today the holiday cruisers may churn up the loch's surface and turn it into a busier thoroughfare than before, and on the shore the tourist industry may peddle the 'monster' trinkets with ever-greater energy. But Loch Ness, the body of water, remains as inscrutable and unchanged as ever it was; our knowledge of what takes place within its many unseen square miles stuck, it seems, in a shallow groove.

For example, no one is really sure yet of the extent of the fish population. In 1988 Adrian Shine moved that aspect of our knowledge forward a little. For several days he worked alongside a small team of scientists from the Department of

Agriculture and Fisheries who were investigating fishing methods aboard their research boat *Goldseeker*, together with a group from the Norwegian-owned sonar company Simrad. It had sent its 100-foot vessel *Simson Echo* to the loch as a floating hospitality and demonstration facility for customers. But when they weren't busy with the men from the ministry and the fishing fleets, the Simrad crew took their array of sonar equipment out into the loch. They made about half a dozen mid-water contacts. One was off the mouth of the River Foyers, at 12.28 pm on 2 August, when the sonar detected TWO targets simultaneously, one at a depth of 150 metres (490 feet), the other at 170 metres (555 feet).

But the more important work concerned the loch's fish population. The Simrad equipment picked up the shoals of char which have long been known to inhabit the loch. The sonar signals were then fed into a Simrad computer which estimates the density of the shoals causing the signals. It concluded that in Loch Ness there are large shoals of char with a density of approximately 1,000 fish per hectare (i.e. per 10,000 square metres). It means that there are many more of these fish in the loch than was previously suspected. It's worth noting that in some fashionable foreign restaurants, char is considered a most unusual delicacy!

It also became clear that there are two quite distinct groups of char in the loch. The big shoals are to be found at a depth of 20 to 30 metres (65 to 100 feet) by day; then there is a second layer which lives very close to the bottom, at a depth of more than 200 metres (655 feet). Specimens of both types have been caught: proof, if more were needed, of the loch's capacity to yield new information about itself. That, indeed, is something which the British Museum (Natural History) has conceded. After one of his earlier expeditions Adrian Shine came away with underwater video pictures of an unusual fish on the loch floor. It was only two to three inches in length, but it prompted Dr Humphrey Greenwood, the Museum's leading fish expert, to remark that it seemed to be something completely new. 'There is,' he said with a smile when I interviewed him about the video, 'a lot more to be learnt about Loch Ness!'

Quite so. And there are, as I've said, signs that more scientists are now prepared to show at least an open-minded interest in the subject. In July 1987 the Royal Museum of Scotland in Edinburgh was the venue for a meeting akin to the one in the Grand Committee Room of the Houses of Parliament in 1975, at which a general survey of the evidence was presented by those who'd been involved in the search. Richard Fitter and Roy Mackal, both directors of the old Investigation Bureau, shared the platform with Tim Dinsdale, Bob Rines and Adrian Shine. The meeting lasted a day; it offered no conclusions, but the fact that Scotland's national museum had opened its doors to the subject was another sign that Nessie was being accepted into the fold of legitimate interest and study.

And yet the doubtful voices are still raised and they are, of course, entirely to be welcomed and encouraged, though it is surely reasonable to expect those who raise them to have done a little basic fact-finding of their own.

A few years ago I met one such sceptic, a man by the name of Steuart Campbell. He was making notes for a book he was hoping to write in which he would reveal Nessie for what, in his opinion, it really was: a load of hysterical nonsense. But towards the end of our conversation the most remarkable thing emerged about Mr Campbell's research. I asked him how many eyewitnesses he had sought out and questioned about their experiences. Not a single one, he told me, and furthermore, he said, he had no plans to meet any. He had made up his mind; they had all been mistaken; there was no need to meet any of these people, look them in the eye and hear from their own lips an account of what they had seen. It seemed a strange and rather unjust way of approaching the matter.

In fact, of course, the sightings have continued; though there do seem to be rather fewer of them these days. Now

199

there is no Investigation Bureau to collect and collate reports – perhaps that is part of the explanation; and on the loch the disturbance from the holiday cruisers is greater than ever – perhaps that is a deterrent to creatures which are said to be so timid. No one knows. But the eyewitness evidence is as central to the mystery now as it was when it began. And occasionally it yields a few feet of film or a couple of photographs to stand alongside the verbal testimony.

On 22 August 1977 two English holidaymakers, Peter Smith, an accountant from Dunstable in Bedfordshire, and his wife Gwen were standing in one of the lay-bys on the southern shore opposite Urquhart Bay. Shortly after 5 p.m. an object emerged from the water about 500 feet away. Gwen drew Peter's attention and he focused a pair of 35 x binoculars on it. In Peter's words: 'The object had what was undoubtedly a thick, rectangular-shaped head with no visible features on a powerful, long neck at least a foot thick . . . the texture, through the binoculars, appeared to be leathery.' They estimated it stood between five and six feet out of the water.

Gwen Smith then grabbed their 8mm cine camera and started to film. Peter was still watching it through binoculars. The object submerged completely, then it reappeared and Gwen continued to film. It submerged and reappeared one more time before disappearing from the Smith's view for good.

But the incident wasn't over: something more startling was to follow. A student from Barnsley in Yorkshire, Christopher Idle, was camping with a friend a few yards away from the Smiths. Chris arrived on the scene a few moments after the object had submerged for the third time. He then got into a small rubber dinghy and started to row out to the spot where it had been. He'd got about fifty yards when, to his very considerable surprise, a head and neck shot up out of the water about eight feet away from the dinghy. It was there for about ten seconds before it plunged out of sight.

200

I met and interviewed the Smiths and Chris Idle. Chris told me the object he saw was about four feet in height; the neck tapered from about eighteen inches in diameter at water level to about nine inches at the head. That, he said, resembled the head of a sheep, though he didn't notice any obvious features. It was certainly not a log, he told me, nor was it an otter, a deer or a water bird.

The film shot by the Smiths is jerky and inconclusive. But it has been carefully studied by the Joint Air Reconnaissance Intelligence Centre of the RAF (the analysts who studied Tim Dinsdale's 1960 film). Their report stated that, judging by the object's movements, it appeared to be joined to something much larger and bulkier beneath the surface. In conclusion, Peter and Gwen Smith told me that they were 'both convinced that what we saw was a live, intelligent animal. Whether anybody believes us is a matter of little consequence to us. We are only happy to have had such extraordinary good fortune.'

In May 1982, a farmer at Lochend, his wife and sister-in-law saw what they described as three separate animals in the loch. Bob Rines and I went to question them about the episode and we took the following details. The farmer said he wished to remain anonymous, but there seemed no reason to doubt his sincerity. He told us they'd seen a large disturbance off Aldourie Castle, which was about three-quarters of a mile away. In one position they saw a 'hump, about ten foot long with a large neck standing out of the water.' A short distance away they said there were two smaller heads and necks. They watched for about five minutes, until a boat rounded Tor Point. The large neck and hump submerged immediately and weren't seen again. The two smaller necks went down, but reappeared twice more.

I asked the farmer if he could have been confused by water birds, swans perhaps. He replied that he had had many years experience of viewing the loch, and he and the others were quite sure they had not been confused by birds and that their estimate of the sizes was an accurate one.

201

On 21 July 1987, Mrs Barbara Grant was being driven home to Drumnadrochit by her neighbour, Mrs Mary Appleby. They'd been into Inverness to take a friend to catch a bus. Just north of the Abriachan turn-off Mrs Grant, who was looking out over the calm surface of the loch, noticed 'a red-brown coloured pillar in the water'. It looked like the thin neck of an animal but she couldn't distinguish a head. A few yards further on they stopped the car in a lay-by and looked out to the loch. There was no sign of the 'neck'; instead there was a shape cutting through the water at speed and throwing up a considerable disturbance. It travelled some distance, and then seemed to submerge.

I asked Mrs Grant several times if it could have been a bird or a seal. She was emphatic that it could not. 'It was too big, and it was going too fast.' She told me she had travelled up and down the loch for twenty-four years but never seen anything. 'Mind you,' she said, 'I've always believed there was something there because too many good people have seen something, and many have seen something and never said anything about it. There is no doubt about it: there is some unusual creature in the loch.'

Four months earlier, at the end of March 1987, Bobo Morrison, a postman in Drumnadrochit, was driving into Inverness with three friends. They were approaching Lochend when he noticed a wash being thrown up about a hundred yards out in the water. Seconds later one of the passengers shouted: 'What's that out there in the loch?' Bobo pulled up the car; all four jumped out and looked down at 'something big, throwing up a lot of spray'. At first it was travelling south, then it circled and headed north again. After nearly two minutes it submerged. Five minutes later a 'long, low hump' appeared again, further out in the loch with a second shape visible a few feet in front of it. The total length seemed about twenty feet. It was travelling fast and headed off down the loch until it submerged out of sight.

'It was something very strange,' Bobo Morrison told me.

'It made the hairs on the back of my neck stand up. I've been in the village for thirty years and I've never seen anything like that on the loch before, never.'

Bobo Morrison is a good witness: he tells his story clearly and factually. There is no attempt to dress up the details. It is a straightforward account of what he and three other adults saw on Loch Ness one morning in March.

'I've always maintained there is something strange in the loch,' he said. 'It's not a monster – a monster is something in a horror movie. It's just something strange in the loch.'

And so there it is: from the legend of what Saint Columba is supposed to have seen in the year 565 to the stories of witnesses in the late 1980s. This account of the Loch Ness story is almost over, but it is my great pleasure to hand over the final pages of this book to a man who's had more cause than most to take an interest in the way the world has responded to the reports which have sprung from this Highland loch.

He is Dr Denys W. Tucker. His name has already appeared in this story. In 1960 he was a Principal Scientific Officer at the British Museum (Natural History). He was an internationally respected zoologist, and something of a free spirit within his profession. He had been fascinated by Loch Ness since he was a child; in the late 50s he took himself to the loch, became convinced there was an important discovery to be made there, had a sighting himself, and then set about trying to persuade his scientific colleagues to support a proper investigation. But the doors were closed to him. And Denys Tucker was not a man to compromise. In June 1960 he was dismissed from the Museum. He was thirty-nine. He was never to find full-time employment as a zoologist again.

Denys Tucker has now broken twenty-nine years of near-silence on the subject to write 'The Zoologist's Tale' for this book. I asked him to set down his memories of some of the things that happened all those years ago and for his theories about what might be in the loch today. They are written with the intensity of a learned man, and with a hint of the passion of one who believes he was wronged.

His conclusion, as you will read, is that in Loch Ness there is quite possibly a small breeding colony of a creature resembling *Cryptocleidus*, a twelve-foot-long member of the plesiosaur family which is supposed to have become extinct many millions of years ago but which he thinks may have survived, unmolested and undetected, rather like the coelacanths off the Comoro Islands, in the dark and deep waters of this Scottish lake.

One day perhaps we will know. His plea, uttered nearly thirty years after he was dismissed from the British Museum of Natural History, is a simple one. It is a plea which everyone who has been associated with this quest – people like Constance Whyte, David James, Tim Dinsdale, Bob Rines and Adrian Shine – would wholeheartedly endorse. It is that a new generation of scientists from our universities and institutions should screw up their courage and curiosity and go and look for themselves.

But if one day they do, and if one day someone produces the evidence which establishes beyond doubt that the eyewitnesses have been right, there is one consideration which must govern every activity at this beautiful place. It is that the animals should always be allowed to enjoy what legend states they were granted many centuries ago by St Columba: the everlasting freedom and protection of the loch.

THE ZOOLOGIST'S TALE

by Denys W. Tucker

To the memory of
Pierre Denys de Montfort
who, because he compiled accounts of the
Kraken and the Giant Octopus in his
Histoire naturelle des Mollusques (1802),
was dismissed from the Muséum National
d'Histoire naturelle and died destitute in a
street in Paris in 1820. He was faithful to
Science in his lifetime and has been wholly
vindicated by Science since his death.

I was an Exeter schoolboy, just 12 and already obsessed with natural history, when the Loch Ness story broke in the autumn of 1933. William Beebe's articles on his bathysphere dives had begun to appear in the *National Geographic* about the same time (1931-34), and these kindled my fascinated interest in the bizarre animals of the deep ocean. As regards Loch Ness, I was fortunate that we took the *Daily Mail* which, for a long time through 1933-34, maintained a more energetic and responsible coverage than most newspapers. Like the whole nation I was vastly intrigued by this mystery and even more so when the now well-known photographs first appeared. Following up both interests, as opportunity offered, I never dreamed that one day I would be making a successful career out of continuing the former or that I would ever have anything material to do towards solving the problem of the latter.

The usual examinations and essential scholarships; a B.Sc. course in marine zoology, interrupted by four years as an R.A.F. officer; a first dogsbody job at Liverpool University. Sixteen years had passed when I was appointed to a post at the British Museum (Natural History) where I could actually handle and study Beebe's deep-sea fishes and eventually earn a London D.Sc. degree for published researches upon them.

I had the exciting feeling that I was now tagging along at the end of a long procession, with all the great natural scientists and explorers still marching somewhere up front and many of their personal effects gathered into the baggage-train which was the Museum. John Gould's hummingbirds, Mary Anning's fossil reptiles, the *Challenger* deep-sea fishes, Darwin's *Beagle* collections . . . all were there, together with original letters, drawings and manuscripts by practically any naturalist I could think of. There seemed, too, to be no book so rare and no foreign journal so obscure that the libraries could not produce it.

Apart from the friendships with some of my colleagues there was a vast stimulation and pleasure from the many international contacts formed through correspondence and meetings with the rich variety of personalities who were my opposite numbers in other institutions and whose often far greater experience and erudition helped to keep me stretched and sharpen my wits. After my study of one fish-group a Russian research-ship down in the Antarctic collected further material and so two Russian colleagues – working in Leningrad, writing in English and publishing in Washington – kindly named a new species *Benthodesmus tuckeri* for their British colleague. Perhaps we were doing rather better than the politicians and diplomats in those days!

It was an accidental turn in a previous research which led me back to the reconsideration of Loch Ness and I think the story is worth telling because it shows, not only

206

that the pattern of events was basically similar in both cases, but also that an 'educated guess' can have useful consequences even when it turns out to be wrong. Indeed, as Professor Karl Popper has pointed out in *Conjectures and Refutations* (1972), the growth of Science is a process which results from the continuing correction of mistaken hypotheses previously put forward by others.

In 1959 I gave a critique of, and a possible alternative to, Johannes Schmidt's classical story of the Sargasso spawning-migration of the European Eel. The spark which initiated this research was a paper by Vedel Tåning (1953) who had discovered that a sudden change of temperature in developing trout-eggs could affect the numbers of vertebrae in the resulting fishes. I knew that numbers of vertebrae were virtually the only difference between European and American Eels and I had a rough idea of the depth/temperature set-up and currents in the Atlantic. The three pieces clicked together into an enticing guess that Schmidt's great saga might be wrong. The adult eels had never actually been captured in the Atlantic; perhaps the 'European' Eels were only the modified offspring of American parents and perhaps they never completed that amazing return journey to the Sargasso.

Given this alternative model to provide the 'European' larvae and juveniles, it was now possible to take a hard look at all the assumptions entailed previously when the return adult migration had been accepted. Thus, the temperatures, salinities and movements of the water-masses at various depths in the Strait of Gibraltar, for example, are in every respect precisely the opposite of the conditions pertaining in the Kattegat. So, whatever physical or chemical stimuli the eels may be navigating by, the basic behaviour-pattern which brought them out of the Baltic would keep them bottled up in the Mediterranean, and vice versa.

Once the idea had gelled there was a vast amount of reading to be done, pros to be looked for, cons even more so, and then the final struggle to bring the whole ragbag of evidence and reasoning into decent order and give it even a kind of elegance. There were now two alternative stories in the field without the conclusive details available to clinch either of them; the verdict was for posterity to decide.

My actual theory has since been shot to smithereens, *but that does not matter*! In a field once rather quiescent it provoked a great deal of research in several countries and has led others to provide, not only a great deal more knowledge, but also many more unanswered questions. The distinctness of the European and American Eels has been proven by shipboard tests on the DNA of larvae freshly caught in the Sargasso. The European Eel has been shown to comprise several races, each, probably, with a distinct spawning-ground. The American Eel does not spawn in the Sargasso at all but probably way back in the Gulf of Mexico. The young stages perform a daily vertical migration, a factor not known or taken into account when Schmidt was putting down his tow-nets. And whereas, sadly, my paper lost me good friends among my Danish colleagues, a new generation of Danish workers have slaved over Schmidt's original research-notebooks and come up with the bald conclusion: 'Schmidt's data do not support his findings'. Thus there is no cause for chagrin or shame at having made a wrong guess. On the contrary: into my obscurity last year came a message bearing the good wishes of an international conference of eel experts and thanking me for all the hard work I had given them!

It was as this previous work was in progress that another cluster of facts clicked together and in due course set me off on a fresh line of inquiry.

Male eels migrate to the sea at 7-12 years and females at 9-19; but there is a reliable record of one living to 88 years in captivity. Migrating eels head for deep water and near-darkness. Eels are cannibals. A conger has been seen swimming on its side at the surface. I thought back to Loch Ness: a large, very deep lake with only a shallow outflow. Could it be that the strange phenomena were due to the occasional surfacing of very large, elderly eels, members of a population trapped in the loch by their own behaviour-patterns and feeding largely on the newcomers which descend the tributary rivers every year?

A mini-submarine has since confirmed that there are indeed large, curiously marked eels in the depths of the loch, with obvious bearing on the food-supply of a hypothetical large predator, but my main theory did not last many minutes. A surface-swimming eel as described would show a pattern of humps moving *backwards* at the same time as the whole group, the entire animal, was moving forward. And the eel has no neck; the skull is rigidly attached to the pectoral girdle so there can be no question of the animal rearing up out of the water and displaying the mobility of head-plus-neck and head-about-neck which some have described in the Loch Ness creature.

Thus we have seen how two pieces of research began in precisely the same way. In the Eel case the proposition put forward was complicated and had to be left for other workers to substantiate or otherwise. In the Loch Ness case we have only a very simple first idea and the evidence was already available for me to destroy its probability; the general line of working is identical in both instances. The ultimate objective in Loch Ness is still far ahead, I fear, but in the meantime it is still possible to worry at the existing evidence in disciplined ways in search of deeper understanding and of raising or lowering the probability of any working hypothesis that may come to us.

In due course I wandered up to the Museum libraries to pick up the book by the late Constance Whyte (to whom belongs the credit for stimulating all the work put into the loch these last thirty years), together with Gould, all the books I knew on the closely-associated sea-serpent problem, and anything else there might be. I had a surprise: the librarian put into my hands a fat packet containing a file of press-cuttings compiled from 1933 onwards under the direction of Dr. W.T. Calman, the then Keeper of Zoology. So much for official indifference!

In fact, as one who has been both an impatient suitor for research-support and a Museum expert in one speciality, I may as well correct a few false impressions. I was in the firing-line when the second Coelacanth story broke and on the sidelines when the Yeti story broke, and with reporters, callers and phone-calls from all over the world, the flood of perfectly legitimate requests for expert information and comment was overwhelming. In the case of the 'Monster' zoologists were hard-pressed and gave doubtful guesses. Collect up the contradictions years afterward and you have a seemingly hilarious scenario like J.G. Saxe's poem 'The Blind Men and the Elephant' in which the protagonists quarrel bitterly over whether the elephant is a wall, a spear, a snake, a tree, a fan or a rope. Having read what my predecessors said at the time I don't find much to blame them for and, unless one has the temerity to admit to the Plesiosaur hypothesis (having had time to consider and to form an opinion that the objections are not quite as weighty as they might first appear), I don't honestly think anyone, coming cold to the subject, could do a great deal better today. That, of course, does not condone the leisured, thoughtless indifference and jeering of subsequent years.

We also learn to be wary of impromptu remarks. A book expresses surprise that a Museum spokesman could announce himself to be 'sick of Coelacanths'. I was that (fortunately unnamed) spokesman, and the important missing detail is that I was taking a call from Melbourne on my bedside phone at home at 3.30 in the morning!

Finally, there is the notion that there is some sort of Establishment conspiracy against Loch Ness. No conspiracy, just indifference, and there is no Establishment; instead various combinations of people come together in ad hoc groups to co-operate in the advancement of some common special interest. Once, for example, it was believed (I think by Edward Forbes) that the deep ocean was lifeless. A transatlantic submarine cable broke and was found to have animals living on the broken ends when they were fished up. A certain amount of deep-sea trawling and dredging was undertaken, with further promising results, and then Sir Wyville Thompson and others eminent in the oceanographic sciences came together to urge upon the Admiralty and the Government that a frigate should be made available to undertake a thorough exploration under their direction. The result was the epoch-making deep-sea exploration by H.M.S. *Challenger* of 1872-76. We do not yet have the same sort of evidence to convince the unwilling; we do not and never will have the opportunity to assemble a committee of accredited authorities in the way Wyville Thompson could. When we honestly consider the increase in knowledge in proportion to the manpower and technology already put into the loch, I sometimes feel that the effort has made it less rather than more likely that we can expect much help on a large scale. The way ahead will most likely be through more ingenious small expeditions and an overdue change of luck.

In the spring of 1958 and again in 1959 I spent most of my vacation-time studying the whole perimeter of the loch, including a few short spells on beaches at night, and shot a 20-minute colour-film which would give a lecture-audience an adequate impression of the types of shore, sparseness of littoral population, inflows and outflow, wake-effects and so on. I met Mrs Whyte and others and a few eyewitnesses and noted the matter-of-fact regard the local population had for their strange neighbours. Off Inchnacardoch on the evening of 22 March 1959 I saw a triangle of foaming water following a hump towards the far shore, where it either sank or melted into the twilight under the opposite bank. Boat it certainly was not, but I plodded around by Fort Augustus checking that there was nothing else on the water nor any boat drawn up on the beach.

Canvassing academic circles from the Royal Society

downwards produced nothing worse than polite interest but little else. The best promise I obtained came through the mediation of Sir Alistair Hardy, F.R.S.: that a Hydrographic Survey vessel would be put through the loch if I could procure another similarly equipped ship to accompany her. But lightning would not strike twice for me, not even in the marine labs of Scotland. My own Keeper of Zoology besought me to think of the press and to think of my reputation. Afterwards I thought his evident agitation might have been one of the issues contributory to my dismissal from the Museum in mid-1960 but, on the discovery stage of litigation, found no evidence, in documentation at least, that this had been so.

I had already given my lecture, 'Loch Ness: the Case for Investigation', and shown the film wherever there was an audience. As a last resort, through 1959 I tried to arouse some interest among the younger generation in the universities, who probably had never heard anything in detail upon the subject and might provide that final but very effective research-tool: manpower. It was with some trepidation, having little lecturing experience at all, much less to such large audiences as came, that I appeared on platforms at Reading, Birmingham, London, Oxford and Cambridge. But the lectures went surprisingly well; a speaker without notes, like a conductor without a score, is halfway home before he starts! The worst thing that befell me was a journey through Birmingham in the rush-hour, riding pillion on a student's motor-cycle with a cine-projector swinging from one hand and a briefcase from the other.

The greatest successes had been at Oxford and Cambridge where, apparently, discussions had gone on in students' rooms until the small hours of the morning. A joint Oxbridge expedition over 100 strong went up to the loch in the summer of 1960 and were evidently well-satisfied with the project because the whole crowd of them, under Peter Baker's leadership, went back the next year. I had been greatly looking forward to going along with these enthusiastic youngsters on the first occasion but unfortunately, on the day of their departure, another event had demanded priority in my social calendar.

In May 1960 a sleek Old Etonian had taken over as Museum Director and promptly announced that he was recommending my dismissal on the grounds of allegations spanning the previous eleven years. He was, it transpired, merely the fall-guy, charged with acting out the role of prosecutor in a case already decided in advance. The General Secretary of the Institution of Professional Civil Servants and I were present that June morning unwittingly to play our parts in a charade which could afterwards be represented as normal Civil Service disciplinary procedure.

In the background skilful persuaders had worked upon the Chairman of Trustees until he had become convinced that half of the Museum would fall down and the rest need to be converted into a mental home if I stayed around a moment longer. Archbishop Lord Fisher of Lambeth had then set about showing that, even without benefit of stake and faggots, he could still do a right professional mediaeval job.

I now began a seven-year fight which, commencing with I.P.C.S. negotiations, went on through a press campaign, debates in Parliament, interviews galore with scientific and political V.I.Ps and, eventually a legal action up to the Court of Appeal. Those who had fondly imagined themselves to be Civil Servants were dumbfounded at Lord Denning's judgement: we were the Servants of the Trustees under the British Museum Act of 1753; we were employed at pleasure and could be dismissed at pleasure and without reason; and in such dismissal proceedings the Trustees were not bound by the principles of Natural Justice! That, with a further ruling that the Director had absolute discretion to exclude me from the libraries and collections of the Museum, was the end of my story and the effective end of my professional life.

But elsewhere there were benefits. The British Museum Bill of 1963 swept aside the Archbishop and the rest of the

Trustees, severed the connection between the British Museum and the British Museum (Natural History) and created new governing bodies for both. How far I helped to provoke this I do not know, but I had certainly discussed with Ministers, been approached for advice by one and was actively briefing speakers in both Houses as the Bill went through.

*

Nicholas Witchell asked for my reminiscences, comments and present opinions. The opinion, as regards Loch Ness, is much the same as it was thirty years ago, and here it is.

General Considerations

1. There have often been delays (Wendt 1956) in the academic acceptance of many genuine animals: e.g. 77 years for de Montfort's Kraken–Giant Squid and 169 years for his Giant Octopus. Long before we reach the country of the Little Green Men there is a large area of suggestively researched and documented 'unknown' animals (Heuvelmans, 1962, 1968). Since it would be surprising if all of these were fictitious it is prudent to be cautious before rejecting any of them.

2. In the family tree of a major animal group the main trunk represents the basic, unspecialised stock. The earlier bifurcations lead to the earliest and most fundamental modifications of structural-pattern and adaptation, in which the main evolutionary thrusts are committed and the main limits of variation restricted for the future. Seals will never evolve into arboreal animals, or whales return to the land, or horses develop webbed feet. In the present state of knowledge an animal with a strikingly characteristic basic construction is likely to belong to an old group already known rather than to a recent group previously unknown.

3. In the 'living fossil' situation the species is usually

one which, through stability of environment and lack of competition or predation, has contrived to survive with very little change. The Tuatera is a new species and genus of a family going back to the Triassic (180 million years). The Coelacanth is a new species, genus and family which links on to a higher group in the Cretaceous (65 million years).

4. Isolated relict populations of large aquatic animals do occur. Thus during the Pleistocene (our Ice Age) Africa was subjected to prolonged heavy rains (pluvials), and the Sahara was a vast swamp. At the end of the period, when the Sahara dried out, populations of crocodiles were isolated in small lakes in the mountainous regions of Tassili, Tibesti, Ennedi and Mauritania and were confirmed by shooting, well into this century. (Guggisberg, 1972.)

5. Loch Ness was open to the sea via Loch Dochfour and the River Ness until the construction of the weir at Dochfour about 1818. The time-lapse until now would need generations of large reptiles well down into single figures for survival. Crocodiles can live to well over a century. Tui Malila, the Seychelles Giant Tortoise given by Captain Cook to the King of Tonga in 1773-74 or 1777 died in 1966, aged at least 189 years (*Daily Mail*, 21 May 1966). There is thus no need for algebraical juggling with 'minimum viable populations', etc.

General Assumptions for Loch Ness
A very large number of witnesses with a wide variety of backgrounds claim to have seen phenomena in Loch Ness which, in their experience, appeared unusual, and various photographs, films, etc., have been produced to support these assertions. When many of these have been disposed of as mundane or inconclusive there remains a hard core of more or less mutually corroborative evidence. This points to the existence of one or more large animals, of a species of which the illustration of the *Cryptocleidus* skeleton may serve as a very general model without pressing the identification further for the present.

215

Elimination of Animal Groups

Invertebrate animals, fishes, amphibia and birds can be ruled out without detailed discussion.

Mammal Groups

The very vast majority of all known mammals have 7 cervical vertebrae; Sloths are exceptional with 9. The Giraffes represent the practical limit of elongation and flexibility of the neck. Of the aquatic groups the Cetacea (Whales, Dolphins, etc.), Sirenia (Dugongs, etc.) and Pinnipedia (Seals, Sea Lions etc.) are locked into special-isations of form, locomotion and habit in which the evolution of a long-necked form would seem virtually impossible and positively detrimental if it were to occur.

Only among the Eared Seals do we find any more promis-ing prospect for our hypothetical long-necked creature. These are compromise-animals whose hind flippers can still be turned forward under the body for locomotion on land. They swim by rowing movements of the front flippers and steer by the hind flippers held close together; the tail is reduced. The neck is relatively long and used a great deal to provide impetus both on land and in the water. But these animals do not swim in a great variety of configurations; they do not submerge for long periods; they come ashore most conspicuously for a long time to breed and are altogether much in evidence and unmistak-able wherever they occur. And in the loch they would be as interested in us as we were in them.

There is, perhaps, something more to be extracted from the evidence of witnesses who have used descriptions expressing extreme disgust in their accounts of the animal. Mrs H. Finley: 'It was horrible! I wouldn't go to look at it if it was exhibited behind six-inch steel bars!' Mr G. Spicer: 'It was terrible . . . dark elephant-grey of a loathsome texture, reminiscent of a snail.' Do we, at the zoo, hear such remarks by the sea lions' pool, or the delphinarium, or in front of seals or otters or deer? But would we, on the other hand, be altogether surprised to hear people speaking in such terms in the Reptile House? Have witnesses who were unable to identify the animal they were watching unconsciously provided a significant pointer?

Reptile Groups

There seems little probability of finding a likely candidate among existing reptiles either. Crocodiles and Marine Iguanas in a hurry swim by using their tails while their feet are tucked in by their sides. Turtles sometimes have a longish neck and swim by paddles but cannot vary the shape of a rigid carapace. In one instance in my experience these too were 'much in evidence': a blissful day in a boat on the Ganges where there were Softshell Turtle heads and River Dolphin backs breaking the surface in all directions.

Thus we have exhausted all the options and must look among the supposedly 'extinct' reptile groups where an apparent candidate awaits us among the Plesiosaurs of the Tertiary period. Ahead the argument runs quite smoothly, but I have made this journey many times in great detail and never cease to be worried at this point. Either we have to go back to the beginning and deny an animal or we have to go on and say that all the indications seem to point towards this:

The Plesiosaur Hypothesis

It was the great naturalist Philip Henry Gosse who in 1860 first put forward the idea that some of the sea-serpent reports might be explained in this way, and in regard to the *Daedalus* and *Umfuli* monsters, and the animal seen in the Sleat of Skye, and others, I would go along with him. I think these, together with the animals reported from Lochs Ness, Morar, and other lakes, are all problems which may have a similar solution in common. But we must be quite clear at the outset that Plesiosaurs are not 'Aquatic Dynasaurs' or any kind of Dinosaur

217

either; the two groups are unrelated for as far back as the fossil record goes. Neither are we likely to find an 'evolved Plesiosaur'; if we have guessed rightly the animal will, like the Tuatera and the Coelacanth, almost certainly turn out to be one very close to a family we already know.

Back towards the beginning of the Triassic a group of rather primitive reptiles gave rise to several offshoots among which were two successful main lines. One line, the Pliosaurs, were large-headed, short-necked animals. The other line embraced the long-necked Plesiosaurs, known as fossils from Europe and Greenland, and the ultra long-necked Elasmosaurs which were worldwide over the same period until the end of the Cretaceous.

There is one basic difficulty to be countered. So far the fossil record indicates that Plesiosaurs were always a marine group (and so, incidentally, lived in the most stable habitat and the one which would have best ensured their survival). This, however is not too worrying because, apart from the incompleteness of the Tertiary freshwater record, it is a fact that modern crocodiles and turtles include both freshwater and marine species; the Estuarine Crocodile *C. porosus* ranges from rivers to far out to sea and so must be able to overcome any physiological problems that occur. The crocodiles are certainly cold-blooded; though they achieved a 4-chambered heart they did not manage the other modifications which the reptilian ancestors of birds and mammals completed. Present opinion inclines to the view that warm-bloodedness was more widespread among ancient reptiles than was once supposed. Thus, if the Plesiosaurs had this advantage, it may well be that some of them moved in from the sea at a late stage to occupy the vacant crocodile niche in certain temperate freshwaters. In cases like Loch Ness the colonisation might have commenced in following up a salmon run.

I intend to proceed by using the *Cryptocleidus* skeleton as a basis for a general discussion of the structure and lifestyle of the Plesiosaurs, with passing reference to the photos by Hugh Gray, the Surgeon, and the one by Rines of the underwater paddle, and introducing at various points related observations which have been made in regard to the Loch Ness animal. Having built up this general picture I will return to the Surgeon's photo and try to show just how much more evidence can be wrung out of it. But take heed; there is many a slip between the photo negative and the printed page and a serious judgement may require comparison of versions in several different books, as well as uncropped original prints.

The Gray photo shows a humped back and the insertions of two paddles breaking the heavy shadow along the waterline. In no pejorative sense it is a naive photo by a naive witness who stated: 'I did not see any head, for what I took to be the front parts were under the water, but there was considerable movement from what seemed to be the tail, the part furthest from me.' It seems probable that the converse was the case; the movement was most likely from the head grappling with a fish in shallow water (to the right) while the tail was relatively inactive to the left. With this adjustment it is now possible to compare the three photos with the skeleton and observe that the information generally available from all four is not inconsistent.

The head in the Surgeon's photo corresponds with the skull in that the profiles of the face and the back of the head are convex and meet on top to form a blunt point; there is no deviation from snout to brow-ridge as there is in seals in which, also, the top of the head is smoothly rounded. The apical point on the skull corresponds to the meeting between the parietal ridge and the converging posterior processes of the squamosal bones. The back of the skull falls away very steeply and its profile thus corresponds to the line of the forwardly-directed neural spine of the second vertebra. The orbits (centre-top of skull) are rather small. Behind these are the larger openings which accommodated the bulging jaw muscles during the closing of the mouth. A very mobile skull-articulation on the neck would account for the apparently 'appearing-disappearing' head reported by some observers.

The nostrils (not shown in our illustration) were carried back up the snout to a position just before the orbits, so that the animal needed to expose only a very small area of its cranium in order to breathe. This, in relation to the 30 square miles of loch surface, would answer the oft-repeated question: 'Why isn't it seen more often?' There would undoubtedly have been fleshy valves over the nostrils but we cannot tell whether they interrupted the profile as projections.

In the Surgeon's later photo, in which the animal is submerging, the angle between chin and neck has changed and the head is turned slightly towards the camera.

The jaws in the skull are armed with simple pointed teeth set in sockets and adapted merely to impaling prey. There could have been no tearing off of pieces nor any chewing. The food – quite certainly fish – would have been thrown about until it was in position to be swallowed, and there would have been the usual reptilian straining (and more) to force it down the gullet. Such head-shaking and general commotion have been described by witnesses.

Flexibility of the neck in *Cryptocleidus* was provided by 31 cervical vertebrae (compare our mammalian 7), and the numbers went even higher in other genera and far higher in the Elasmosaurs. A large animal rowing itself at speed could hardly manoeuvre and brake well enough to capture mobile prey and a long flexible neck would compensate for this deficiency. Most likely feeding would have occurred with the body slow-moving or stationary and the neck allowing the swift sudden strike at approaching prey. Fishes are sometimes attracted to the cover of floating objects, and some herons and whole fleets of pelicans exploit this propensity by spreading their wings to provide the necessary shadow. Such behaviour would explain the loitering humps seen on Loch Ness, and the presence of two or more individuals account for some of the more baffling hump-configurations which have been observed and photographed. If reptilian intelligence did not allow co-operation the presence of small fishes near one animal might well serve to attract a second to join it.

How the neck was carried during swimming is anyone's guess, but any configuration would have probably resulted in small secondary humps appearing in an animal swimming at the surface. It might, as in the slow-flying heron, have been drawn back between the shoulders. It would, if carried extended, have performed undulatory movements to counter flow-turbulence, as in flying swans. It might have performed surging actions to give added impetus, as in sea lions: we cannot tell. It would, as we shall see below, certainly have been useful in the event of the animal coming ashore.

Early in the last century Dean Buckland described the Plesiosaurs as resembling 'a snake threaded through a turtle's shell'. The skeleton is built like a battleship to provide a rigid framework for the powerful muscles of the paddles. The ventral elements of the limb-girdles are expanded into great broad plates, there is a massive sternum and the body-wall is reinforced by stout abdominal ribs. The animal would not collapse under its own weight as whales do when stranded; if it came ashore the ventral skeleton would serve as a gigantic skid, and if the creature dived to the depths which sonar says our animal does, it would be well able to resist the pressure.

To understand the motion of the paddles stand with the right arm extended horizontally to the side, palm down, thumb (leading edge) forward. Sweep the arm forward from the shoulder until the fingers are pointing ahead: this is the recovery stroke. Now twist the arm until the thumb is pointed down and the palm vertical. Sweep the arm back to the side and you have the propelling backstroke. (Pedants can perform the exercise lying on their tummies.) The sequence of movements would probably involve diagonally opposite limbs moving together (the usual

221

reptilian sequence), with the tail (shortened to avoid fouling the rear paddles) acting as a rudder to prevent the animal yawing. To my eye the Dinsdale film shows a regular left-right-left-right splashing up front of the hump, which confirms not only what the above analysis would expect but also contradicts the idea that the film shows a motorboat.

Another point of explanation. In reptilian limbs the bones of the upper arm (humerus) and thigh (femur) are articulated so that they swing to and fro to the sides of the body like oars. In the mammals, however, they have become rotated downwards so that they swing to and fro beneath the body like pendulums. All patterns of locomotion, on land or in the water, are affected accordingly.

In Plesiosaur paddles the humerus and femur are relatively long, the distal bones of the limbs shortened and the five digits very long and many-jointed (hyperdactylous). Note this in the *Cryptocleidus* skeleton.

We are now ready to consider the Rines underwater photos of the paddle. These are profoundly important. Note first the tuberculated skin on the flank. Compare the description in the account of the Spicer sighting on the B862 road on 22 July 1933: ' . . . dark elephant-grey of a loathsome texture, reminiscent of a snail'. Is this not a striking mutual corroboration? On this occasion two photos were taken with an interval of a minute between. In the second the limb is carried perpendicular to the surface of the flank in typical reptilian fashion and at an angle which indicates that it must be midway through a recovery stroke. Since the taper of the body is behind the trailing edge of the paddle (to top of photo) it must be a tail rather than a neck, so the paddle can be identified as a hind one. The earlier photo shows the same paddle in a slightly more retarded position, and also gives a much clearer image of the ridges of two ribs showing through the skin of the flank anterior to the root of the paddle. We can now deduce:-

1) Confirmation that we are dealing with a hind limb

since in the *Cryptocleidus* skeleton the ribcage does not extend forward of the forelimb;

2) Since the abdominal rib-series does not approach so close to the hind limb these two ribs must certainly belong to the dorsal vertebral series. Thus we are able to deduce that the two photographs show a dorsal view of part of the body and right posterior paddle;

3) Since the mammalian ribcage ends far short of the hind limb and girdle we have firm evidence that the photos show part of a reptile.

The limb-skeleton of *Cryptocleidus* would fit nicely into the photographed paddle towards the leading edge, with the main axis corresponding to the light off-centre line running along the paddle. Since such a paddle is seldom if ever feathered out of the water its structure has to combine rigidity for the propulsive backstroke and a streamlined cross-section for the recovery stroke through the dense medium of water. Thus we have the surface extended into a wider non-skeletal flap at the trailing edge so that it provides a smooth water-flow without the turbulence which would result if the trailing edge merely followed the contour of the main spar. The paddles making recovery strokes would also act as hydrofoils, giving excellent lateral stability, while slight variations in the angle of the blades would introduce a controllable element of drag and assist the tail in steering. However the neck was carried there would not be much chance of adverse effects due to torque. (In the locomotion of whales torque is considerable: on the occasions when a Narwhal develops a second tusk (canine tooth) both tusks spiral in the same direction.)

The Spicer story of a beach-landing as far as the B862 (given in full elsewhere) is at once the most extraordinary story in the entire saga and one of the strongest supports for our present theory. It is either a true report or an incredible fabrication; there are no possible mundane explanations in between. However, an animal like *Cryptocleidus*, designed as a wholly aquatic vehicle with no

Pinniped compromises would, if it dragged itself ashore, display a body pitching and rolling and yawing in all directions as it obtained the necessary clearances for paddles to move and inch the body forward. In these efforts the head and neck, in various configurations, would be used as an adjustable mass to overbalance the body in the desired direction (it has been said that a Sea Lion could not move on land were its neck half as long) while the tail would be used to the best of its capacity in the same way. The Spicer account of a bulky body moving in a series of jerks, apparently without visible limbs, with a rapidly undulating head and long neck showing two or three arches, and a tail held high at the rear, is to my mind a truthful and utterly convincing description and corresponds entirely with what we would expect in the Plesiosaur we have been considering.

The Loch Ness animal may on occasions create a considerable commotion, yet on others it can sink without so much as a ripple and without displaying the tail in a surface dive as a mammal would. In this regard we can invoke a mechanism which modern crocodiles and ancient Plesiosaurs have in common. Cott (1961) showed that the Nile Crocodile swallows pebbles which then serve a hydrostatic function, providing an anterior counterpoise and ventral stabilising force, giving neutral buoyancy in association with the inflation of the lungs for lying at the surface, and enabling the animals to dive easily and rest for long periods on the bottom; young crocodiles cannot dive until they have taken ballast aboard. (cf. von Humboldt in 1852: 'The Indians have come up with the absurd idea that these lazy animals weigh themselves down in order to dive more easily.') Such gut-stones or gastroliths are found in association with fossil Plesiosaurs, and not fortuitously; one from Texas contained pebbles from North Dakota 600 miles away.

Such a mechanism, including possible diverticula from the lungs, could explain many things about the Loch Ness animal: the floating at various elevations above the surface, the ability to submerge with no disturbance and the propensity to die without leaving an apparent corpse which, as in the crocodiles, would sink to the bottom and be dealt with by putrefaction and scavengers.

There are occasions when the Loch Ness animal, in normal locomotion or in one of its occasional orgies of violent splashing, causes the water to foam, as when I saw it. Seals have an oily wake but do not produce such phenomena. A reptile, however, voids its kidney and intestinal wastes through a common cloacal opening and aquatic reptiles, having no need to conserve water, are prodigal of it in flushing their kidneys. Our animal therefore, almost certainly a large piscivore, may well be creating both the substance and the agitation of the foam it produces.

Finally, let us return to the image which has intrigued so many for more than half a century that it is widely known as '*The* Surgeon's Photograph' of '*The* Head and Neck'. We have already commented on the form of the head, its resemblance to *Cryptocleidus* on the one hand and its dissimilarity to seal-heads on the other. The long neck is patently suggestive of the Plesiosaur. Now, with the foundations laid, we can try to understand the rest of the image, if necessary checking the versions published in other books.

Between the base of the neck and its reflection the image is transected by a dark horizontal bar which is much longer to the left of the picture. In this longer portion note that the left half has a clean, hard upper edge which descends into the water as a rounded tip. Towards the animal the said hard edge makes an obtuse angle with a light diagonal area which descends towards the surface of the water. Between the light area and the base of the neck the remainder of the dark structure is vaguer in shape and less intense in tone. I suggest that in following these observations the reader will now have clearly made out the form of the right anterior paddle of the animal, carried with its face perpendicular to the surface of the

225

water, and seen its highlighted inner trailing edge and attachment to the right shoulder. The paddle has just completed its backstroke and is lying back against the animal's right flank. Compare the form of the right posterior paddle in the second of the Rines photos; the trailing edge is towards the top of the photo.

Next consider the dark mass to the right of the base of the neck. Part of this is reflection in the water, but the position and form are commensurate with the tip of the left anterior paddle 'feathered' on its side and lying in the position from which it will rotate and commence its backstroke.

Now let us try to make something of the water movements (cf. Tricker, 1964). There is a broadly elliptical or circular area around the animal in which the general wind-drift has been disturbed, and this disruption comprises three separate elements:

1) the most disturbed area, corresponding to the most recent event, the completed backstroke of the right anterior paddle;

2) a similar area, corresponding to the earlier backstroke of the left anterior paddle, in which the disturbance has had time to travel outwards and subside, and where the longer wavelengths of the basic wind-drift are beginning to reassert themselves;

3) the expected configuration of the back of the animal, revealed in the arched and transversely corrugated form of a sheet of water cascading off the hump in much the same way as it does from the hull of a submarine (e.g. *The Times*, 17 February 1964).

*

So there, in a short space, it is, and no justification for: 'Scientist says Monster Plesiosaur' or 'Eel-man Believes Monster' or even, 'Poor old Tucker, have you heard? He's gone back to the Bush!' Let us look at it this way, avoiding words like 'fact' and 'truth' and 'belief' which are much more complicated than they at first seem.

A scientific statement is one with so high a degree of probability that for practical purposes it may be accepted as a certainty. That is implicit in a paper in which a statement is made on the authority of, say, 'Smith (1938)' or 'Jones (1954)'. It is explicit when a worker, anxious to know how far the sample he has studied gives a fair picture of the population as a whole, applies arcane (probably correct!) mathematical formulae and announces that his results are 'significant at the one percent level'. By this he means that there is only one chance in a hundred that a random sample would have given the picture he has found if that picture were not representative of the population at large, and that his results are, in effect, 99% certain.

A theory, or hypothesis, or model, is an educated guess. It has sufficient probability to merit further thought, observation and experiment, but not enough to qualify as a scientific statement as yet, and it is the job of the scientist to see whether he can raise its probability to the point where it becomes acceptable or lower it to the point where it can be safely discarded.

So on these lines I might give my Plesiosaur hypothesis a rating of 20 percent, thus admitting how far short it falls at present, and go on to give 9 to the seal, 4 to the otter-circus and so on, indicating my relative opinions of the other candidates in the field. If it were known that there were surviving Plesiosaurs elsewhere in the world I might well have rated the Loch Ness chances at 70 or 80 percent; if one were certainly present in Loch Morar I might have been justified in going as high as 95 or 98 percent in the case of Loch Ness.

The irony is that, unrecognised among the 573 sea-serpent sightings documented by Heuvelmans (1968) and the equally painstaking survey of lake monsters by Costello (1974), there may well have been the material evidence to reinforce our Plesiosaur hypothesis for Loch Ness. The corollary is that the Loch Ness investigations, having the advantage that they are pursued in a confined space, must, whatever their outcome, carry implications for the probable interpretation of the many reports elsewhere.

Loch Ness is a legitimate subject for proper scientific investigation: there is a solution of a kind to be found and no professional stigma should attach to any who seek it in a properly professional and scientific way. The shame, if any there be, attaches to the men who dominated my profession during my maturity and who, even in their armchair speculations, did not extend themselves to consider the evidence collected by others or fully engage the intelligence, expertise and knowledge which they undoubtedly possessed.

As for me? Once I was a schoolboy naturalist, and now I am an old boy naturalist, and the curlew still call as sweetly over the marshes as ever they did.

SUGGESTED READING

Bright, M., 'Meet Mokele-Mbembe', *B.B.C. Wildlife* **2** (12) 596-601 London, 1984.

Burton, M., *The Elusive Monster*, Rupert Hart-Davis, London, 1961.

Campbell, E.M. & Solomon, D., *The Search for Morag*, Tom Stacey, London, 1972.

Carr, A., *The Reptiles* (Life Nature Library), Time-Life International, 1968.

Costello, P., *In Search of Lake Monsters*, Garnstone Press, London, 1974.

Cott, H.B., 'Scientific results of an inquiry into the ecology and economic status of the Nile Crocodile', Trans. Zoological Society, **29** Part 4, London, 1961.

Dinsdale, T., *Loch Ness Monster*, Routledge & Kegan Paul, London, 1961.

Gosse, P.H., *The Romance of Natural History*, James Nisbet, London, 1860.

Gould, R.T., *The Case for the Sea-Serpent*, Philip Allen, London, 1930.

Gould, R.T., *The Loch Ness Monster*, Geoffrey Bles, London, 1934.

Guggisberg, C.A.W., *Crocodiles*, David & Charles, Newton Abbot, 1972.

Heuvelmans, B., *On the Track of Unknown Animals*, Rupert Hart-Davis, London, 1962.

Heuvelmans, B., *In the Wake of the Sea-Serpents*, Rupert Hart-Davis, London, 1968.

Holiday, F.W., *The Great Orm of Loch Ness*, Faber & Faber, London, 1968.

229

King, J.E., *Seals of the World*, British Museum (Natural History), London, 1983.

Mackal, R.P., *The Monsters of Loch Ness*, Macdonald & James, London, 1976.

Mackal, R.P., *Searching for Hidden Animals*, Cadogan Books, London, 1980.

Mackal, R.P., *A Living Dinosaur? In Search of Mokele-Mbembe*, E.J. Brill, Leiden, 1987.

Oudemans, A.C., *The Great Sea-Serpent*, E.J. Brill, Leiden, 1892.

Romer, A.S. *Vertebrate Palaeontology*, University Press, Chicago, 1947.

Tricker, R.A.R., *Bores, Breakers, Waves and Wakes*, Mills & Boon, London, 1964.

Tucker, D.W., 'The Loch Ness Monster', *New Scientist*, 27 October & 17 November, London, 1960.

Wendt, H., *Out of Noah's Ark*, Weidenfeld & Nicolson, London, 1956.

Whyte, C., *More than a Legend*, Hamish Hamilton, London, 1961.

Wood, F.G. & Gennaro, J.F., *An Octopus Trilogy, Natural History*, **80** (3), New York, 1971.

INDEX

234